Intuition
and
Success

THE SECRET OF INNER GUIDANCE

Dr. Ivan ERENDA   ⊙   Aleksej METELKO

www.inner-success.com

INTUITION AND SUCCESS: The Secret of Inner Guidance

www.inner-success.com

Publisher: Selfpublished, Dr. Ivan Erenda and Aleksej Metelko, Novo mesto, 1st edition
Publication Date: 2018
Language: English
Document type: Paperback
No.of copies: Print on demand, 300 copies printed in Slovenia
Cover design: Aleksej Metelko
Cover image: Jani Pavlin
ISBN: 978-961-288-486-4

ivan.erenda@gmail.com or aleksej.metelko@gmail.com

CIP - Kataložni zapis o publikaciji
Narodna in univerzitetna knjižnica, Ljubljana

159.956

ERENDA, Ivan
    Intuition and success : the secret of inner guidance / Ivan Erenda, Aleksej Metelko. - 1st ed. - Novo mesto : selfpublished I. Erenda : [selfpublished] A. Metelko, 2018

ISBN 978-961-288-486-4
1. Metelko, Aleksej
295095040

"I've read tons of books on personal growth and I truly believe that Intuition and Success belongs at the very top of the list. The message, scale and originality of the examples that the authors obtained through research and interviews is simply unprecedented."

—Boris Vene, Best-Selling Author
and Founder of Health Super-Boosting Method "Body Reset"

"This book literally has the power to change your life for the better, 100 percent. Intuition and Success will make you pause and rethink the meaning of your life - this is the best gift you can ever get. Share it with your loved ones."

—Oskar Kogoj, world-renowned industrial designer,
academician and artist

"Intuition and Success will enrich you with a deeper understanding of this great inner power we all possess and which can be awaken and developed at any time. The authors take the very understanding of success in life to another level: it's a pioneering work."

—Ivo Boscarol, founder and CEO of Pipistrel

"If you are searching for the missing link that connects everything and everyone, read this book and rediscover your life again."

— Victoria Lynn Weston,
renowned business psychic-intuitive consultant

"Knowledge is vital, but nothing can compare with that special feeling of total truth which completely overtakes you, and you simply know what you should do. I cannot overstate my regard for this book."

—Dejan Zavec, 4x world boxing champion

"Intuition and Success offers you an opportunity for self-discovery and a framework for success. If you want to live a more meaningful life, this is a MUST-READ."

—Edward Clug, internationally renowned choreographer

"If you are going to read one book on intuition, search no more - this is the one. Intuition and Success is a very valuable read for anyone who is looking for true and lasting success."

—Dr. Ivan Misner, New York Times bestselling author
and Founder of BNI

"This book will teach you how to feel your intuition, how to listen to your heart and control your ego. When we achieve this, we are like a medium that transmits the pure truth and creation from which big things arise."

—Simon Robinson, renowned conductor,
pedagogue and composer

YOU ARE HOLDING A POWERFUL BOOK IN YOUR HANDS. A BOOK ABOUT AN INNER POWER WE ALL POSSESS – INTUITION. IT CAN CHANGE THE WAY YOU EXPERIENCE YOURSELF AND THE WORLD AROUND YOU IN A HIGHLY BENEFICIAL MANNER.

INTUITION, THE INVISIBLE POWER THAT LED SO MANY AMAZING PEOPLE TO ACHIEVE GREAT THINGS, THE POWERFUL FORCE WHICH WAS BEHIND ALL GREAT INVENTIONS, THE FACULTY THAT PRODUCED SOME OF THE MOST INFLUENTIAL BOOKS, MEMORABLE SONGS AND, MOREOVER, HAS LITERALLY SAVED MANY, MANY LIVES.

FIND OUT HOW SUCCESSFUL PEOPLE FROM DIFFERENT FIELDS USE THEIR INTUITION. DISCOVER HOW TO FIND AND HARNESS YOUR INTUITION IN ORDER TO REACH YOUR FULL POTENTIAL AND ACHIEVE TRUE AND LASTING SUCCESS, AS MANY OTHERS HAVE.

This book will help you find the way to do the right things in the right way and at the right time. You will gain a deeper understanding of intuition, backed not only by esoteric teachings, but also by scientific principles.

*"Perhaps the most important thing
we can ever do in our lives is to
find a way to our intuition."*

Dr. Ivan Erenda

*"Learn to hear your inner voice,
be led by your heart and never stop giving —
this way, you will always walk the right path
and you will never walk alone."*

Aleksej Metelko

Acknowledgements

We would like to acknowledge and thank everyone who participated in the research we conducted; thank you for sharing your stories, your insights and your victories with us. We are deeply grateful for your generosity, inspiration, wisdom and trust. We would also like to acknowledge and thank all who contributed in any way toward organizing the interviews. We are profoundly grateful for your belief in and support of this project.

A very special thanks also goes to our families, who have tolerated the long hours of absence while we were doing research, interviews and writing. You are our greatest treasures and we are deeply grateful for the gift of your love in our lives.

Contents

A Secret Weapon… Even for "Unintuitive" People

WE USUALLY ASSOCIATE intuition with the activities of the right side of the brain, which is responsible for giving us a direction in life, for imagination, expansion, a broader view of the situation, abstraction, and similar functions. The domain of the left hemisphere is logic, analytical ability, order, systematization.

This kind of thinking, the concept that each half of the brain has distinct and separate skills, reveals a simple solution that we can apply when we do not know how to proceed when solving a problem. When we get stuck on some point, it usually means that we have fallen into a trap – we are depending exclusively on the activity of either only the left or only the right hemisphere. It follows that dreamers and visionaries need to "get their feet on the ground" by using defined steps, protocols and systems, left hemisphere activities. Analytical people, on the other hand, who perceive events through logical sequences, predictable activities and rational predictions, need the right-brain "view from the top of the mountain" which extends the horizon and offers new approaches and solutions.

With that being said, we may conclude that intuitive insights help us when we are looking for a fresh idea or solution that goes beyond existing patterns of thinking and activity. For example, when the time comes for a change and, mostly out of habit, we still continue to cling to our old ways of thinking and acting. At a first glance, one may also assume that intuitive insights are reserved for people with a more highly developed right brain hemisphere. However, this point of view is not entirely accurate. People who consciously monitor and develop their intuitiveness can learn to use their intuition in a variety of different ways - even if they usually operate in a predominantly analytical fashion, they can find ways to apply intuition within their logical frameworks and their rational view of a given situation.

So, being intuitive doesn't necessarily mean that we must forget everything we are familiar with and step into the unknown. We can stay within our accustomed frame of mind, but with the help of intuition, we start making better decisions. What we need to do is just relax and identify the intuitive flash when it appears.

Through the stories and examples of successful people from all over the world and from all walks of life, this book will show you how they have used intuition on their way to success. Sometimes this occurs within the context of an existing way of thinking and acting, and sometimes it provides help for discovering new ways and ideas.

For example, Lisa Nichols, from the hit movie "The Secret", one of the world's most-requested motivational speakers and New York Times bestselling author, reveals how to tell the difference between intuition and mental chatter.

Debra Cafaro (Ventas, Inc.), nominated for the "Top 50 Best-Performing CEOs" by Harvard Business Review, describes how to lean on intuition in the field of employee selection.

Author and former director of the Düsseldorf office of McKinsey & Company, Inc., Dr. Peter Kraljic, points out the importance of collective intuition for reaching "tremendous breakthrough results, unattainable by a single individual".

Riccardo Illy, former Business Director of the famous coffee brand Illycaffè and current President of Gruppo Illy (the holding company of the Illy family which owns illycaffè) presents examples of how he used intuition when making some of his most important decisions, including the choice of diversifying the family business, and in employee selection.

Even more specific is Dr. Robert Samuel Langer, Jr., the most cited engineer in history, who was awarded the Queen Elizabeth Prize for Engineering. He explains how, exactly through the use of intuition, he has solved certain scientific problems.

Dr. Shirin Ebadi, the Nobel Peace Prize winner and "one of 100 most powerful women in the world" according to Forbes, reveals the connection between intuition and the collective consciousness, available to anyone.

An interesting story was also shared by Branko Lustig, Hollywood film producer and two-time Oscar award winner. It was intuition that turned the original, average story of the film "Gladiator" into a world-class mega-hit.

People in the highest positions also use intuitive approaches. Stjepan Mesic, the 2nd President of Croatia and the last President of the Presidency of Yugoslavia, reveals a behind-the-scenes story about $2 billion of humanitarian aid that took place during the war in Croatia, and in which the main role was played by intuition.

One of the most unusual examples of the extent to which a person can capitalize on his intuitive potential is by playing chess while blind-folded - against several players at the same time! This is the art that has been perfected by "The Blindfold King", chess grandmaster Timur Gareyev. He shares his insight on the role of intuition in his game.

In short, the book you are holding in your hands is not just a kind of an exclusive collection of interviews and research, or an overview of the practical use of intuition. It not only discusses different esoteric and scientific points of view, offering you a deep understanding of this phenomena and its widespread use. It is also a guide that reveals some practical steps toward mirroring and modeling the intuitive approaches of the world´s most successful people. Intuition and Success also brings forth a fresh concept of success, and will impress you with the message it holds.

So, keep on reading with an open mind and a pen in your hand – to write down your own intuitive insights as they arise during your reading.

Boris Vene, Bestselling Author and Founder of the Super Health-Boosting Method, "Body Reset"

PS: One more thing. It is extremely important to be aware, as Ivan and Aleksej point out in a visionary way, that we are living in an interesting time, with rapidly advancing technology and the Fourth Industrial Revolution on one side, and a growing human awareness on a planetary scale leading to the use of latent human potentials on the other. Both factors are capable of dramatically changing the world. Can intuition be the possible answer to the growing threats of rapidly developing artificial intelligence? The authors propose that we must nurture our intuition and include this faculty as a basic concept in our global culture, paving the way for future generations who will need it even more.

The Other Truth About Intuition

ELCOME TO "INTUITION and Success". For some of you, this book will open up new horizons about the nature of reality, the universe and mankind. For others, it will add details to your already expanding understanding of what is possible in your life, helping you to see more clearly to what extent you can control and create the world around you.

Interspersed with the authors´ text, this book includes comments from many successful people, and their responses to some of the questions in the survey that we have conducted during the 7 years of research about the correlation between intuition and success. In order to maintain clarity, and to avoid too much detail, we didn't include the complete results of every interview here in the book. Even so, we advise you to pay careful attention to the quotes we have included.

When many of us think of the word "intuition", we associate it with something mystical, supernatural. We may have been taught to think that receiving ideas from an unknown source, located either inside or outside ourselves, is mysterious, inexplicable, even impossible. Not many generations ago, and even today to a certain extent, the word "intuition" was always included as part of the phrase "women´s intuition", and was considered to be a purely feminine characteristic. But none of these traditional views happen to be correct. This book will show you that, in spite of the different opinions that our civilization has used to label intuition, it is a natural faculty of all human beings, a basic part of our nature, although for one reason or another we may have been led to forget this fact. And we may begin to see that all the viewpoints once separated into the wide variety of sciences, religions, esoteric philosophies, magic and superstition are just describing different ways of looking at a single, underlying reality.

While there are many ways of classifying our perceptions of the things around us, one of the most useful is to divide the world into the visible and the invisible. It may have been from this perspective that the terms "natural" and "supernatural" came into being – what our senses perceived got labeled as belonging to the natural world, and things that we couldn´t perceive directly with our senses, even though we could see their effects all around us, or even inside us, were classified as being supernatural. Even the wind may once have been considered to be supernatural, because we cannot see the air or the forces which cause it to move and blow things around. But as science progressed and learned to develop instruments which extend the possibilities of our senses so we can detect things which had been "invisible" before, from the atom and microbes to magnetism and electricity, we have learned that the realm of the invisible is just another side of nature, lying outside of our limited physical perceptions but still influencing our lives.

We have always had other, inborn "instruments" for detecting certain types of invisible influences on the world around us, and one of the principle tools in our "kit" is intuition. Some rare people have other abilities, and can see or hear things that others don´t seem to detect. But intuition, the ability to know something without knowing why we know it, is a gift that belongs to everyone. We make a choice, and often know which choice to make without having a logical reason for choosing that option; it just seems right. Something inside us led us to go in one direction instead of another, and we either listened to it or we didn´t. But that inner sense, which has been referred to as a "still, small voice", is always there, giving us pointers about what to do and what to avoid – all we have to do is learn to listen. Terms like "voice" and "listen" confuse us sometimes, because they are just metaphors for another level of perception which modern society teaches us to distrust. But with attention and practice, we can learn to confide in this inner guidance.

What causes these feelings of what we should or shouldn´t do? Over the centuries, there have been many explanations: God, or the gods, Guardian Angels, the Universal Mind, the Supreme Consciousness, disembodied beings, invisible messengers, Ascended Masters, the spirits of the dead, extraterrestrials, and countless others. Life demonstrates that, behind everything, there is a single unifying force that ties everything together. While each of us leans toward one or another of the many explanations available, depending on what culture we have been raised in or what influences we have come across in our lives, it is still difficult to define the exact cause or the specific process that brings intuitive information to us. But one thing is clear – through trial and error, we can learn to use it to benefit our lives and the lives of others.

Some people use rituals, either religious, magical or personal, to concentrate the energy of their attention and thus strengthen their internal contact with the nameless force behind things. Part of the process is usually focused on "purification", removing either the physical impediments to our internal perceptions or the psychological barriers and learned behavior which limits their functioning. It also helps by improving our "tuning" with the source of hidden knowledge. The heightened awareness which results can be applied to strengthening our intuition as well as other "occult" abilities.

Looking once again at the title of this book, there is another key word that we need to think about – success. What does success really mean? For some people, it means becoming wealthy, having enough money to do whatever you want. This is an extreme of Financial Success. For others, it means being highly respected, or acquiring enough power that you can tell others what to do. This may be defined as Social Success. On those terms, not many people can be considered successful, and seeking that kind of goal will leave the rest of us who don´t achieve it frustrated for our entire lifetimes. But for other people, success can mean something very different. Having the things you need, meeting people who will become important to you, discovering your true mission in life, your reason for being – these are all forms of success which are highly attainable and which can make your life a real joy to live, called Spiritual Success by some. And intuition can help you reach them all, both the traditional material goals and the more customized personal objectives.

One factor that defines our view of success is our view of what we really are. If you consider yourself to be separate from the rest of the world, the only one who matters, the center of the universe

– and let´s be honest, all of us feel this way sometimes – then success will mean achieving goals to make yourself happy. But that kind of happiness doesn´t last long. The old saying "no man is an island" contains more wisdom than most of us give it credit for. If your goals, your definition of success, only goes as far as your own self, you´ll be missing out on something beyond everything that you can imagine. Often, by expanding our awareness to strengthen our intuition, we also end up expanding our perception of ourselves to include the idea that we are part of a greater whole, an entire universe filled with life and consciousness and light. If we can learn to increase our scale of what deserves our attention, our concern, our love and compassion, we open our hearts (and our intuition) to receive information from a wider base, and to contribute to a larger collectivity that includes our natural environment, other races and nations, and someday, maybe even other worlds. And if we reach this bigger picture, we see that real success means doing our part to contribute to the whole, whether we see that whole on the level of our family, our community, our country, our world or the whole universe. So when we start to use our intuition to lead us to success, we can also use our intuition to tell us what success means to us, instead of just accepting the popular images of success that are thrown at us from all around us. Intuition can tell you not only what to do, but why you should do it, and knowing that is real success.

Ivan and Aleksej

I. Introduction

DID YOU KNOW that all four airplanes which crashed on September 11, 2001, at the World Trade Center (WTC), the Pentagon and in Pennsylvania were unusually empty? As much as 74 to 81 percent of the seats on those planes were unoccupied. The most surprising fact was that the average absence of passengers who had booked reservations on the four planes was no less than 21 percent! Think about it, almost a quarter of the passengers who had paid for a plane ticket did not take the flight! This staggeringly high absence of passengers seemed strange and suspicious, even to FBI investigators. When they started investigating and asking those people for the reasons for their absence from the flight, they faced a lot of unexpected and interesting answers, full of synchronicities, coincidences, premonitory dreams and intuitive hunches. As many as a quarter of the people who had carefully planned to attend those flights found what they considered to be a good reason for not entering those planes on that particular day. Could it be possible that those people were somehow aware of those catastrophic events in advance? Some of you may answer yes and some may not. There are probably some among you who may even have some personal experience of a similar nature, when you avoided some dangerous situation in your life. And even if there was no life-threatening situation involved, we all have certainly experienced that mystical feeling of knowing something without knowing how we know it. We have all felt the urge to do something that might not be reasonably explained, yet we knew that it was the right thing to do.

Sometimes things just happen - or do they? Sometimes events follow each other in what seems to be a perfectly normal way, at least at a first glance, but if we look at them more closely, we discover that something special has guided the sequence of those events to occur exactly as they did, instead of taking the usual flow and following the routine we are accustomed to. It is a little known fact that Academy Award-winning actor and director Robert Redford was in New York the day before September 11 for a Sundance Channel meeting. And United 93 was *"the early morning flight from Newark to San Francisco that he normally favored";* but as the meetings ended earlier than usual, he somehow decided to fly back on September 10. United 93 was the hijacked plane that crashed in Pennsylvania the following morning. [1]

Mark Wahlberg, Hollywood's highest-paid actor in 2017, should have been on American Airlines Flight 11 on that same fatal day. He was scheduled for that flight with some friends, but changed his plans at the last minute and took a flight to Canada on another plane. Flight 11 was the first plane to hit the North Tower of the WTC that day. *"We certainly would have tried to do something to fight. I've had probably over 50 dreams about it,"* said Wahlberg. [2]

Let's look at the other side of the story, from the point of view of those who were supposed to be in the WTC at the time of this tragic event, but weren´t. It's quite a handful of people, above average; actually, so high that conspiracy theories started to crop up. Why is that so? Somehow, these people made seemingly inconsequential decisions such as taking a different subway route, or stepping out for a smoke and being late for work, which resulted in avoiding certain death or serious injuries. One of these is Greer Epstein, an executive director at Morgan Stanley, who rarely left her office during working hours; and yet, just a few minutes before a plane hit the building, she suddenly made what was, for her, an uncommon decision – to go out for a smoke. As soon as she stepped outside of the building, she was shocked to see what was happening to the North Tower. And just at the moment when she was staring at the fire and smoke billowing from the hole made by the first impact, the second plane flew through her office in the South Tower. This *rare* morning break saved her life. *"I never took a break before noon,"* she said. *"It was something that happened that day."* [3]

Speaking of Morgan Stanley, we must mention another name, Rick Rescorla, who was the second vice president for corporate security, a retired Army colonel and decorated veteran of three wars. His story is one of true heroism led by the power of intuition. Rescorla, main character of the 2002 History Channel film *"The Man Who Predicted 9/11"*, has received credit for saving almost 2,700 lives that day, only to lose his own. The story behind his act is simply astonishing: after the bombing attacks on the WTC back in 1993, his gut feeling about a future recurrence of the attack just didn't go away. He had developed a detailed evacuation plan, and when the fateful day arrived, he organized and directed the evacuation. [4] Ian Thorpe, highly decorated Australian swimmer with 5 Olympic gold medals, 3 silver and 1 bronze medal, along with 11 World Championship gold medals, was out for a jog and on his way to the observation deck at the WTC. Suddenly, he realized that he had forgotten his camera in his hotel room. He took a cab back to his hotel, and when he turned on the TV in his room, he realized what had just happened. [2]

"Intuition is something that is 'installed' into every human being."

—Branko Lustig

"We sometimes have a feeling that something is going to happen and that we should not go on a certain trip we had planned. This happens rarely, but it does happen, and then you read in the morning newspaper about some accident that happened in connection with that trip. And most of the time, we are not even aware of the fact that our intuitive decision has actually saved our lives," entrusted us Branko Lustig, Hollywood film producer who won Oscar awards for producing the hit films Schindler's List and Gladiator. Lustig said that, throughout his life, he has been following his feelings and "listening" to his intuition. *"I enjoy mountain climbing, and prior to going to the wall, you look at the mountains, and it might happen that you say to yourself, 'today I am not going'. You simply sense this feeling that today is not the day to go."*

Another fascinating fact, closely related to this very same tragic day, has to do with the study performed by the Global Consciousness Project (GCP) led by Dr. Roger D. Nelson, who founded the GCP back in 1998. The GCP contributed toward expanding the concepts of consciousness field research to global dimensions. The GCP's researchers have created a worldwide network of detectors to record the effects of major "global events" on a hypothesized global consciousness. [5] For this purpose, about 70 detectors have been set in different parts of the world to continuously acquire data in the form of random numbers. What they have found is that there is a subtle but indisputable correlation between important global events (such as the US Embassy bombings in Africa, earthquakes in Columbia, the New Year´s Variance in 2000, Pierre Trudeau´s funeral, the terrorist attacks on Sept. 11, 2001, world-wide meditations, the Wellstone plane crash, the Chechen hostage tragedy, Global Peace demonstrations, the Athens Olympic opening, the Russian school hostages, Pope John Paul's funeral and the attacks in Gaza [6]) and human mental activity at the specific time of each event, as well as the deviations in a set of random number generators (RNG). In the case of 9/11, as much as several hours before the first plane crashed into the New York Twin Towers, a big change in GCP data was noticed. *"The GCP results are of relevance for the study of mind and brain because they bear directly on fundamental questions of consciousness. Research in conventional brain science tends to focus on the neural correlates that give rise to consciousness, and tacitly or explicitly assume that consciousness reduces to brain activity. The GCP results urge us to ask a harder question: Are there direct correlates of consciousness to be found outside the brain? The question is challenging because it posits or points to phenomena that are anomalous and hence mysterious from a conventional stand-point. The search for understanding of mind and brain obviously must change dramatically if consciousness correlates are found in the broader world."* [7] By studying the concepts of consciousness, intention and the effects of the human mind on the physical world, Dr. Nelson's work successfully integrates two very distinctive areas: the fields of science and spirituality. We shall talk more about individual human consciousness, global consciousness and some interesting examples of mystical phenomena in later chapters.

When making decisions, people usually rely on their knowledge, "evidence," experiences and conscious reasoning – using available facts and figures to come to a conclusion. Intuition is just the opposite – it's the ability to acquire knowledge without understanding how the knowledge was acquired, it's knowing without knowing. Yes, that IS possible, and has even been proven scientifically! In addition, numerous testimonials to this experience exist, including those of some highly successful, charismatic, famous and highly fulfilled people from around the world.

Through the research which we conducted during the *Intuition and Success* project, some of these people personally entrusted us with their own experiences, insights and wisdom concerning intuition. This project began seven years ago with studies of all available sources on intuition and closely related research areas. An additional dimension was given to the project by dozens of in-depth interviews with some of the most successful people in the world (from business, the arts, sports, politics, science and many other fields). This book contains exclusive revelations of the insights and amazing stories they shared with us. These stories and similar cases from recent and older history, along with scientific and esoteric sources, have been influential in our personal and business lives, and we are very confident they will have an important positive impact on yours, too. We firmly believe that tapping into intuition brings positive change and inevitably leads to a more prosperous life – studies confirm this. Wouldn't you agree that it is best to learn from the best?

Dr. Ivan Misner is considered to be one of the world's leading experts on business networking and has been a keynote speaker for major corporations and associations throughout the world[1]. He is called the "Father of Modern Networking" by CNN and one of the "Top Networking Experts to Watch" by Forbes. Being also a New York Times Bestselling author who has written 21 books, there is absolutely no doubt that Dr. Misner is an exceptional person with many interesting and enlightening stories to tell. We are very pleased that he was one of a few dozen highly successful people who participated in our *Intuition and Success* Project and entrusted us with their personal experiences with intuition. Here is one of Dr. Misner's unique experiences with intuition that can be easily recognized as a powerful intuitive flash. *"I cannot consider myself to be the most intuitive person, but I remember one time reading some information about a bank where I did business. That article did not say anything that should have upset me, but I became so nervous reading it, almost fearful, that I immediately knew I had to get my money out of that bank. I*

---

1 Dr. Misner is Founder and Chief Visionary Officer of BNI, the world's largest business networking organization. BNI has over 220,000 members in 8,000-plus chapters worldwide. In 2016, BNI members generated more than $11.2 billion in closed business.

withdrew everything except what was insured, and within a week or two that bank went bankrupt."

Such experience can have a great influence on our lives and our decision-making models. Our perception of the world and of our lives can change forever in a fraction of a second. We start to process what we feel and start making final conclusions based not only on reasoning but also on our gut feeling. This is the moment when we add a totally new dimension to our life, and it starts to flourish in all areas of activity and existence. Sometimes intuition reaches us in a very subtle way; often, we don't even realize that we were touched by this divine force: but then again, its voice can be very loud and clear, usually when we are facing important life-changing decisions.

As the project *Intuition and Success* was gaining more and more public notice, we also started to receive quite a few e-mails from people who identified with the essence of the project and who were generous enough to share their experiences with us.

Susan is one them. She is a successful entrepreneur, loving mom and active athlete in her mid-forties from Austin, Texas, USA. She lives a completely *ordinary* life, but that doesn't mean she doesn't have an amazing story to tell. She doesn't want publicity, and we respect that. You might think of her as the "average Joe" who has found her way through life with the help of intuition. Susan´s story is fascinating and inspiring, and very easy to relate to.

Here is Susan´s complete and unaltered letter to us:

"Dear sirs. I'm writing you because I found out that you are studying intuition and you might find my story interesting. First, I have to say that I was never a believer in anything that I couldn't touch or see, and everything that I did in my life was somehow connected to the pure facts, analyzed, rationalized, like we were taught all the way from elementary school onwards. Many times in the past, I've heard stories about a so-called "gut feeling", intuition and unbelievable coincidences, but I rejected them at once, seeing them only from my logical point of view, and they were nothing but a waste of time for me.

However, today, almost ten years after what happened to me, I see them in a completely different light, I feel they are a blessing. I know now that they happen for a reason, to help me, and if I'm ready and able to accept them, great things fall into place. Being aware of the fact that my intuition appears out of nowhere, I became a much better observer and pay more attention. Through the experience that I'm about to speak of, I discovered that my intuition helps me in all kinds of small daily situations, as well as in the most important decisions I have to make.

Back then, my business was kind of stuck, I just couldn't find the right path, I was struggling and wasting too much energy just to keep my head above water. I had pretty much the same situation in my private life and my personal relationships. I used to look at them according to the law of "cause and effect"; I did everything the way I was supposed to, or the way I was taught to do, but the only results were disappointments, one after another.

I remember it like it was yesterday. Strangely, that morning I woke up much earlier than I had set my alarm clock for. My mind was clear and my thoughts were unusually sharp. I woke up and went through my morning routine, accompanied by pretty much the same thoughts all the time. I was thinking about my mother in many different ways. We hadn't seen or heard from each other since the previous Christmas. I went to my office, had a cup of coffee with my colleagues and became occupied with the urgent work I had planned for that day. Throughout the day, my inner thoughts were overwhelmed with thinking about my mom, and I couldn't get her out of my head. I unsuccessfully tried to put it aside, but I finally picked up the phone and called her home number. Since she didn't respond, I thought she had gone to a local store, and I decided to call her again later. And so I did, I called a few times afterwards, but got no response again, so I felt the urge to call her next-door neighbor, Margaret. She told me that my mom was taken to a hospital with a stroke after she had called 911 earlier that morning. I was speechless.

Luckily, my mom recovered after the stroke; and as for myself, well, I finally realized that we as humans are capable of far more than we are normally aware of. Far more than we were ever told we are, at least in my case. That morning, I had gotten an alert; somehow, I got a pretty direct message that something was about to happen to my mom, but I ignored it. At that time, I couldn't have believed that something like that was even possible. After that day, I learned to trust that inner voice, and I received many different insights which gave me some much-needed break-throughs in my business; I even won a car in local drawing. I was really grateful for that, but that was actually nothing compared to avoiding a plane accident. Some of my friend didn't believe me when I told them that I supposed to be on that plane, but you know, I really don't care anymore. This is my life and I know perfectly well now what I feel and sense. I don´t want to go into detail, it´s very personal, but what I want to say is that I learned that I have to say YES to my instincts. I learned to be aware of all the different details, feelings, thoughts, sensations, hunches and even dreams; all of them brings us more or less important messages, but it is up to us to be able to recognize and accept them. In the beginning, I was still trying to find the answers - how does it work, where does it come from, how can I sharpen it, who is sending me these messages... Today, I don't think like that anymore; what is important to me is that I stay on course. Regardless of what we may think of it, the important thing is to follow it, no matter what."

Intuition usually follows our natural priorities, and as we are all unique, our intuition also shows itself in very unique ways. We have done our best to make this book a faithful companion to all who are or were on the same path as Susan, so they can become more successful and live a more meaningful life. That's what our project is all about. We try to find answers to the questions that bothered Susan and countless others through the alchemical process of merging science and spirituality. We try to open new doors to understanding the hidden power which we all possess and offer a much deeper insight into intuition than ever before.

What can we learn from Susan's story? Susan perceived her inner guidance, like most people when they reach a certain level of awareness; that is, the time when they are finally ready for it. We can say that human life is divided into three main stages. In the first stage, we are more or less enjoying ourselves and developing mentally and physically. In the second stage, we are occupied with establishing an adequate material existence, while in the third stage, we are moving from survival and material matters to a more spiritual view of life, focused more on finding our inner self, achieving happiness and inner peace. This third stage is when we are most likely to consciously get in touch with our intuition. In a nearly independent manner, we are finally able to start to "get to know ourselves". In this stage, we may find our true calling and purpose more easily if we have already made a connection with our intuition. Intuition can help us improve our decision-making process and lead us to greater prosperity in life.

"I wish I'd had the courage to live a life true to myself, not the life others expected of me." [8] This is the number one most common regret among those people who discover they don't have more than 12 weeks of life remaining.[2] Knowing that you are facing death and that you have no more than a few weeks left in your life is hard to ignore; it's a force which can crush people. All the regrets comes to the surface - it must be one of the most painful things possible. It´s hard to imagine the remorse one can feel over something that you know you should or you shouldn't have done, when you made the wrong choice even though your inner voice was telling you differently . And now, even though you

---

2 Collected by Bronnie Ware, a palliative nurse.

are aware of it, you can't really do anything to change it as your life is almost at the end.

Living in alignment with your intuition will make you feel proud of yourself and will leave you with no regrets at the end. You will be satisfied and calm about the way you've lived your life. Is there anything else that's more important than that?

Tip: When we make a decision, intuition gives us an instant confirmation of whether or not we made the right choice – you have that unique and pleasant feeling of "knowing".

It's not always easy to follow your intuition. But if you want to be successful, if your true intention is to understand yourself and the world around you, if you really want to overcome the obstacles that prevent you from reaching your highest potential and living a full life, you have to get to know yourself, you have to get tuned to your life´s purpose and you have to find your way to your intuition. Hopefully, this book will inspire all you "seekers" and give courage to those who think and act through their heart, because that's the only thing that really matters. And yes, it takes *guts* to follow your gut feeling!

Intuition Throughout History

"All human knowledge thus begins with intuitions, proceeds thence to concepts, and ends with ideas."

—Immanuel Kant

THE WORD *INTUITION* comes from the Latin, *intueri*, which means "to look within". [9] Another interesting thing; if we split the word intuition into the words *in* and *tuition*, we cannot overlook its significance in relation to *inner tuition*, inner teaching. Without a doubt, this word has to do with our inner self.

Intuition can be described in many different ways, such as:

⊃ inner voice
⊃ inner wisdom
⊃ gut feeling[3]
⊃ hunch
⊃ instinct
⊃ sixth sense
⊃ second sight
⊃ premonition

---

3 Is the similarity in pronunciation of the phrases *gut feeling* and *God feeling* just a coincidence?!

⊃ third eye

⊃ inner guidance

⊃ "aha" moment

⊃ extra-sensory perception (ESP[4]), etc.

Although these names are broadly used as synonyms for intuition, each of these terms has a slightly different meaning and may be associated with some other area of competence as well.[5] In spite of this fact, and in order to keep this book as simple as possible, we are going to use them all as meaning more or less the same thing.

Throughout history, Eastern and Western philosophers have studied intuition. According to Plato, for example: "…*intuition is the immediate perceiving of ideas. This may be supernatural intuition or rational intuition. The first is perceiving ideas seen before birth, the second is recollection of knowledge or cognition of ideas in the mind. The aim of intuitive knowledge is the definition of the essence…*" Aristotle, on the other hand, "…*used intuition to formulate the first principles of science or to define the goals of activity… ,There are differences between the types of intuition. First of all, they concern whether the object is natural or supernatural, its intersubjectivity, and the sources of intuitive cognition.*" [10]

"*Confucianism does not proceed along the path of science nor does it subscribe to principles of science. As a mode of thinking, Confucianism is not based on demonstrable proof or evidence (lunzheng). Rather, it relies on intuition (zhijue).*" [11]. Studies on intuition can be also found in Hinduism, Buddhism and Islam.

Another example is Immanuel Kant (1724–1804), the German philosopher who is the central figure in modern philosophy and who stated that "*Intuition and concepts constitute... the elements of all our knowledge, so that neither concepts without an intuition in some way corresponding to them, nor intuition without concepts, can yield knowledge.*" [12] In the literature on mathematical intuition, one can find research papers on, among other topics: (1) **numerical intuition** (Linchevski & Williams, 1999; Raftopoulos, 2002); (2) **geometric intuition** (Piaget & Inhelder, 1963; Fujita, Jones & Yamamoto, 2004); (3) **intuition of infinity** (Fischbein,

---

4 Reception of information without using any of the five physical senses.

5 Instinct, for example, can also be understood as the inherent inclination of a living organism towards a particular complex behavior (hunting, reproduction...) and hence related to a lower level of intuitive phenomena. It is a way of knowing without having been taught, direct knowledge.

Tirosh & Hess, 1979; Tsamir & Tirosh, 2006); and (4) **intuition of probability and combinatorial concepts** (Fischbein & Grossman, 1997; Fischbein & Fischbein, 1997) [13]

Just as has happened in the last few decades, we can expect new facts and explanations of the concept and origins of intuition in the future. This will occur in a variety of different scientific disciplines, such as cognitive science, psychology, modern quantum physics, new biology and so on.

Debunking Intuition Stereotypes

STEREOTYPES ARE BY their very nature a simple, easy way of understanding something much more complex, and for this reason they are widely and quickly spread among people. It's possible to find them in correlation with almost everything and, of course, intuition is not an exception; but the problem is that some stereotypes are simply wrong. We consider it important to address some of these, and they will be discussed under the following subheadings: Intuition is Some Kind of "Voodoo" Thing, Either You are Rational or Intuitive, and Women are More Intuitive than Men.

Intuition Is Some Kind of "Voodoo" Thing

Truth be told, despite growing interest in researching the phenomenon of intuition, it's still unclear where this valuable phenomenon comes from and what is the operating mechanism behind intuition. There are also numerous astounding examples of intuitive power with a mystical, almost divine character, which may in the end even partly justify this stereotype. But this mysterious aspect is only prevalent at first sight, and is largely due to the lack of understanding. As a matter of fact, intuition is just the opposite, it is the most natural and basic human faculty possible. Humans have lost this sensory ability over time, but now we are rediscovering it.

Intuition, synchronicities and coincidences are phenomena which leave people with a deep impression of mysticism, especially when these predict future events or give them a hint about something they could never possibly have known. The lack of understanding is part of a perfect recipe for "voodoo" soup. We believe that, from time to time, everyone has experienced certain situations which leave them with mixed feelings. For example, let´s say you are thinking of someone you haven't heard from in a long time, and in a minute or so you receive a call from that person. Or another example; you are driving a car, and a strange thought suddenly pops into your head and makes you take another direction, and you meet someone very important for you at that time (or even escape from a car accident you would have had).

This is how Victoria Lynn Weston, respected business psychic and intuitive consultant, who has been successfully offering consultations to businesses and individuals for more than two decades now, described her personal experience with intuition, while driving on two different occasions: *"I tend to hear my 'intuitive voice' when there is something negative about to happen —this hasn't happened often. In my twenties, I briefly worked as an Advertising Director for a business magazine. I sensed the female vice president, who was much older, didn't like my style. Ninety days later, I was driving to work and I heard my intuitive voice say, 'Today, you are going to lose your job.' Initially, I shrugged it off, only to learn minutes after I entered my office space that I was no longer needed. Another example was when driving in the city of Atlanta: I got lost and turned into a rough neighborhood, and I heard my intuitive voice say, 'What are you doing here? You need to turn around now!' Seconds later, I was stopped by a police officer who told me to turn around because I was in a heavy crime and drug area."* As Victoria explained, our intuitive voice can surely save us from bad situations and warn us of negative circumstances. *"I believe these things happen not only to guide us, but to help us prepare emotionally for negative news or circumstances, helping us to logically think through a situation."*

These are not Voodoo-like experiences, but profound moments of intuition.

Either You Are Rational or Intuitive

Absolutely not true! Intuitive people are also rational, and vice versa. Those who belong to the category of rational people are also intuitive. In fact, many of the greatest minds in history like Nikola Tesla, Thomas Edison, Albert Einstein, Steve Jobs, Richard Branson,

Elon Musk and many, many others who, because of their professions, should apparently be ranked at the top of the "rational" group, do acknowledge the great potential intuition is offering us and have on one or more occasions clearly stated that it played a huge role in their lives.

> *"In the same way that I tend to make up my mind about people within thirty seconds of meeting them, I also make up my mind about whether a business proposal excites me within about thirty seconds of looking at it. I rely far more on gut instinct than researching huge amounts of statistics."*

—Richard Branson

In general, the classification of the two ways of operating (rational/intuitive) is causing huge damage to individuals *in each of these groups*. It is providing people with an unfounded excuse to remain faithful to only one mode of operating. This way, we are burdened by false boundaries and limits to our development and performance. It may seem to you that at least professionals in the hard sciences think that rationality is the only true way to arrive at conclusions, but you would be surprised at how many of them actually do think differently. Take famous English theoretical physicist and cosmologist Stephen W. Hawking, for example, who was quite aware that new ideas also demand a great measure of intuitiveness: *"There is no prescribed route to follow to arrive at a new idea. You have to make the intuitive leap."*

We agree, one may be more keen on intuitive guidance than rationalism, or the other way around, but that doesn't mean that one doesn't have the inborn capacity to exploit both. Human nature is such that it leads us along the path of continuous development; we are always striving for more, to excel (personally, professionally and spiritually), and from that point of view, suppressing the capacity for intuitive power isn't really a smart thing to do.

Why not apply both aspects in combination, one complementing the other? Successfully dealing with different challenges in all kinds of areas should be based on the proper combination of intuitive and rational activities, such as (1) defining a problem and setting a goal, (2) gathering the relevant facts and information on a given subject, (3) paying attention to many different cues, (4) searching for different insights, (5) capturing an intuitive idea or a hunch, and (6) backing up intuitive ideas and hunches with further studies and research.

Women Are More Intuitive Than Men

> *"So ingrained is the idea of female intuition that it is tempting to think this social stereotype must contain a kernel of truth".*
> *[14]*

False, more or less. Gender doesn't play a big role when speaking about intuition. Stereotypic thinking about sex differences and intuitiveness has provoked many researchers to test that prejudiced assumption and to find out what's the role of sex regarding intuitive predisposition. Without going into details concerning these findings, a number of studies indicated equal intuitiveness in either gender; however, the bottom line is that there is actually a barely noticeable difference in favor of the gentle gender.

We have found in one study[6] which we conducted ourselves among managers in the automotive industry that, on average, women do decide more intuitively (M = 4,0) than men (M = 3,6). Statistically significant differences were noted between the two groups (α < 0,05).

Intuitive decision making according to gender				
		Arithmetic mean	**Standard deviation**	**t**	**Sig.**
Intuitive decision making	Men	3,6	0,7	−2,431	0,021
	Women	4,0	0,6		

But, if women do make more intuitively guided decisions, this still doesn't mean that they are actually more intuitive in their core: they might only have a slightly higher tendency to listen to their inner voice.

---

6 This study was performed among Slovenian managers within the automotive industry in 2013.

This may be due to cultural conditioning. Maybe social preconceptions permit womem to perceive (or to act on their perceptions of) intuition more than men, while men are discouraged from trusting in this "feminine" trait, and so may not even be aware when they DO rely on it.

Another indisputably noticeable tendency that we found in other studies while doing one-on-one interviews for the purpose of writing this book was that women are actually more open about their past intuitive experiences in comparison to men, and report them more frequently. Women are more courageous about sharing their intuitive experiences and they accept them at once, or at least faster than the majority of the men interviewed. In conclusion, we believe that both genders are equally perceptive of intuitive signals, meaning that women are not more intuitive than men, even though they are slightly more willing to accept these signals and consequently more willing to take action accordingly.

Intuition Makes No Sense, or Does It?

"Intuition is something that comes in a flash, and whenever I have relied on intuition, I was right."

—Stjepan Mesic

IN WESTERN SOCIETY, we are mainly raised and taught to be rational, logical and analytical. We are prepared for our lives in a way that leads us to consider only pure facts and to make choices accordingly. We are told that the things that we don't understand have no real value, and it is best to avoid them. Fortunately, we are constantly alerted by numerous amazing people from many different areas of life that there is something more than just the rational side of life. Looking back, we may say that the majority of the real "breakthrough ideas" in history were purely intuitive and often made absolutely no sense to their contemporaries, because of the very unique nature of intuition, which is future-oriented, directed toward long-term success.

Intuition is constantly in touch with us, or more precisely, on the subconscious level, we are always 100 percent in contact with our intuition. In our conscious state of mind, we are incomparably less aware and less able to recognize the intuitive information that we actually do have access to. The strength of our connection with this information only depends on our awareness of it. Our intellect determines both our level of consciousness and our perception, the way we look at the world. Consequently, when we open our mind to new information, it helps us a lot. We instantly get access to increased perception and a better understanding of certain events around us.

Introspection and retrospection are of crucial importance: introspection to better know yourself and retrospection to get another opportunity, a second chance, if you will, to do the introspection after the fact (to look back on what happened once again, or as many times as needed).

When we are struck with an intuitive flash, a certain idea, hunch, inner voice or however we may call it, and if we are trying to understand it only through rational eyes, most often we find ourselves in quite a paradoxical situation. Quite often, our first thoughts are something like, *"This just doesn't make any sense"*. Or does it, we may ask ourselves? Although intuition gives us an incredible and unique feeling of total truth, accompanied with a perfectly peaceful and calm state of the mind, most of the time intuition makes absolutely no sense (to our conscious mind), it's completely illogical and irrational.

But how come something which feels absolutely right makes no sense? This is the veil of mystery that covers intuition – you perceive the veil, you know that there is something behind it, but you can't really see through it with your own eyes. You feel it, it's that familiar sensation of knowing without knowing. Let's try to explain this further with a very simple example from our everyday lives; most of us have been in the following situation (maybe some of you are at this very moment). Imagine that you are in a relationship with a partner who meets all of your criteria. You are even deeply in love with that person, but somehow you can feel that this relationship is not going to be what you are expecting it to be in the long term. Right now, you are not able to see through your rational eyes what the reasons for that are and why you feel that way (you just have this odd feeling in your gut, this tingling…). If you look at that particular intuitive insight and try to analyze it, you often find that it makes absolutely no sense. For obvious reasons, just the thought that this relationship might not be promising can absolutely unbalance you, it can even trigger hatred towards these thoughts. But after a certain time, when things starts to take place and prove that your feeling was correct, reasons slowly come to mind, and finally you discover what you have known to be true from the very beginning. Thoughts, feelings and images all come together; now you can connect the dots, and finally you can see the whole story very clearly.

Most of the time, intuition resides outside of our rational perspective, but as we saw in this example, and as you will be able to notice in many others that are still to be revealed in coming pages and chapters, it may provide exceptional assistance if implemented into our decision-making process.

Boris Vene, best-selling author, one of the leading authorities in the fields of holistic health[7], leadership, motivation, communication and development of human potential (also a dear friend of ours), revealed to us how he used one of his intuitive flashes (which he fortunately managed to recognize instantly) to prepare a very special health program that resulted in unimaginable success. This example also nicely depicts the very essence of intuition. For more than a decade, Vene has been adhering to a special program that includes ten different health-maintenance protocols. Not only did these protocols literally "raise him from the dead" (after a severe illness and a doctor's prediction that he might have only half a year left to his life), but they also helped him to maintain his youth, drastically increase his level of energy, relieve stress immediately and offer him other beneficial effects. With all the activities he has been performing for his clients, he actually never thought of offering this complete program to the public. But then the intuitive insight struck him like a bolt of lightning. *"After the intuitive impulse, I immediately got down to work. I broke down the elements, created the modules and finished the program which I named "The Body Reset". People literally grabbed it; in fact, the number of applications exceeded the program's capacity by exactly 300%, it was a huge success and we need to repeat it four times in a row. But the greatest success was still to be seen later. Carefully documented testimonials showed that the desired effect was achieved in all 100% of the participants - which is a unique record for the health area."* As Vene explains, from the intuitive impulse that can show us a new vision of the future, we can continuously draw enormous amounts of power,

---

7 His latest book is called *Zdravje je v nas* (roughly translated as *We Control Our Health*) and is co-authored with his long-time collaborator, Nikola Grubisa (as are most of his other works).

About Vene and Grubisa's best-selling book, *The Millionaire Mindset*, the famous Dr. Joe Vitale wrote: *"...It was like the best of every business and self-help book I had ever seen while still being entirely fresh, new, inspiring, and practical..."*

energy, inspiration and motivation throughout our entire journey through life. Without that foundation, to which we can occasionally return, it's very difficult to maintain our motivation for realizing the goals we set. If we don't have that, it is possible that every effort will turn into a nightmare. Yet people keep insisting on continuing this kind of destructive situation, no longer because of the joyful expectation and desire they feel, but rather due to their own stubbornness and because they want to prove something.

Intuition can help us to read people's true intentions and even to see people's true nature (our own or others); it can help us to detect a possible trouble spot or help us come up with a new solution to a vexing problem.

Tip: You should not allow your logic to completely override your intuition, not even when you haven't any solid reason for trusting your intuition at all.

Trusting Intuition Takes Courage

"You can never cross the ocean until you have the courage to lose sight of the shore."

—Christopher Columbus

ABSOLUTELY THE TOUGHEST part of the "process" is to trust your intuition. Many people report that they do "receive" intuitive signals, but not so many take action accordingly. How many times have you preferred to listen to the advice of others (your friends, family, colleagues...) instead of following your own gut reaction? How many times have you done something without that joyful expectation, just because others expected you to do so (or maybe because you just felt that way), but it was not your true desire? How often have you been struck by a strong inner message to avoid someone or something, but you still kept heading toward them and later deeply regretted it? How often did you absolutely know that something would happen, but did nothing to prevent it?

Imagine for a moment, that you feel you need to tell your boss something like, "*We are going in the wrong direction, I believe we should do this and that instead,*" or to say to your loving partner, "*I don't know why, but I have an odd feeling about us, can we please talk about it?*" Yes, it takes courage to follow your intuition! In many cases, it's not easy to understand what our intuition is saying to us and we are unable to interpret it in a way that we can fully understand it (at least, at that moment), but it's absolutely necessary to be aware of the fact that it is your intuition which is always correct, and you should find the courage to follow it in order to live a blissful life. This is easier said than done, but if you have a desire to change, you will also find the strength to build up your courage.

John Bramblitt, a blind painter told us, *"One of the things that I tell people in my workshops is that it's very important to learn how to accept intuition. Because that's the hardest thing to do, but also very important. It's important to know that anything you do is fine, you get that feeling of "right" and everything is flowing in the right way. Soon you get an overall feeling that you can't do any wrong."*[8]

How to fully develop courage is still a real "million-dollar question", but what we have found is that a very important part of the process is to dedicate some time and energy to investigating and analyzing your own past experiences with regard to intuition, so you can learn to trust it.

A very simple method, which we have named the *APE method*, might help you a great deal with this. The abbreviation "APE" stands for "Analyzing Past Experiences", and all you need to do is to follow three simple steps: (1) keep your own intuitive diary, (2) retrospect (recall relevant moments from your life) and (3) find patterns from your own past.[9]

Another practical and valuable recommendation in developing the courage to follow your intuition is to take full responsibility for your decisions and, eventually, for your life. Regardless of the situation you are in right now and the circumstances, no matter what your background and education is, etc., each one of us needs to accept the fact that our life is our own personal responsibility – no one is responsible for your life and your choices but you. There are really no wrong decisions, only our unique way of getting through life, of achieving our personal best. It doesn't matter how many times we make what seem like wrong decisions as long as we are moving forward and learning along the way. Matty Mulins, American rock musician, once said: *"The only person you should try to be better than is the person you were yesterday."* [15]

---

8 We discuss the connection betwen intuiton and blindness in the chapter "The Role of Intuition in Blindness".

9 More details on registering intuitive experiences will be covered in the chapter entitled "An Intuitive Diary Allows Deeper Retrospection and Insights".

We must keep sharpening our intuition and keep getting familiar with our inner being, keep improving – really, that's all that matters. The only competition we have is with ourselves; think about this, and remember the words of Zenkei Shibayama, Japanese Rinzai[10] who was the head abbot of the entire Nanzenji Organization, overseeing the administration of over five hundred temples and a significant contributor to the establishment of Zen Buddhism in America: *"A flower does not think of competing with the flower next to it. It just blooms."* This is a very powerful and enlightening concept.

It's important to be aware that, no matter how much you have developed in following your intuition, some kind of uncertainty is almost always to be expected. The *risk feeling* before deciding to actually act according to your intuitive insight will be present, and this is completely normal.

Self-observation (Body, Mind and Spirit)

> *The centre that I cannot find*
> *Is known to my unconscious Mind;*
> *I have no reason to despair*
> *Because I am already there.*

> —W.H. Auden

One of the most important aspects when speaking of tapping into intuition is self-observation and understanding that everything is going on within you. Every experience and sensation is happening inside of you, never outside; the activities of the outer world can only act as stimuli, but the experience itself is always happening within.

Sadhguru (Jaggi Vasudev), Indian yogi, mystic and founder of the Isha Foundation , a volunteer-run, international non-profit organization dedicated to cultivating human potential, said that we may be stimulated by external situations, but that the source is always within. *'Pain or pleasure, joy or misery, agony or ecstasy, happens only inside you. Right now, you are holding a book. Where do you see the book? Use your finger and point to where you see it. Do you think the image is outside you? Think again. You remember how it works? The light is falling upon the book, reflecting, going into the lens of your eyes, and is projected as an inverted image on your retina—you know*

---

10 Rinzai is the Japanese name of a school of Zen Buddhism.

the whole story. So, you are actually seeing the book within yourself. Where do you see the whole world? Again, within yourself. If someone touches your hand right now, you may think you are experiencing their hand, but the fact of the matter is you are only experiencing the sensations in your own hand. The whole experience is contained within. All human experience is one hundred percent self-created." [16] *With that said, there are three sub-aspects you need to pay attention to: your body, mind and spirit. These will help you to recognize, improve and develop your intuition.*

"Your amicable words mean nothing if your body seems to be saying something different."

—James Borg

Intuition can reveal itself on a physical level, through different body cues or body sensations. Physical cues, or what's going on with your own body, is almost a palpable aspect of this super power. Your stomach hurts, you get indigestion, cold or sweating hands or feet, tension in the body, headache, a pounding in the head, an electric zing, chills up the spine – these are some of the many possible physical messages that occur. The body's signals are in many cases (but not always) accompanied by certain intuitive insights or intuitive flashes.

An interesting example was shared with us by children's author and screenwriter Lois Wickstrom in an interview we did with her: *"I'm working on a screenplay called Mr. Barsin's Toy Store. A character who wants to kill dragons simply popped into my head. She is now an important character in the story, even though she was never part of the original outline. I'm re-doing the outline to see where she contributes to the story. This sort of thing happens at random. Many stories happen with unexpected characters or events or scenes. The fact that they do happen is part of the fun of intuitive writing."*

While in a relaxed state, when our mental chatter is at a lower volume, we are more receptive of intuitive flashes. One of the authors, Ivan Erenda, once had the following experience: *"One Saturday morning, I was driving from a country house to the center of a town in which I had lived for almost three years, when suddenly I had a thought which seemed completely out of context - I had never had any bad experience with the police, like getting a speeding ticket. This thought seemed so strange to me that I took it as a sign that I should instantly decrease the speed of my driving, and after a few moments, I noticed a police patrol measuring my speed with their radar pistol."*

The same principle that applies to our bodies and minds also applies to our spiritual insight. We may perceive a sign or message during dedicated spiritual practice: for example, it may come as a warning; or on the contrary, as a deep feeling of rightness when we feel an unstoppable urge to do something.

PART I

II. Understanding Intuition

"I think that humans possess many more abilities than we think they possess. It's not just what we can see, smell, taste, touch or hear: we are capable of much more. I think our body is only able to detect one small part of reality."

—Riccardo Illy

WHAT IS INTUITION? Does it really work, and if so, why and how? There has always been a huge interest in this topic, and based on numerous scientific works as well as other less verifiable explanations that have been published both recently and throughout history, we can most certainly say that intuition exists and certainly works. But the answers to why, how and what mechanisms are in operation are more complex and require a deeper understanding. While there are many different theories, and an even greater variety of definitions for this phenomenon, we are still unable to reach a clear scientific answer to these basic questions. Every scientific and non-scientific school explains this matter more or less differently; and of course, everyone defends their own point of view. Regardless of the fact that a consensus has not been reached concerning exactly what intuition is, the bottom line is that we can say that it is the ability to acquire knowledge without rationally understanding how this knowledge was acquired. Many agree that intuition is an inborn gift we all possess; furthermore, it is also more or less agreed that this powerful force within us can help us improve our decision-making process and lead us to greater prosperity in life.

Intuition is the power or faculty for attaining direct knowledge or cognition without evident rational thought and inference. And that's what makes intuition one of the most mysterious psychic experiences sensation that occur within us, right next to phenomena such as telepathy[11], psychokinesis[12], remote viewing[13], out-of-body experiences[14] and others. Intuition is also the most common of all of these phenomena.

Victoria Lynn Weston, recognized intuitive/psychic consultant, described to us her view on intuition: *"Intuition tells us, 'Go,' or 'Don't go, I have a feeling about something.' Intuition is our sixth sense; it is knowing without facts or logic. It is also an element of ESP. Parapsychologists use ESP (extra sensory perception) as an umbrella term that includes intuition, mental telepathy, clairvoyance, and precognition."* Victoria also confided to us about her childhood intuitive experiences: *"For myself, I became aware of knowing when events would happen. At the age of 9, I had a premonition that my uncle was going to die unexpectedly. Shortly after his death, I had the ability to know what family members were going to say before they spoke. During dinner, I knew what they were thinking and told them, often finishing their thoughts/sentences before they did."*

One thing that keeps intuition on the edge of science is the fact that it's extremely difficult to prove scientifically. The nature of evidence for intuition is highly subjective, and for that reason it does not meet all the necessary criteria of scientific research. But nevertheless, as we shall discuss in coming chapters, there are some serious studies which are confirming its existence with great credibility. Many people consciously or unconsciously know that "there is something to this", and therefore the number of researchers who keep on "digging"

---

11 Telepathy is a way of communicating thoughts directly from one person's mind to another person's mind without using words or signals. [140]
12 Psychokinesis is movement of physical objects by the mind without use of physical means. [141]
13 Remote viewing is a mental faculty that allows a perceiver (a "viewer") to describe or give details about a target that is inaccessible to normal senses due to distance, time, or shielding. [142]
14 Out-of-body experience typically involves a feeling of floating outside one's body and, in some cases, the feeling of perceiving one's physical body as if from a place outside of this body. [143]

and researching in this direction is increasing. There was a period in our history when we believed that the Earth was in the very center of our universe; or during the Middle Ages, both scholars and uneducated people believed the Earth to be flat. In more recent times, many other "myths" have been proven by science to actually be "truths", but they could only be proven now, with advanced technology and interdisciplinary knowledge.

It is only a question of time before some of the newest technologies or methods will furnish all the necessary requirements of proof and provide indisputable evidence for demystifying intuition, too.

Remember how many times you have caught yourself asking: "Why didn't I listen to what my 'gut feeling' was telling me?!"

Tip: Even though we might not fully understand our intuition, we should pay attention to it and never dismiss it.

Where Does Intuition Come From?

"Intuition functions in a quantum leap."

—Osho

THE STRAIGHTEST AND most honest answer would be: "No one knows"! But, resuming the results of past studies, we may consider the three major concepts about the origins of intuition to be: (1) the subconscious mind, (2) a collective field of consciousness, or (3) a higher power. Let's briefly review each of these.

The Subconscious Mind

The fact is that we are only aware of a small percentage of what's going on in our brain[15]. It is estimated that, through the sensory system of the human body, the brain gets eleven million different bits of information each second, which is far more than the amount of information we are able to handle. We can process only between sixteen and fifty bits per second [17].

Thus, the majority of the hard work of collecting, sorting and processing data, and even the making of countless different daily

---

15 Scientists don't share the same opinion about the percentage of the human brain that we use, but most frequently, the data found in relevant literature is from 5 to 10%.

decisions, is a function of our subconscious. The main role of the subconscious mind is to process huge amounts of gathered information in order to form our judgments and decisions, and at the same time to protect our conscious mind from collapsing under such massive amounts of information.

This kind of data-processing relationship is happening all the time, when we are awake or even when we are asleep. The subconscious perceives the majority of this information and does all the "hard" work. We can understand our subconscious to be like a giant recording machine with a fascinating capacity and astonishing speed for making decisions. When needed, our subconscious mind combines all our past experiences, diverse knowledge, multiple feelings, thoughts, assumptions, pattern recognition, dreams and many other types of information and generates something which we can call an intuitive flash or hunch. Through this intuitive hunch, formed by our subconscious, our conscious is advised to make the best possible decision at a particular moment. Therefore, for us, it is often absolutely impossible to recognize any logic in these intuitive hunches.

A huge example of the power of our subconscious mind over the body can be seen in the incredible phenomenon of sleepwalking – a combined state of sleep and wakefulness. For instance, various studies of sleepwalking activities show that while sleepwalking, people are able to make certain physical movements which they are not able to do when they are awake. Another interesting thing is that during sleepwalking, people tend to be much faster, more accurate and proficient in their motions, despite the darkness. It seems that darkness becomes an absolutely irrelevant element during sleepwalking.

One of the important roles of the subconscious mind is also to transform "big data" into meaningful information. You can imagine this as being a process through which the subconscious is completing the incomplete data by filling in what's missing and producing the necessary information, which now becomes "readable" and meaningful to our conscious mind. For example, it can complete the missing data and information of spoken language with data and information from highly complex non-verbal communications (facial expressions, especially micro-expressions[16], body language, etc.), by combining

16 Micro-expressions are a special kind of facial expression that occur within only 1/25th of a second and exposes a person's true emotions – they are involuntary and come from conscious suppression or subconscious repression. We can also learn to spot micro-expressions consciously.

those two groups of data into valuable messages that come to us in an intuitive way. Thus, the unconscious mind provides us with numerous "superhuman" services and performs all the hard work for us.

Speaking of "superhuman" capabilities, the real *Superhuman*, Gabriel Dechichi Barbar, multiple Rubik's Cube record holder and the winner of Discovery Channel's *"Superhuman Showdown"*, was pushed further than ever before when he was challenged to solve three Rubic's cubes, blindfolded. And he succeeded, of course. When talking with him about intuition, he entrusted us with his experience and insights regarding this "super–power". For him, intuition is a *natural* process which all people have and which involves a mix of the unconscious and the conscious processing inside our brain. *"When we are consciously, and sometimes emotionally, invested in a problem, it seems that our brain embraces it, and starts processing it in the background, even when we aren't consciously thinking about it. Sometimes it finds an answer and communicates it to us in the form of a gut feeling. I call this intuition."* As he explained further, intuition always comes to him as an unpolarized emotion, not necessarily having to be "good" or "bad", but just different from the other emotions he feels at a particular moment. *"I believe that's the way our subconscious communicate with us… It's like a "genius" who can't talk, so it has to show you what it found."*

One of the most prominent supporters of the belief in the subconscious as the source of intuition is a German psychologist, Dr. Gerd Gigerenzer. *"Gut feelings are tools for an uncertain world. They're not caprice. They are not a sixth sense or God's voice. They are based on lots of experience, an unconscious form of intelligence."* Based on his experience while working with large international companies, about 50% of all decisions made by decision makers in these companies are, in the end, gut decisions.[17] [18]

---

17 We discuss this topic in more detail in the chapter "Intuition in Business – a New Concept of Success"

The human brain is a two-tier system (conscious and unconscious mind) for collecting and processing data and making decisions. Both of these parts are of crucial importance for successful functioning in complex human societies.

Tip: It's important that we keep on developing and stay willing to open ourselves to the input of both parts. Don't allow one to dominate the other. The key to successfully tuning into oneself, each other and the environment lies in the full coherence of both parts of the mind.

The Collective Field

"There is no place in this new kind of physics both for the field and matter, for the field is the only reality."

—Albert Einstein

Is it true that everything is connected in a single, illusive field? Does everything, from the smallest particles to the galaxies, vibrate in the subtle and mysterious quantum field? If an invisible universal energy exists, what kind of energy is it and where does it come from? Is the brain the only place where data and knowledge are stored, and if so, how come so many great discoveries appeared at the same time but in different locations? How can we know something that we have never learned or experienced? How can a mother know when her child is in danger, and what is the role of the human heart? What happens with our consciousness when we die?

Some of the new scientific findings of the past few decades have turned science fiction into reality. Completely new areas of knowledge have been opened up, and our understanding of some of the most fundamental aspects of our lives is being radically changed. New discoveries, especially in the field of quantum physics, provoke some completely new explanations of the world that we live in. This transformational process is probably going to continue at a very fast pace through the coming years and decades.

Sir Isaac Newton's ideas of isolated and unconnected particles is slowly being replaced by the theory in which everyone and everything is connected by a universal energy field, which is the essential foundation of all matter – just as it was believed in philosophy, religion and science for thousands and thousands of years before Newton. The findings of quantum physics indicate that, at the quantum level, we are all made of the same basic substance – quantum energy, and that this energy connects everyone with everything else in the universe. Through this invisible quantum energy, which forms a subtle net or matrix, we are able to constantly exchange information through thoughts, feelings and other cognitive functions. It could be said that we are "plugged in" to the universe. With our conscious mind, we are not able to recognize most of the information that we receive, but it still makes the necessary impact on our perception system and consequently results in our intuitive performance and the conscious actions that follow this sequence of events. This might explain the synchronicity of many important discoveries concerning the same problem (sometimes even in the same way) but made independently by different scientists in different parts of the world.

One of the most illustrative examples of drawing inspiration and "knowledge" from the collective field is the Newton-Leibniz formula, also known as the "fundamental theorem of calculus". We are speaking about one of the most widely known mathematical formulas, which represents the very foundation of modern mathematics. It was discovered simultaneously and independently by Isaac Newton and Gottfried Wilhelm Leibniz. Since it was impossible to judge who was the first to actually discover this formula, it was named after both of them. Another example would be the Saussure–Fortunatov law. Linguists Filipp Fedorovich Fortunatov and Ferdinand de Saussure formulated this law of intonation completely independently of each other [19]. Elisha Gray and Alexander Graham Bell both worked independently on discovering the phone and even filed their patents for the discovery on the very same day. Hans von Ohain (1939), Secondo Campini (1940) and Frank Whittle (1941) independently invented the jet engine. Takaaki Kajita and Arthur B. McDonald independently proved that neutrinos have mass and shared the 2015 Nobel Prize in Physics [20].

We had the opportunity to talk to Jain 108, international lecturer, author and researcher of vedic mathematics and sacred geometry, who also happens to be "the first person ever to have adopted a numerical surname". 108 told us about his experience with regard to different intuitive insights in mathematics, geometry and physics derived from the "collective field". *"I find when a great piece of knowledge comes down to Earth through someone like an Einstein, it actually goes to five or six people. That transmission of knowledge gets sent to many minds, it's never to one individual, I believe. Because I keep meeting people, gypsies and travelers and scholars that come to Australia, and they could be from Germany or the USA, and as we start talking we realize that we have received the same information in the same year, it could be even on the same day. So bit by bit, [we discover] one piece in the puzzle, that we all are connected, and the knowledge comes to many, many people."* In the same way, he explained, he may have been intuitively writing something, not being aware that it was already in a book by another author. And further, he says that it took him quite a few years to realize that he always possessed this knowledge, it's nothing really new, it's actually ancient knowledge in his opinion. He believes that we do not discover anything, we just rediscover formulas and patterns. *"When I rediscover something for myself, it gives me a beautiful feeling to know that I'm sort of connected."*

Many other similar cases exist, but we don't think it's necessary to extend the list further since these few examples are already sufficient to show a clear pattern. This kind of synchronicity can be observed throughout our history and clearly supports the theory that, at certain times, certain information is available to us and if we are able to get aligned with the field which contains them, we can receive them intuitively.

The theory that the contents of our minds and even our memories themselves are not stored in the brain but in some kind of web of information in space was proposed by physicists Carl Pribram and Walter Schemp. They postulate that when we need this information, we simply access it. [21]

"I think that everything that exists and all human beings are joined to one another with some kind of common energy. This energy connects all of us and links everyone within this existence. I believe that anyone can actually access information through intuition, but in order to do that, they need to get away from materialism

and strenghthen the spiritual side in them. Any human being, regardless of their faith and ideology (he could even be an atheist), as long as he is working on his spirituality, can awaken this faculty in himself, he can actually tap into this energy," the Nobel Peace Prize winner, Dr. Shirin Ebadi, confided to us when we were talking to her about how intuition functions. Dr. Ebadi is an Iranian laywer, former judge and human rights activist who was awarded the Nobel Peace Prize for her significant and pioneering efforts for democracy and human rights (especially in the field of the rights of women and children). She became the first Iranian and the first Muslim woman to receive the prize (2003), and she was listed by Forbes magazine as one of the "100 most powerful women in the world". She lived in Tehran, but she has been in exile since 2009.

She kindly and generously open the door to some very private and painful moments of her life, and explained to us how strong her "gut feeling" was at that time. She was about to fly to Spain for a three-day seminar in June 2009, *"and I had actually booked a flight to return after those three days. I remember when a taxi came to pick me up at my home and give me a ride to the airport, and my husband came with me to the door to say goodbye. It was about midnight, and I remember that suddenly I got a very strong and precise feeling that I would never return to my home again. This intuition, this gut feeling in me was so strong that I turned around, opened a drawer and to took out my US Green Card. My husband said to me, 'Oh, but you are only going away for three days in Spain, why are you taking a US Green Card with you?' And it was because I was so worried and I felt that I might need my Green Card. Unfortunately, my intuition proved to be correct, I can no longer return to Iran for political reasons, and also my husband and I have been separated since."*

For thousands of years, the wisdom of ancient civilizations from all over the world included the knowledge that space itself is not empty, but rather that it is full of connective energy. We are all interconnected, to each other, to nature around us and to the universe itself. Throughout different periods during human history, the importance of communicating beyond the five physical senses (taste, sight, touch, smell, and sound) was more or less widely accepted. People believed that a human being is far more than just a very complicated machine, and that we have a soul which is somehow able to provide us with experiences that our physical senses are not capable of. They *knew* that we are all part of the same unified whole, and that we have a much greater potential than we normally use or are even aware of.

They believed in prophecy, necromancy[18] and the supernatural[19] ; they were scientists, priests and occultists all rolled into one, and used this mixture of knowledge to explain the complexity of Nature.

When speaking about a collective field, we must mention one very familiar name, Lynne McTaggart. The efforts and work of this amazing woman deserve great credit for the worldwide awareness of the field theory. In her book "The Field", she presents a variety of scientific studies, and states that the universe is unified by an interactive field and that there is a quantum connection between the Earth, all living things and this field. *"Some scientists went as far as to suggest that all of our higher cognitive processes result from an interaction with the Field. This kind of constant interaction might account for intuition or creativity - and how ideas come to us in bursts of insight, sometimes in fragments but often as a miraculous whole. An intuitive leap might simply be a sudden coalescence of coherence in the Field."* [22] Furthermore, in her later book, "The Intention Experiment", she discusses how, through the effects of quantum mechanics, this field and the world around us can be influenced by our thoughts; more precisely, by our intentions. Some esoteric philosophies speak of a process of (1) intention (choosing a specific goal), (2) attention (feeding that goal with the energy of our focused thoughts and efforts), and (3) creation (making the goal materialize).

Some Western philosophies which claim to be based on Oriental concepts also refer to the collective field or collective mind by the name "Akashic Records". Supposedly, when ideas come to more than one person, those ideas come from these Akashic Records, where all human ideas and memories are said to be recorded on a non-physical plane. Based on this concept, it can be said that when an idea comes into our mind, we are not discovering something new, we are remembering it (for example, Columbus believing that there was a westward path to the East may have been based on memories of older civilizations, and not a new idea originating in his mind alone). Edgar Cayce and other clairvoyants may have been given a way to contact these memories in order to orient people concerning forgotten experiences in past lives.

---

18 Process of communicating with the dead, especially in order to anticipate and predict the future.
19 Phenomena which lie beyond the commonly understood limits of nature.

A Higher Power

*"It is a highly personal and subjective experience, possible only
if we are searching for greater truths about ourselves and God."*

—Jimmy Carter

Another theory about the source of intuition is based on the hypothesis that intuitive insights come from a God, Spirit Guides or that they represent some sort of communication with our non-physical part - our Soul. In this theory, intuition is understood as being some kind of "direct message" from the so-called Higher Self, Authentic Self, Inner Being and so on. That theory explains human consciousness as the spirit of God. By praying, we are getting in contact with a Divinity - our inner spirit, which is talking back to us in the only way we can understand, revealing knowledge beyond logic and helping us to make correct decisions about difficult problems. Because of its religious aspects and thousands of years of tradition, this explanation of the intuitive mechanism is very widespread.

Interestingly, even though today we perceive an abyss between science and religion, with this new knowledge and awareness, the boundaries between these two areas may slowly become less and less. Discoveries in the last decade have proposed new hypotheses about God and the very nature of the universe. *"Science without religion is lame; religion without science is blind,"* said Albert Einstein, who later in life was convinced that there must be some form of intelligence behind the universe. Many researchers in the hard sciences believe in God or some higher intelligence, or have a greater or lesser tendency to explore spirituality and seek esoteric knowledge. Many scientists today also state that there is no conflict between their faith and their scientific work. An older example, Sir Isaac Newton, the well-known physicist and mathematician, has left behind many works that would now be classified as occult studies, discussing alchemy and theology.

Victoria Lynn Weston believes that intuition is another level of our self, our soul, talking to us. She told us: *"Intuition, those flashes of insight that seem to come out of nowhere, those gut instincts, those voices you hear when you're taking a shower or driving to work, is your physical self communicating with your soul. Your soul speaks to you in an intuitive voice to guide and assist you in life. Our intuitive voice often strikes when we are faced with danger, giving us strength and guid us out of danger. We often hear of individual experiences, like: 'I had no idea where I came up with the idea, what road to turn onto to avoid a car accident, canceling an air flight only to hear that the plane was in danger or delayed.' "*

An important aspect of the theory that intuition comes from a Higher Power is the fact that intuitive messages are in most cases accompanied by a divine feeling of total harmony and a sense of energy. This leaves us with a strong feeling of the presence of something with far greater power than that of any human. Charles Hard Townes, the founder of laser science and Nobel laureate in physics, replied to the inquiry, "What do you think about the existence of God?" with the following answer: *"I strongly believe in the existence of God, based on intuition, observation, logic, and also scientific knowledge."* [23] Sources say that Gregor Mendel, called "the father of modern genetics", Galileo Galilei, called "the father of modern physics" and even Rene Descartes, called "the father of modern Western philosophy", as well as Guglielmo Marconi, Johannes Kepler, Michael Faraday, Nicholas Copernicus, Robert Boyle, and many others, all believed in God. [24]

And last, but not least, one of the questions we asked in our numerous one-on-one interviews (which were conducted specifically for the purpose of writing this book) was also about the origin of intuition: *"Where does intuition come from?"* The statistics showed that as much as 37% of those interviewed answered that intuition comes from God. Being intuitive might also mean being able to hear God's words. Communication with God isn't necessarily one-sided.

Lisa Nichols is one of the world's most-requested motivational speakers, a media personality and New York Times bestselling author, as well as the founder and CEO of a global personal-development company whose world-wide platform has reached and served nearly 30 million people. She believes in her intuition more than anything else. She was able to transform herself from a struggling single mom on public assistance to a millionaire entrepreneur, and become an inspiration for millions of people around the world. Lisa was also one of the interviewees in the outstanding movie, *The Secret*. We talked to her about her experience with intuition, and she shared quite a few amazing insights. *'I believe that our intuition is our internal GPS system, or as I nick-named it, my internal "God Placement System". And my intuition is that part of me that's always whispering in my ear and reminding me that, regardless of my skill set, regardless of my bank account balance, regardless of my status, of my relationships, my intuition is giving me insight of what I love, what I adore, what I appreciate and what I really want to happen in my life."*

How to Distinguish Intuition
from Our Monkey Mind

VEN PEOPLE WHO live hand–in–hand with intuition are constantly developing their ability to recognize and tune in to this gift. It's not always easy to distinguish whether a certain *message* is a result of intuitive insight or misleading mental chatter. This distinction is of crucial importance: we cannot stress enough how important it is to identify and separate these two, right from the very first phase of learning how to use your intuition. Well, the good news is that everyone can learn to do this. On numerous occasions, people have told us how they followed their "inner voice" but found out it was misleading them. In many cases, when these same people learned to distinguish between their true inner voice – intuition – and their mental chatter, they quite rarely fell into this trap again, and their lives seemed to improve significantly. As we are all unique and different, our way of identifying our intuition is also very individualized and personal.

The overwhelming and constant chatter of our mind, which Zen Buddhists refer to as our "monkey mind", is quite often a big distraction that interrupts and distorts the true inner voice. This is an exemplary animal metaphor, representing the fact that our minds are in constant motion – like monkeys that are jumping from one tree branch to another with nonstop chattering. "Monkey mind" refers to our conscious mind, which is *programmed* to be rational and *"designed to keep score, to keep track, to take notice of what worked and what did not worked... She (intuition) is talking to all of us, but some of us have our intuitive volume turned so low, because the chatter in our head is so high, that intuition can't get through,"* as Lisa Nichols says. Our mind is constantly provoking fear, both real and imaginary, recalling hurtful experiences from the past, projecting them into the future, judging the present and keeping us entrapped with "what if" scenarios. Monkey mind doesn't leave us any space to slow down, to feel, and doesn't encourage a relaxed, non-stressful state of mind, which is of great importance for getting in touch with our intuition. If you learn to tell the difference between your intuitive communication voice and your mental chatter, then you are much closer to living a more meaningful and successful life.

"Intuitive communication and your mental chatter are very, very different, and you have to be still enough to feel and hear yourself. My intuitive guidance is always pointing to my highest calling and my highest contribution. My intuitive guidance is always encouraging me or commanding me to expand myself - to step into the next version of me. My intuitive calling is always moving me forward and expanding me. My mental chatter on the other hand is always questioning how it will work, will it even work, what if it doesn't work, and you have to push that mental chatter away in order to hear your intuition. Therefore, we find there is always an internal struggle going on, because the chattering mind wants to have the dominant space, so the only way to deal with that noisy chatter would be to say to your mind, "I hear you, I feel your presence, and now I'm gonna move you out of the way," then go back to listening to your intuition, go back to your growth, the expansion, and ask, "What's my calling, how do you want me to serve" and other breakthrough questions," as Lisa Nichols very nicely explains.

Due to mental chatter, it is very important to know how to relax and let go. And another important thing is to know ourselves, to establish a connection with our true self and put away the ego, with all its fear, judging and other inhibitors of intuition.

It is of the highest importance to discern between the voice of intuition and other voices like beliefs, doubts, fears, and conditioned thinking.

Tip: Search for signs such as an increased sense of being enlivened and energized, accompanied by inner peace – these are considered to be true indicators of the presence of intuition.

Generally speaking, when we are trying to distinguish whether the signals we receive are intuition or not, there are two basic laws of nature which are of great assistance; (1) the Law of Individuality and (2) the Law of Change.

The Law of Individuality. According to the most recent numbers on the current world population, there are approximately 7.5 billion people living in the world right now [20] [25]; yet, we can't find any two who are exactly alike. Although we were "made" according to the same "model" and are seemingly similar in terms of our body features, that's just a superficial observation. Each and every one of us has our own unique external and internal physical features. And there is also another unique world, the world of our inner self - each and every one of us has our own unique personality, character and perceptions of the world around us, and we all perceive and understand ourselves differently. Each and every one of us is a completely unique individual, and as such, each of us also has a completely unique way of communicating with our intuition. This is very important to know; you should not blindly follow the "rules" you read or hear somewhere, or be disappointed if they don't work for you. It just means that you are unique and special in terms of your inner world, too.

From the extensive research, numerous interviews and the many stories and testimonials we have received in regards to intuitive phenomena, we can conclude that human access to intuition is very hard to model in a way that suits everyone – no single process works

---

20 The data refers to March, 2017.

for all cases. We will present a pretty long list of intuitive signs (you'll find it at the end of this chapter) that may work just perfectly for you, but due to the law of individuality, you might have to find your own recognition signs, too. The best advice we can give is to get in tune with yourself and find your own way of identifying your intuition.

We can use one's path to enlightenment as an example. There are many gurus out there, explaining "how to reach enlightenment", but none of them can ever give you the exact steps, a complete and full instruction manual on exactly how to achieve it. It's not that they wouldn't want to give it to you, they just can't, because enlightenment happens only through each individual's unique experience. Thus, these spiritual teachers can only share their own experiences, which doesn't necessary lead YOU to the light. They open the door, but it is you who needs to step through it and see what's on the other side; they can show you the road and teach you about the rules and signs on the road, but you will have to go on the journey yourself. You can only reach enlightenment by knowing yourself better and better, through your own experience. The same is true with intuition.

The Law of Change. Due to our uniqueness, we are each changing and developing ourselves in different ways and with different dynamics. Already some 500 years B.C., a philosopher by the name of Heraclitus of Ephesus discussed ever-present change as being the fundamental essence of the universe. As he stated in the famous saying:

> *"No man ever steps in the same river twice, for it's not the same river and he's not the same man."*

> —Heraclitus of Ephesus

The continuous flow of the river always renews itself, and in the same way, we are today different from what we were yesterday. We can resume Heraclitus´ philosophy in just two words which you already know very well - *panta rhei*. Everything flows; everything is in constant change, from the smallest grain of sand to the biggest stars in our universe. We are reinventing ourselves over and over again. As with the law of individuality, the law of change is also highly influential in your personal experience with intuition. We are subject to constant change, and because of this, we think, act, feel and perceive things differently today from the way we did yesterday - and from the way we will tomorrow. The techniques we used in the past may not work as well for us in the future, so we have to constantly search and develop new ways of doing things. The good news is that the changes we are subject to exist because we continue to grow, personally, professionally and spiritually, every hour of every day.

To get back to the question of how to distinguish intuition from the mind's chatter, we have listed below some of the most common ways through which the *true* intuitive voice reaches us.

Here are some of the ways you may recognize your intuition:

- usually it's something that comes into your mind before other ideas, like a strong first impression or feeling;
- it appears rapidly and all of a sudden, without any effort on your part, and you are not able to know how you know this thing, you just know that you do;
- an intuitive idea has a character of discontinuity (it surges forth with a leap, unexpectedly, beyond your control) [26];
- it's a very quiet and peaceful way of knowing, tolerant and persistent, leaving you with absolutely no doubts;
- it's not connected to any kind of fear; you feel calm and peaceful about your decision or idea, even though your rational mind *thinks* you shouldn't be feeling like that – you still continue to perceive a pleasant, fearless feeling of correctness;
- you feel completely connected to yourself, the universe and to the present moment;
- you feel deep relief and peacefulness, in many cases even an enthusiastic feeling or a feeling of being in the flow;
- the intuitive voice always addresses our highest calling, encouraging us to move forward, to expand ourselves, to step into the next version of ourselves;
- intuition comes from "deep inside"; you feel the flow, warmth, from the navel upward, while everything that comes from your mind, arises in your head and proceeds downward.

On the other hand, ideas which do not arise from our intuition most often come from our ego, past experiences and fears. If you pay attention to the signs, you will notice this difference quite easily, and once you've done that, you will immediately feel that you have made a giant leap towards tuning in to your intuition, perceiving its reality faster, easier and with greater confidence. You will become aware that you are now a new, better version of yourself.

The Scientific View toward Intuition

The Definition of Intuition

THE ETYMOLOGICAL ROOTS of the term *intuition* stem from the Latin word *intueri*, which can be translated as "to look within". Many different researchers have conceptualized intuition in a number of different ways [27], and we may say that there exist at least as many definitions as there do researchers. Some of the most significant definitions are gathered in table on the following page.

Authors and definitions of intuition (in alphabetical order) [27]

Source	Definition of intuition
Bastick (1982)	"A powerful human faculty, perhaps the most universal natural ability we possess."
Bowers et al. (1990)	"Intuition is a perception of coherence, at first not consciously represented, but which comes to guide our thoughts toward a 'hunch' or hypothesis. Intuition has two stages: a guiding stage involving an implicit perception of coherence that guides thought, unconsciously, toward a more explicit perception of the coherence in question. By a process of spreading activation, clues that reflect coherence activate relevant associationistic networks, thereby producing a tacit or implicit perception of coherence. A second stage involves integrating into consciousness a plausible representation of the coherence in question; it occurs when sufficient activation has accumulated to cross a threshold of awareness."
Dane and Pratt (2007)	"The defining characteristics of intuitive processing are that: (1) It is non-conscious… it occurs outside of conscious thought. While the outcomes of intuiting and intuitive judgments are clearly accessible to conscious thinking, how one arrives at them is not. (2) As a holistically associative process, it may help to integrate the disparate elements of an ill-defined problem into a coherent perception of how to proceed. For this reason intuitive judgments are said to become more effective relative to rational analysis as a problem becomes increasingly unstructured. (3) It involves a process in which environmental stimuli are matched with some deeply held non-conscious category, pattern or feature. (4) Intuitive processing has speed when compared with the rational decision-making processes."
Dreyfus and Dreyfus (1986)	"Intuition is manifested in the fluent, holistic and situation-sensitive way of dealing with the world."
Jung (1933)	"A psychological function that unconsciously yet meaningfully transmits perceptions, explores the unknown, and senses possibilities which may not be readily apparent."

Miller and Ireland (2005)	"Intuition can be conceptualized in two distinct ways: as holistic hunch and as automated expertise. Intuition as holistic hunch corresponds to judgment or choice made through a subconscious synthesis of information drawn from diverse experiences. Here, information stored in memory is subconsciously combined in complex ways to produce judgment or choice that feels right. 'Gut feeling' is often used to describe the final choice. Intuition as automated expertise is less mystical, corresponding to recognition of a familiar situation and the straightforward but partially subconscious application of previous learning related to that situation. This form of intuition develops over time as relevant experience is accumulated in a particular domain."
Polanyi (1964)	"Intuitions are implicitly or tacitly informed by considerations that are not consciously noticed or appreciated."
Reber (1989)	"Intuition may be the direct result of implicit, unconscious learning: through the gradual process of implicit learning, tacit implicit representations emerge that capture environmental regularities and are used in directly coping with the world (without the involvement of any introspective process). Intuition is the end product of this process of unconscious and bottom-up learning, to engage in particular classes of action."
Rowan (1986)	"Intuition is knowledge gained without rational thought. It comes from some stratum of awareness just blow the conscious level and is slippery and elusive. Intuition comes with a feeling of 'almost, but not quite knowing'."
Sadler-Smith and Shefy (2004)	"Intuition is a capacity for attaining direct knowledge or understanding without the apparent intrusion of rational thought or logical inference."
Shirley and Langan-Fox (1996)	"A feeling of knowing with certitude on the basis of inadequate information and without conscious awareness of rational thinking."
Simon (1987)	"Intuitions are – 'analyses frozen into habit'."
Smolensky (1988)	"Intuition has the characteristics of being implicit, inaccessible and holistic. Intuition and skill are not expressible in linguistic forms and constitute a different kind of capacity, reflecting 'sub-symbolic' processing."

Vaughan (1979)	"Knowing without being able to explain how we know. Intuitive experiences have four discrete levels of awareness: physical, which is associated with bodily sensations; emotional, where intuition enters into consciousness through feelings - that is, a vague sense that one is supposed to do something and instances of immediate liking or disliking with no apparent reason; mental, which comes into awareness through images or 'inner vision' - this is an ability to come to accurate conclusions on the basis of insufficient information; and spiritual, which is associated with mystical experience, a holistic understanding of actuality which surpasses rational ways of knowing."
Westcott (1968)	"Intuition involves awareness of things perceived below the threshold of conscious perception."

We may conclude that the reason for the wide variety of definitions is based on the specific research interests and experiences of certain scholars, as well as because of the fact that intuition is an innate competence (ability), which all humans possess in a variety of specific forms and intensities.

When making decisions, people usually rely on their knowledge, "evidence," experiences and conscious reasoning – using available facts and figures to make a decision. Intuition is just the opposite – it's the ability to acquire knowledge without understanding how the knowledge was acquired. We have the capacity of knowing something without actual knowing why it is so. While some speculate that intuition is a sixth sense, we believe quite the opposite; we believe that intuition is actually a primary sense - the first sense, as a matter of fact, because with its dominating insight it offers us a far greater experience than any other known sense, a basis for decision and action. Intuition is able to show us the way, when all other recognized senses only have a secondary function, which is to help us when we are already on that way[21]. Somehow, it seems that human civilization lost the awareness of the importance of intuition and the understanding of how to fully use it to our own benefit. According to legends in several older cultures about Golden Ages in the past and new archeological findings which push the dawn of human existence further and further into the past,

---

21 A very plastic example would be a person who is blind, but his intuition guides him in ways that his eyes could not, and there is of course also a non-physical, spiritual dimension to it, in finding a life path.

one can assume that history has not been a linear progession from a low caveman state to our supposedly advanced civilization of today. Not everyone agrees with this view of history, and this is not the place to discuss this matter in more detail, but we believe it is certainly worth thinking about. It is supposed by some that there was a time when humans had a more complete connection with other levels of reality, both inside and outside themselves, when what are now considered to be "mysterious psychic powers" were seen as pretty much normal abilities, when consciously communicating with beings in other dimensions was a daily experience, when we could judge what was good or bad for us by "seeing" the energy field (for example, to know what medicinal plant would adjust a specific imbalance in us, or what location had the correct energy for us to live there or to give us access to other planes), and so on.

Researching Intuition

"Your vision will become clear only when you can look into your own heart. Who looks outside, dreams; who looks inside, awakes."

—Carl G. Jung

Intuition is amongst the hardiest of bounded rationality's perennials, appearing and re-appearing in various guises from the 1930s to the present day, and has spread to different fields of scientific inquiry (i.e. behavioral, biological, and brain sciences). [28] Intuition has been studied by both Eastern and Western philosophers, such as Plato, Kant and Confucius and can be found in Hinduism, Buddhism and Islam. Some of the extremely negative attitudes towards intuition formed during the history of researching its concepts are still present to this day. And some of the modern philosophers of the mind are still defending the belief that intuition is misleading and that a man should use only pure facts, critical thinking and reasoning. [29] One of these was the famous neurologist and founder of psychoanalysis, Sigmund Freud, who stated: *"There is no other source of knowledge but the intellectual manipulation of carefully verified observation – in fact, what is called research... and no knowledge can be obtained from revelation, intuition or inspiration."* [30]

Still, that didn't stop the wide interest in the phenomenon of intuition, not even that of his close colleague, C. G. Jung, who was considered to be his successor at that time.

The concept of intuition appeared for the first time in scientific articles back in 1916. The article *"How to Learn Easily: Practical Hints on Economical Study"* was published in the *Psychological Review* by George van Ness. Despite the fact that serious research on intuition was started much later, interest in the phenomena of intuition and its potential benefits has been growing ever since. Truly pioneer work was done by famous Swiss psychiatrist and psychoanalyst, Carl Gustav Jung (1875-1961), who is called the "father of analytical psychology". *"In such doubtful matters, where you have to work as a pioneer, you must be able to put some trust in your intuition and follow your feeling even at the risk of going wrong,"* stated Jung, who believed that when an inner situation is not made conscious, it appears from the outside to be fate.

Jung is most recognized as an author of the terms and concepts of collective unconsciousness, archetypes and synchronicity. The term synchronicity[22] has been described by Jung as *"temporally coincident occurrences of acausal events"* [31]. Synchronistic events are acausally connected, that is, they are not connected by the law of cause and effect in a detectable way. Usually, they have a strong symbolic nature, especially at transitional points – important milestone in our lives. Deep emotional experiences may also accompany synchronistic moments, or even appear later, after the event. This is how Jung himself described synchronicity in one simple sentence: *"Synchronicity is the coming together of inner and outer events in a way that cannot be explained by cause and effect and that is meaningful to the observer."*

"Synchronicity is arguably the most recognizable term of analytical psychology, and yet there has been virtually no methodical treatment of it. It is as if most writers are seduced, or perhaps inspired, by the implications of synchronicity, which point towards a non-statistical, non-rational, and for some, a spiritual realm, and therefore leave behind its systematic and scholarly examination". [32]

"We often dream about people from whom we receive a letter by the next post. I have ascertained on several occasions that at the moment when the dream occurred the letter was already lying in the post-office of the addressee." [33]

---

22 The term "synchronicity" was mentioned for the fist time by Jung in the year 1934 (during a lecture at London's Tavistock Clinic), but was only to be published for the first time in 1952.

Another important researcher of intuition was Chester Irving Barnard (1886-1961), an American business executive and public administrator, who was also one of the pioneers in management theory and organizational studies. Barnard was one of the writers who attempted to articulate what intuition is and speculated on its nature and origins, as well as on the circumstances and particular job roles to which it is relevant. He separated mental processes into two distinct categories: (1) logical and (2) non-logical. [28] *"By 'logical processes' I mean conscious thinking which could be expressed in words, or other symbols, that is, reasoning. By 'non-logical processes' I mean those not capable of being expressed in words or as reasoning, which are only made known by a judgment, decision or action."* [34] Barnard's contribution in researching intuition lies especially in the field of the "practical benefits of intuition", since he was a practicing executive for a long time. His findings were compatible with the existing psychological theories, as well as being easily understandable and highly useful. His work anticipated by several decades Polanyi's (1958) and Reber's (1969) theories of tacit forms of knowledge and implicit learning, respectively, as well as perhaps containing intimations of automatic versus controlled processing. [28]

Herbert Alexander Simon (1916-2001) was another great researcher who followed Barnard. He was among the pioneers of some of today's most important scientific areas, like AI (Artificial Intelligence), information processing, decision making, problem solving, organization theory, complex systems and computer simulation in scientific discovery. Among other top-level honors, he was also awarded the Nobel Prize in Economics in 1978 for his contribution to the organizational decision-making process. Simon defined intuition as "analyses frozen into habit"; ergo, intuition explains an aspect of expertise or tacit knowledge which is drawn upon with varying degrees of automatic reaction, depending upon the interaction of the individual and the context. [35]

Many other studies of intuition have been conducted, either as experimental research into intuition or as studies investigating intuition in daily life. Still, both general and specific domains for applying the understanding of intuition are underdeveloped, and there is plenty of room for expanding knowledge in this area in the future.

Neuroscience Increasingly Recognizes Intuition

As time has shown, neuroscience is developing rapidly, especially in the last decade or so. Scientists are constantly discovering new evidence which supports the existence of intuition – the human capacity for knowing without knowing. Although their definitions of intuition may vary and they are still far from a scientific explanation of the phenomenon, at least it is now perfectly clear (even to mainstream science) that this amazing human ability does exist. Intuition works on a non-rational basis: it's about knowing something without a logical explanation of how you know it, therefore it might never be fully explained in scientific terms. Science will only recognize intuition (and many other types of phenomena) when it learns to understand areas of knowledge which still lie outside our present perceptions. Improvements in technological instruments have permitted advances in previously "invisible" physical phenomena (electricity and software, for example), and adequate instruments will appear for studying other "invisible" phenomena, even if WE are those instruments.

One could mistakenly think that this is a unique case, but that's far from true. Just take love, for example; love doesn't necessarily have a rational explanation nor can it be logically explained, yet it does exist; we all know it and we all feel and enjoy it. Intuition and our ability to perceive its signals are becoming more and more evident to science. The more we become aware of its existence, the more we will be able to use and enjoy this incredible inner power which we all possess - just like love.

A very interesting study that clearly demonstrates the existence of intuition as an invisible inner faculty was done using a simple card game where the goal was to win the most money; but what the subjects didn't know was that the game was rigged from the start (one deck was stacked to produce big wins followed by big losses, and another produced small gains with almost no losses). After about 50 cards, the subjects began to feel a hunch about which deck was safer, and after another 30 cards or so, they could give an explanation of the difference between the two decks. But the most amazing thing was that around the tenth card, they unconsciously started to favor the "safer" deck. What is even more fascinating is that measurements indicated that their palms began to perspire slightly every time they reached for the "dangerous" deck (also from around the tenth card on). This clearly indicates that our intuition warns us and guides us towards safety long before our analytical brain can realize what is going on. Other studies have found that trusting your intuition leads to better outcomes when major life decisions are at stake (buying a house, marriage…). And what Kelly Turner found in her own research on Radical Remission cancer survivors, again and again, is that intuitive decisions on future actions save many lives from cancer. [36]

Dr. Joel Pearson, psychologist and neuroscientist, published findings on measuring intuition from studies which he conducted with a team of researchers from the University of New South Wales in Psychological Science, saying, *"This is the first time we have been able to show strong evidence that something like intuition does actually exist… This data suggests that we can use unconscious information in our body or brain to help guide us through life, to enable better decisions, faster decisions, and be more confident in the decisions we make."* During the process of making decisions, participants were exposed to different emotional images that were outside their conscious awareness. Even though being unaware of these images, they were still able to make accurate decision using the very information from these images. Another interesting finding arising from this study is that intuition can be improved with practice and over time. [37]

We have all experienced moments when we made certain decisions based on our gut feeling, and later on it turned out that we couldn't have made a better decision. Usually, we don't have a reasonable explanation for our decision, but we just know this is the right decision and we go for it – just like with love.

While we are on the subject of neuroscience, we would also like to point out the staggering findings within the field of neuroplasticity in recent years. Scientists used to believe that the adult brain is unchangeable and physiologically static, but that's not the case anymore – it is now being shown that our brains can change and develop during the course of our lives. Neuroplasticity examines how and for what reasons the brain changes[23]. In other words, we all have the ability to rewire our own brains through mental training (repetition of a thought or emotion) with which we are able to reinforce a neural pathway. Step by step, these frequent repetitions lead to physical changes in our brains, and consequently to general physical and mental changes. If

---

23 Brains are much more plastic during the early years of our lives, till 6-7 years of age, but a certain level of brain plasticity remains throughout our entire lifetimes.

some part of the brain is missing or damaged, undamaged areas of the brain can take over control of the function that was previously managed by the damaged area.

Multiple ground-breaking studies have been done by Dr. Richard J. Davidson, neuroscientist at the University of Wisconsin, in cooperation with the Dalai Lama, who studied the brains of Buddhist monks during meditation. His findings undoubtedly confirm the human ability to alter the structure of the brain through the practice of different techniques of meditation. [38] Other well-known studies demonstrating experience-based structural alterations in the brain and other positive effects of meditation were led by Dr. Sara Lazar, neuroscientist from Harvard University. In one study, they compared ordinary people (not even meditation teachers) who practice meditation for about 30-40 minutes a day with a demographically matched group who don´t meditate. *"And what we found is this: That there were indeed several regions of the brain that had more gray matter in the meditators compared to the controls. One of the regions I'm going to point out to you is here in the front of the brain, it's the area that's important for working memory and executive decision making."* [39]

Another amazing example is the work of Dr. Edward Taub from the University of Alabama at Birmingham, another pioneer of neuroplasticity. With his colleagues, he developed a special form of behavioral therapy that helps patients regain a significant amount of limb use. In the U.S. alone, there are hundreds of thousands of patients who have experienced a stroke and are facing the consequences of impaired limbs. But through a therapy known as constraint-induced (CI) movement, they are able to develop new neural pathways in the brain so the patients learn to use handicapped limbs again. This therapy consists of restraining the less-affected limb for a certain period of time, during which the more-affected limb is trained and exercised intensively. [40]

Another pioneer in neuroplasticity who is developing methods for putting our brain plasticity to practical use, especially for improving speech, language and reading deficits, is Dr. Michael Merzenich[24]. *"The point is that you can train your brain out of this. A way to think about this is that you can actually re-refine the processing capacity of the machinery* [author´s

---

24 Dr. Michael Merzenich has been awarded the highly recognized 2016 Kavli Prize in Neuroscience for his pioneering work on the brain's plasticity. He also designed clinically proven brain training called BrainHQ.

comment: the brain] *by changing it. Changing it in detail. It takes about 30 hours on the average.''* Their success is enormous: they had accomplished this in about 430,000 kids by the year 2004, when Dr. Merzenich presented the talk. He also pointed out that with the same approach they can also address problems in aging, like declining memory, cognitive functions, postural ability and agility. He concluded his speech at TED by emphasizing brain aerobics, which he believes is going to become part of every life, just like any other physical exercise. He suggested that we consider how to nurture ourselves, *"...now that you know, now that science is telling us that you are in charge, that it's under your control, that your happiness, your well-being, your abilities, your capacities, are capable of continuous modification, continuous improvement and you're the responsible agent and party."* [41]

Drago Plecko[25], researcher of unconventional scientific disciplines who studied the systems of thought of yogis and Tibetan lamas for several decades, also a close and trusted friend of the Dalai Lama, has created 39 varieties of subliminal CD's for reprogramming neurons. On one occasion when we were drinking coffee at a table in his favorite restaurant in his hometown, we asked him how he is affecting the brain with subliminal messages and how, in his opinion, a person can develop or improve his intuition, he put it like this: *"With a pretty simple exercise that deprograms the learned conditioning at the subconscious level. The point is to reprogram the neurons and the subconscious understanding of the past, present and future as all being something different and separated from each other. In reality, time flows in both directions at the same time, and only NOW is real. It is impossible to change that perception through a logical process, using analysis and mathematics. Real spiritual experiences that all lie within the domain of intuition are only possible due to the deprogramming which I mentioned, and of course that is not easy. What I do is create individually directed subliminal CD's, based on a detailed questionnaire and other specific personal data. As experience has shown, after listening to subliminals and doing some exercises that I suggest, people report not only receiving spiritual insights but also, for example, improvements in malignant diseases, mental disorders, and other illnesses. In order for intuition to exist, there must be an observer. And the observer could not exist without time and space."*

---

25 Drago Plecko personally met nearly all of the world's authorities on spiritual teaching during the last 35 years. He is the author of more than 300 TV films, 6 books and a series of subliminal CDs for self healing, as well as a unique self-healing disc called Vortex Mirabilis.

The Bridge to Our Intuition

But science doesn't stop there: new findings even demonstrated the ability to generate new neurons during adult life (adult neurogenesis), meaning that we are not only capable of re-wiring neurons, but that, through certain brain training techniques, we are also capable of creating perfectly new neural cells.

This new concept of understanding how our brain works has far-reaching implications and possibilities for numerous aspects of human life – from early-age learning to rehabilitation to personal growth and spiritual enlightenment. At the moment, it is impossible to define how far the limits of these possibilities may extend. That being said, and considering the interconnection between intuition and the frontal cortex, then we may ask the speculative question: Can specific brain training help us build a bridge to our intuition, too? According to the latest scientific data, the answer is yes, we can literally do that. Taking this idea one step further, we may be able to *build* intuition completely from scratch (actually, we believe that intuition is an inborn capacity of all human beings, but for people who have been unable to perceive it in their lives so far, whose capacity for intuition has been latent up till now, they may consider themselves to be "starting from scratch"). If we are able to re-wire and create new brain cells and neurons during our lifetimes, then this opens up the possibility for reinventing ourselves. This renewal can definitely be performed to a certain extent, but we may even be able to bring about the complete manifestation of intuitive capacities where none were perceived before. We know of lots of successful people who follow their strong intuition, but there are also those who don't even believe in such a faculty. Even someone who has spent thirty, forty or more years in *dis-belief* and have not even once felt intuitiveness may have the capacity and tools to literally build/create his intuition from *nothing*.

Neuroscience is sending us a very strong message in relation to this idea.

Can We Measure Intuition?

Measuring intuition is an area with a huge lack of consensus among scholars, and there is little agreement as to the methodology through which intuitive information is received. While different methods for measuring intuition use different techniques, the basic aims of researchers in general address the same two goals: (1) to determine how intuitive insights are processed and (2) to identify in what forms intuitive judgments appear.

There are a number of subjectively reported preferences for measuring intuition. One of the best known among these is the Myers–Briggs Type Indicator (MBTI; Myers, McCaulley, Quenk, & Hammer, 1998). MBTI is based on Jungian theory [42], which may be one of the reasons for it's widespread application.

There are also many different instruments used to measure intuition in general; some of them are presented in chronological order by year of publication in the table below. A common characteristic of the great majority of these instruments is that they are based on psychological theory [43].

Instruments for Measuring Intuition

Year	Instrument	Author(s)
1961	**Problem Solving**	Westcott
1974	**PSI Game**	Dean, Mihalasky, Ostrander and Schroeder
1983	**Myers-Briggs Type Indicator (MBTI)**	Myers-Briggs
1983	**Are You Intuitive**	Goldberg
1984	**The Keirsey Temperament Sorter**	Keirsey-Bates
1989	**Test Your Management Style (AIM Survey)**	Agor
1989	**Hermann Brain Dominance Instrument**	Hermann
1993	**Personal Style Inventory: Gateway to Personal Flexibility**	Taggart and Taggart-Hausladen
1994	**The Cappon Intuition Profile (IQ2)**	Cappon
1994	**Intuitive Quotient Checklist**	Emery
1994	**Questionnaire**	Parikh
1994	**I-OptTM Survey**	Salton
1999	**Rational Experiential Inventory (REI)**	Pacini & Epstein [42]
1999	**Perceived Modes of Processing Inventory**	Burns & D'Zurilla [42]
2000 / 2001	**Intuitive Behavior Questionnaire**	Raidl & Lubart [42]
2004 / 2008	**Preference for Intuition and Deliberation Scale**	Betsch [42]
2007	**The Types of Intuition Scale (TIntS)**	Pretz & Totz [42]

Note. Partly adapted from *Decision-Making using Organizational Engineering Methodology* (page. 40), by A. F. Fields, 2001, Wayne Huizenga Graduate School of Business and Entrepreneurship of Nova Southeastern University.

Empirical research on intuition remains largely fragmented in terms of how intuition is measured. Further work is thus necessary to better understand the most effective approaches for capturing intuition empirically. [44]

While you may never have considered the question before, we believe that now you are probably asking yourself, "How intuitive am I?". Take a pencil right now, complete the following checklist and find out how developed your intuition is (according to one of the techniques used for this purpose – see table below). We have prepared this very simple questionnaire to enable you to find the current level of your intuitiveness in a matter of minutes. All you need to do is answer "yes" if you can easily identify with the statement, otherwise answer "no". There is no right or wrong answer, you only need to pay attention and be completely honest in answering. This way, even such a simplified questionnaire will help you get an accurate perception of your level of intuitiveness at your present stage in the process of its development, so you can be in the best position to advance further and reach a higher level of intuition.

Discover Your Level of Intuitiveness

Intuitive Checklist	Yes	No
1. My first impression of people usually turns out to be right.	☐	☐
2. I have no trouble understanding the non-verbal messages of other people.	☐	☐
3. I often know what people think when I look at them.	☐	☐
4. I pay attention to the tone of voice of the people I speak with.	☐	☐
5. Empathy with other people is easy for me.	☐	☐
6. When my mood changes without reason, I pay close attention to it.	☐	☐
7. I do not ignore physical signals and sudden pains in my body, but rather try to understand what my body is trying to communicate to me.	☐	☐
8. Because of sudden physical symptoms and unusual pain in my body, I am prepared to cancel even the events which are most important to me.	☐	☐
9. I pay attention to any sudden drop in my energy level – it alerts me that I am about to do the wrong thing.	☐	☐
10. I pay attention to unusual cues and signals from my surroundings.	☐	☐
11. Coincidences and synchronicity between certain events usually get my attention.	☐	☐
12. Normally, I know instantly whether or not some idea or decision is right.	☐	☐
13. From time to time, I surprise myself by knowing something that I have never learned or been in contact with before.	☐	☐
14. An instant "illumination" and a sudden flash of understanding is something that I can always count on.	☐	☐
15. Facing some difficult situations, I ask myself "What should I do?" and believe I get the answer.	☐	☐
16. Decisions made suddenly, but with great internal conviction, mostly prove to be true.	☐	☐

17. Usually I make decisions which I consider to be right, although I do not have any arguments or facts to support them. ☐ ☐

18. Often, I think of someone and soon after that same person visits me or calls me on the phone. ☐ ☐

19. I find myself good at estimating the time, distances, etc. ☐ ☐

20. In certain situations, I feel like I´m "being led" by someone or something. ☐ ☐

21. Having premonitions and anticipating future events are not unusual for me. ☐ ☐

After completing this checklist, count the "yes" answers and find the corresponding description below.

Up to 7 "yes" answers:

Your intuitive awareness is probably underestimated. Like many people, you consider yourself to be rational and only follow your intuition without realizing it. You do not value your intuition very highly and do not give it its proper credit and space in your life. You should give the guiding force in your life a chance, perform some intuitive exercises and practice, and soon you will be able to raise your intuitive awareness, reclaiming it and developing your natural intuitive abilities to the next level. It is highly probable that once you "let go", you stand a good chance of experiencing rapid progress in your intuitiveness.

Between 8 and 14 "yes" answers:

You are already in tune with your intuition. You have learned through some of your experiences to trust your inner guidance and to benefit from the use of a proper balance between rationality and intuitiveness in many areas of your life. Many times, people at this stage of intuitiveness find they are having an inner struggle over some major decision, about whether they should follow their intuition right away or think things over, as well as questioning themselves as to whether they´re experiencing real intuition or just wishful thinking. In order to make better progress to the next level, you should practice quieting your mind, your inner critic or the voice of ego. An intuitive breakthrough on some major decision will give you the needed self-confidence to reach the next level in your intuitive awareness. It is highly probable that only a small step separates you from the giant leap and amazing experience which is awaiting you, just around the corner.

More than 15 "yes" answers:

Congratulations, you ranked in the highest category! You have managed to reclaim the most powerful guiding force in your life. Paying attention to what's going on inside you - your inner feelings and dialogues as well as external signals and messages — has made you capable of an instant insight into situations and gives you an amazing ability to connect with others. Remember, most successful people follow their intuition, and you are among them! But never forget that there is always room for further development. Of course, most of the people in this category already know that and are doing the best they can to achieve an even greater connection with their intuition. There is actually no known limit to how deep this connection can become or how in tune with intuition we can get, so keep exploring and keep living a meaningful life. We also encourage you to share your experiences and stories with us, and maybe in this way, together, we can help others on their path to success.

The heart as the Essence of Extra-Sensory Perception?

In contemporary, "realistic" science, the heart is known as a muscular organ. Its function is to pump blood through the blood vessels and thereby provide our body with oxygen and nutrients — the heart keeps us running, it keeps us alive. It seems to be one of a kind, as it has also taken on another very important role throughout history: It has always represented the center of every living being, its essence, the very core of sensory perception and more. Many religions use the image of the heart to express human and moral qualities and as a temple of the human soul. Even today, it symbolizes the moral, emotional and spiritual essence of a person.

Is there really something more going on here? Can the heart have some other vital role in addition to its most obvious function? We believe so. In modern science, the heart has a much greater role than just that of a pump that sustains life. In the last few decades, we have been experiencing a shift from mind intelligence to heart intelligence. Hundreds of independent researchers from different fields such as psychophysiology, neurocardiology and others have been studying the role of the heart in relation to the functioning of the whole organism and its surroundings. They are addressing heart intelligence, i.e., awareness that arises from the heart.

"When educating the minds of our youth, we must not forget to educate their hearts."

—the Dalai Lama

Scientists at HMI (HeartMath Institute) and other research centers have conducted a number of studies exploring the role of the heart in human performance. At HMI, they have come up with a very precise description of the heart - it is, in fact, a highly complex information-processing center with its own functional brain, commonly called the "heart–brain", which communicates with and influences the cranial brain via the nervous system, the hormonal system and other pathways. These influences affect brain functions and most of the body's major organs, and play an important role in mental and emotional experience and the quality of our lives. [45]

"Heart intelligence is the flow of awareness, understanding and intuition we experience when the mind and emotions are brought into coherent alignment with the heart. It can be activated through self-initiated practice, and the more we pay attention when we sense the heart is speaking to us or guiding us, the greater our ability to access this intelligence and guidance more frequently. Heart intelligence underlies cellular organization and guides and evolves organisms toward increased order, awareness and coherence of their bodies' systems." [46]

It has been proven that the heart communicates with the brain in four major ways: neurologically (through the transmission of nerve impulses), biochemically (via hormones and neurotransmitters), biophysically (through pressure waves) and energetically (through electromagnetic field interactions). [45]

Constant two-way communication:
heart → brain; brain → heart

Communication along all these channels significantly affects the brain's activity. Moreover, research has shown that messages which the heart sends to the brain can also influence its performance.

One study has shown that the heart's afferent neurological signals directly affect activity in the amygdala, an important emotional processing center in the brain, and the nuclei associated with it, [45] which together are vital to the maintenance of cardiovascular stability and efficiency.

In addition, the "heart–brain", also called the intrinsic cardiac nervous system, has both short-term and long-term memory functions and can operate independently of central neuronal command. The heart's intrinsic nervous system is vital for the maintenance of cardiovascular stability and efficiency, and without it, the heart cannot function properly. The neural output, or chain of messages from the intrinsic cardiac nervous system, travels to the brain via ascending pathways in both the spinal column and the vagus nerve, where it travels to the medulla, hypothalamus, thalamus and amygdala and then to the cerebral cortex. [45]

Another branch of the extensive 'heart–brain' communication system is via the hormones. The heart produces a number of hormones and neurotransmitters that greatly impact the body. Some of these are oxytocin, atrial peptide, norepinephrine, epinephrine and dopamine.

In the 1990s, the concept of emotional intelligence was introduced. This concept shifted attention from mind intelligence to heart intelligence, explaining that a high intelligent quotient is far from a guarantee of success in life and work. Success is also very much dependent on human qualities like empathy, intuition, creativity, passion, self-control, self-awareness, honesty, courage and others. Facing life's different challenges requires emotional and cognitive skills, and when these two are in sync, our potential for success increases.

The key to successful coherence between the mind and the emotions lies in increasing one's emotional self-awareness and the harmonious functioning and interaction between the neural systems that underlie cognitive and emotional experience. [45]

For humans to function at our optimum level of performance, it is vital that we possess inner balance and coherence. This includes coherence between the physical, mental, emotional and social systems. When this balance is achieved, a person is much more susceptible to receiving intuitive signals and hunches. *However, the heart and cardiovascular system have far more afferent inputs than other organs and are the primary sources of consistent dynamic rhythms.* [45] Because of this, the heart proves to play an important role in regards to intuition.

*"Since emotional processes can work faster than the mind,
it takes a power stronger than the mind to bend perception,
override emotional circuitry, and provide us with intuitive
feeling instead. It takes the power of the heart."*

—Doc Lew Childre

In addition to utilizing the nervous system, the hormonal system
and its neurotransmitters, and the biophysical system with its pressure
waves as means of communication, our body uses its own electromagnetic field for this purpose, which is referred to as cardioelectromag-
netic communication.

The heart's magnetic field is the strongest rhythmic field produced
by the human body. Its electrical field is about 60 times greater in
amplitude than the electrical activity generated by the brain and
not only surrounds every cell of the body but also extends outside
us[26]. Research conducted at HMI suggests that the heart's field is an
important carrier of information and suggests that magnetic signals
generated by the heart have the capacity to affect individuals around
us. [45]

The heart's electromagnetic field is a carrier of the individual's
emotional frequency, and using this capacity, communicates through
the body and into the person's surroundings. One common example
of this phenomenon is when someone present in a room perceives
the energy of another person who has just entered, without knowing
anything about this person. The electromagnetic field works in both
directions, as a transmitter and as a receiver of information. Another
example is our everyday perception of being watched. Normally, we can
"feel eyes on us" without previously seeing the person who is showing
interest in us. It is very likely that these signals are perceived by the
electromagnetic field of the heart and are then further processed in the
body. This kind of energetic communication between individuals may
play a role in therapeutic interactions between clinicians and patients
that have the potential to promote the healing process. [45] In other

---

26 This may be the energy responsible in part for the aura, the part of the human
energy field which some esoteric schools refer to as the "etheric body" or "vital
energy", that layer of the energy surrounding us which is closest to the physical body
but usually invisible to the physical senses. Or it may be related to the "astral body",
which is also called the "emtional body". Or both of these may be connected with
different aspects of the heart. There is a great need of further research into this area.

words, our "heart energy" can have a direct influence on other people's "heart energy" and vice versa. This cardiac field can reach out up to 10 feet from where we are positioned.

You'll be surprised by some of the facts about the human heart - here are some of the most amazing ones:

Recapitulating:

⊃ The heart has it's own brain, consisting of 100,000 neurons.

⊃ The heart produces some important hormones and neurotransmitters.

⊃ It communicates with the rest of the body through pressure waves, nerve impulses and an electromagnetic field.

⊃ The heart is the most powerful generator of electromagnetic energy in the body.

⊃ The heart's electromagnetic field is about 60 times greater in amplitude than the electrical activity generated by the brain.

⊃ The electromagnetic field produced by the heart is more than 5000 times greater in strength than the field generated by the brain.

⊃ The electromagnetic energy of the heart not only envelops every cell of the body, but also extends out in all directions into the space around us

⊃ Our cardiac field touches those within 8-10 feet of where we are positioned

[47]

"Our heart is our greatest instrument, and if the heart is pure, then it will "tell" you everything you want to know. But as soon as some resistance appears, the communication ends in a moment. How can we achieve [and maintain] that connection? We need to become children again, pure, playful and loving. This is the recipe for the development of the soul, intuition and creation that drives the world forward," says Oskar Kogoj, world-renowned industrial designer, academic and artist, who is living a very spiritual life. As he told us, the heart always knows.

Professionals who work with people in the areas of personal development and enhanced brain functions confirm the importance of personal and business decisions associated with the authenticity and consistency of the whole of human activity. Failing to consult our "heart", sometimes also called "gut feeling", leads to major difficulties later on in life - and oftentimes, deep unhappiness. The observations of therapists confirm that people who have only been using their logic in life arrived at their clinics feeling utterly suffocated and were some of the unhappiest people - despite their degree of career success. [48]

It is a common mistake to base our decisions only on our mental body systems, such as using only logic. Instead, we should learn to listen and connect to different parts of our overall functioning and base our decisions in accordance with them.

Making good decisions depends on our ability to use our emotions, self-control, our consciousness, cognitive abilities and our intuition, or as referred to earlier, our intuitive intelligence. It is therefore important that we consciously direct our attention from the brain to the heart, from logical thinking to the intuitive.

Considering all of these facts, we can say that the heart is an organ that is capable of self-consciousness and transmits its perceptions to all other parts of the body, affecting them in profound and subtle ways.

Dreams

There was a very interesting study done by a scientist from Stanford University which ended with somewhat scary results. In the experiment, they prevented a group of people from dreaming for 14 days. As soon as dreams were detected by the applied measuring instruments, the scientist stopped them. And what happened was that they actually had to stop the experiment, as it showed that this elimination of dreaming caused some serious personality changes in the experimental group. A pioneering sleep researcher, William C. Dement, also the head of this experiment, stated that more than 14 days without dreams could even cause the death of a human. [49]

So, it's not just sleep deprivation that causes serious psychological and physical effects, but also the deprivation of dreams themselves. That's a very interesting and important finding, indicating the importance of dreaming.

Freud, one of the pioneers in dream research, considered them to be "the royal road to the unconscious". The renowned psychologist, G. H. Estabrooks[27], claimed that dreams are a safety valve for

---

27 G. H. Estabrooks was chairman of the Department of Psychology at Colgate University and an authority on hypnosis during World War II, known for hypno-programming U.S. government agents during World War II.

releasing excess pressure. Dreams play a vital role in our lives, and yet many people are not even aware of this; most of the time we do not even remember our dreams. Another interesting concept related to dreams was that of Jung, who believed that it's not just the past that can be expressed through dreams, but also the future. The first person to systematically study dreams that reveal the future – precognitive dreams - was J. W. Dunne, a British soldier, aeronautical engineer and philosopher who experienced precognitive dreams himself. He believed that our experience of time as having a linear flow is an illusion created by our consciousness, and argued that the past, present and future are interconnected in a higher-dimensional reality[28].

> *"I saw in a dream a table were all the elements fell into place as required. Awakening, I immediately wrote it down on a piece of paper; only in one place did a correction seem necessary."*
>
> —Dmitri Mendeleev

Due to our busy everyday lives, not many people have the time or the desire to study this interesting field, but anyone who starts digging into it very quickly realizes a well known fact: that many successful people and great inventors claim to have had dreams in which they envisioned their decisions or inventions. They directly connect their dreams with future events in their lives, either showing or causing those events. *"The sewing machine, for instance, invented by Elias Howe, was developed from material appearing in a dream, as was Dmitri Mendeleev's periodic table of elements"*, [50] along with the elements which were at that time unknown. One of the most prominent European chemists, Friedrich August Kekulé, saw the solution to the atomic arrangement of the benzene molecule in his dreams. Another amazing invention which was the result of inspiration from dreams was the discovery of insulin by Frederick Grant Banting.

A very special case that we must point out is that of the highly respected scientist, Nikola Tesla, who claimed to have had a constant dream in which he saw detailed drawings of his inventions, based on which he was able to build his machines directly, without any blueprint or special knowledge of mechanics. These machines were built with

---

28 Dunne further eleborated the concepts of "serial time" and "serialism" in his theory on time.

precision, and in most cases they were working perfectly right from the start or after just a few small adjustments, which is incredible.

Dreams have also been a great "source" for many famous writers: take novelist Stephen King, for example, whose books have sold more than 350 million copies and who revealed that his inspiration for the novel *Misery* came from dreams: *"Like the ideas for some of my other novels, that came to me in a dream. In fact, it happened when I was on a Concord, flying over here, to Brown's. I fell asleep on the plane, and dreamt about a woman who held a writer prisoner... I said to myself, 'I have to write this story.'"* [51]

Srinivasa Aiyangar Ramanujan was hailed as one of the greatest mathematicians in history, despite his lack of formal education. Ramanujan was known to be a devotee of the Goddess of Namakkal, and he claimed that the Goddess appeared in his dreams and inspired him to bring forth new formulae. [52].

> *"While asleep, I had an unusual experience. There was a red screen formed by flowing blood, as it were. I was observing it. Suddenly a hand began to write on the screen. I became all attention. That hand wrote a number of elliptic integrals. They stuck in my mind. As soon as I woke up, I committed them to writing."*
>
> —Srinivasa Ramanujan

Jain 108 operates like a psychic detective looking for the truth in mathematics. *'My kind of prayer to God or to the Universe is 'I wanna be shown the truth.' So I use my inner knowing, my intuition, perhaps in daydreams, to consciously navigate, to get an answer for my question. When I go to sleep, I want to be shown through an image, a song, or something I read in a book, so when I wake up in the morning I want to have a solution, and I do."* As he said, he wakes up in the morning and when he opens a book or listens to some song on the radio, there is the answer. *"So it comes in very mysterious ways, and that's why I keep doing this, because I wanna have full knowledge, I wanna have full access to the records, some call them the "Akashic Records" (also called the Zero Point Field) and intuition is crucial here,"* explains 108. The Zero-Point Field is the collective energy field of all particles existing everywhere, which may be connected in a single universal energy field. It is a concept used in Quantum Physics, but also seems to be related to the concept of a Universal Mind which interacts with our individual minds, both bringing us ideas and information from other apparently isolated sources and receiving our ideas and intentions and sending them to other parts of the whole. In some way, it may help our intentions to materialize in the physical world. Some see this concept as the ultimate connection between religion and science.

As Peter Baksa says, *"If thoughts equal energy and energy equals matter, then thoughts become matter."* [53]

Despite the huge interest in the phenomenology of dreams, their purpose and concept are still not fully explained by science[29]. Dreams have also been the topic of scholars (beginning with Sigmund Freud's "The Interpretation of Dreams") who showed philosophical and religious interest, along with the related topic of dream interpretation as searching for possible underlying messages in dreams. One of the categories that has caused much interest among esoterics as well as scholars are lucid dreams,[30] which have also been found to be associated with mindfulness,[31] and it has been discovered that the same regions of the brain are occupied during both.

Dreams are considered to be one of the most important factors when speaking about intuition. As we saw in the examples above (and there is a much longer list than what we are presenting here), dreams can bring us direct visions and ideas about the problems which we are occupied with at the moment or show us some indirect or symbolic situations, metaphors, images, sensations and feelings. Dreams can give us that one essential spark needed to boost our work or provide us with courage to start some particular action or activity. With the help of dreams, we can receive insights on certain issues, or they may provoke us to think more deeply about some situation and consequently help us to solve complex dilemmas.

Coincidences or Synchronicity?

At first glance, coincidence and synchronicity might appear to be two different things, but when we look at them a little bit closer, we realize that these are just two different words for describing the

---

29 The scientific study of dreams is called oneirology.

30 In lucid dreams, the dreamer is aware that he or she is dreaming, and it is possible to wake up deliberately, to influence the action of the dream actively, or to observe the course of the dream passively. [136]

31 Direct attention on the present moment with a non-judgmental attitude. [138]

same sequence of events - striking occurrences of two or more inter-connected events at one time. The main difference between the two is actually only in the personal perception of such sequential events, where coincidence is understood as being determined by chance or luck, while synchronicity on the other hand is perceived as the presence of a "higher intelligence" at work. In other words, one who believes in coincidences as random events is the kind of person who probably believes that life is simply happening to him, imposed on him by external forces, and can hardly find a connection with his own inner world, while those who look at these same sequential events as being synchronicities usually perceive that there is more than just a "physical form" of life. They are convinced that some kind of interconnectivity exists between everyone and everything.

Drago Plecko put it very simply: *"There are no coincidences in life, only synchronicities; remember that,"* he told us with a great sense of knowing.

It is common that, at first, people understand the phenomenon of striking occurrences of two or more events at the same time to be purely coincidental, but sooner or later they begin to notice the other side of the story. If we allow ourselves to think about these "strange" coincidences without the filtering applied by our rational side, we soon conclude that there is something more to it. These unusual events disrupt our causal paradigm of the world, but at the same time we find them very valuable, enlightening, and we are left with no more room for doubt. Extraordinary incidents that we witness eventually stir us to think about our capacities and our role in this world. Yet, we are still unable to note more than a small part of the synchronicities that go on around us, even if they are quite obvious sometimes. Because of this, we miss valuable guidance and hints which might be able to lead us to a more meaningful life.

The most common forms of synchronicity are those that announce something special in our lives. By being fully receptive to these announcements, we can expand our possibilities and deliver brilliant new ideas in many different situations.

There are many facts which show that everything in the universe is connected and that nothing happens by chance. And everything that happens has some impact on the overall environment in which we live.

Tip: If you experience a coincidence or synchronicity, do not ignore it; accept it and follow where it leads you, even if it's impossible to see some direct benefit as a result.

Collective Consciousness

According to Dr. Rupert Sheldrake, it is possible to observe some kind of collective consciousness in certain species of social animals, such as ants, bees, wasps, termites and several others. Sheldrake has presented the theory of an inner connection within these groups of animal, which can be perceived in the synchronous movement of a school of fish or a flock of birds. Numerous experiments have been performed which prove that this is not due to physical influences, but that some kind of collective consciousness, more specifically a "morphic resonance", actually does exist.

"Morphic resonance is the influence of previous structures of activity on subsequent similar structures of activity organized by morphic fields. It enables memories to pass across both space and time from the past. The greater the similarity, the greater the influence of morphic resonance. What this means is that all self-organizing systems, such as molecules, crystals, cells, plants, animals and animal societies, have a collective memory on which each individual draws and to which it contributes." [54][32]

Dr. Sheldrake claims that many animals such as elephants and bison survived the Sri Lanka tsunami of 2004 by climbing into the mountains a few hours before the destructive wave hit.

---

32 James Cameron's 2009 science fiction movie, Avatar, shows a speculative form of this concept on another planet, but in the 1960s, Dr. James Lovelock theorized that all life on Earth was interconnected as a living system, including human society. This idea was expanded on by Dr. Lynn Margulis.

Although these findings refer to animals, this same concept is very interesting and important for understanding the so-called collective intelligence in human beings.

"Researchers from Princeton University and the New Jersey Institute of Technology report for the first time that the "living" bridges that army ants of the species Eciton hamatum *build with their bodies are more sophisticated than scientists knew. The ants use collective intelligence to automatically assemble when they detect congestion along their raiding trail, and disassemble when normal traffic has resumed."* Although these ants don't follow any perceptible orders or directions, they instinctively form "living" bridges across breaks and gaps in the forest floor to travel more efficiently. They do this as a colony; each individual ant only has its own localized information, so to be able to achieve something as amazing as this, they are using a collective intelligence. [55]

Expertise Enhances Intuition

EVIDENCE SUGGESTS THAT intuition tends to be more accurate when decision makers have accrued significant levels of expertise in their specific field so that their cognitive schemas are complex and domain-relevant. [56]

Cognitive schemas are mental structures or patterns of thought which organize information and interrelate it with other information to help us interact with the world around us. The ways in which these are developed was discussed by the Swiss psychologist, Jean Piaget. According to the Componential Theory of Creativity, a scema can be said to be domain-relevant when a person's mental structure contains adequate references for judgments, based on experience in that person's area of expertise. These references seem to help us to arrive at intuitive conclusions without conscious analysis of a situation.

One of the clearest results that came out of our research is that intuition and expertise are in a highly positive correlation to each other, they go hand in hand.

Dr. Marta Bon, successful handball coach who has lead a few national handball teams, is considered to be a special phenomenon in Slovenian sports. She has succeeded in several different areas - first as a top athlete, then as a coach and later as a teacher and researcher. She openly discussed the phenomenon of intuition with us and revealed to us quite a few interesting stories where trusting her intuition had very positive outcomes. In sports, quick and effective decision making is of great importance, and often there is no room for hesitation. *"When you make a decision,"* she says, *"it'd better be the right decision, as you have to go forward with full power."* Dr. Bon uses her intuition practically every day, in both personal and business life. She believes that intuition grows with awareness of it and trust in it. The more you are dedicated to your work and the more you are developing your intuition, the more you will gain from it. *"Intuition grows with you; by developing your confidence in it, intuition grows and serves you better as well."* We couldn't agree more; the more time you devote to your area of expertise, the more you develop the direct link between expertise and intuition. You can imagine it as a muscle - the more you train it, the more it grows.

"I experienced cases of something just coming into my mind, a kind of intuitive knowing, in my youth and during the first years of my professional life as well. However, back in those days, I was just too scared to use it. It's bizzare when you know that something should be done in a certain way, but since you are afraid of loosing, afraid of other people's attitudes and judgments, you decide to do it in the opposite way and obviously regret it afterwards. I think this is the way that most people act, but with experience and expertise you become able to shed your 'cloak of fear' and finally decide to act according to your inner knowledge and higher wisdom, which is most frequently expressed as intuition."

She recalls one very important handball match in France, which had literally been the decisive moment in the fate of the club. *"We played against the Metz Handball team, the most decorated French handball club. The goalkeeper we had wasn't very successful that season, and everybody in the club was uncomfortable about having her in the club. The night before the deciding match, I prepared and presented a very bold plan to our team — I decided that this very goalkeeper would play and defend our net at the goal. I risked my position with that decision, but deep inside I felt that it was the right choice."* Believe it or not, this goalkeeper played her best game ever and they won in magnificent style. *"She defended everything, completely 'locked the doors', as we like to say,"* explains Marta with a smile of pride on her face.

And this is far from being an isolated case. We also received very firm confirmation that expertise advances intuition from two different sources in the medical sector. In personal conversations, two highly experienced doctors (very respected European surgeons) both confided to us that their intuition and intuitive decision making had improved greatly with their years of expertise in medical practice. It is not uncommon, they say, for them to make decisions based on their "gut feeling" in their everyday work. *"But this is something I don't like to talk about, especially not publicly, and is certainly not something I would say to my patients. They might not understand it the way we are discussing it, and might get unnecessary and unjustified feelings of uncertainty. Even though it would sometimes be hard for me to explain my intuitive decisions, the fact is that they are the correct ones."* Due to the sensitive nature of this topic, we are not able to reveal their identities. But the fact remains that their testimonies reinforce our conclusions.

Another interesting case showed up during our research, recounted to us by none other than the highest political representative, the President of a country himself. Stjepan Mesic, the 2nd President of Croatia and the last President of the Presidency of Yugoslavia, revealed to us the importance of intuition in politics and diplomacy in general, and also how his intuition helped him at some crucial moments in his political career. He has no doubt that expertise enhances intuition: *"In diplomacy, intuition is of great importance, but of course it is also important to apply a serious analysis. Having been in many different political functions, a judge, mayor, Prime Minister, President of the Parliament, President of the Republic and the last President of the Presidency of Yugoslavia, I have met and dealt with a lot of people. And I can say that I have developed a sufficient level of intuition to provide me with a very accurate first impression of people, which consequently leads me to take the right steps in further communication with them and everything else that goes with it."* Mesic also shared a very specific personal experience from the times when Croatia was in a very turbulent situation. *"To be led by intuition in the best possible way, one also has to have adequate knowledge. That way, intuition can help us even more to create the best possible results in any given situation. At the time, when I was the President of the Parliament, Croatia had been struggling through very difficult times: we were in a war. One day, I met a gentleman, neat, decently dressed, and he said he had a proposition for Croatia, a very significant proposal, which if realized would be of great benefit, not only for the nation's defense, but also for the reconstruction of Croatia. He said that he had a connection to some American humanitarian fund of two billion dollars and that Croatia was included in the program of this fund, and that the money could only be used for humanitarian purposes – no purchasing of weapons. He wanted me to recommend him to certain institutions in Croatia, so he could start implementing the assistance he offered. Everything this man said was perfectly logical and correctly presented, there should not have been any doubt about it: yet, at the same time, it was immediately and perfectly clear to me that this was a scam."* Because his intuition had warned him, Mesic managed to avoid possible confusion, scandal and difficulties.

Let's finish this chapter in high gear. Paul Bonhomme, the most successful pilot in Red Bull Air Race history, also thinks intuition is somehow connected to experience and expertise. *"I do consider myself to be intuitive, but when asked about it, I wonder whether I am naturally intuitive or whether my reaction to an event is based on experience. I reckon if I was to compare myself to others, then I am possibly more intuitive than the average, but when that personality trait is added to my experience, then it can be a very powerful tool."* Bonhomme, who is the only pilot to have won three World Championship titles, also confided to us about how intuition communicates with him. It comes as a feeling, he said: *"I find intuition to be a feeling, positive or negative, which occurs without conscious thought. In my case, it is normally signaled by an emotion before I have had the time to think… either a 'fantastic' or an 'oh, no' feeling, which starts the thought process of wondering what has happened or is happening."* His reaction to what happens around him, or possibly his anticipation of what will happen in the next instant, is guided by this feeling, which mixes with what his body and mind remember from previous experiences, leading him to make those decisions and responses that make him a winner, and the same thing can work for you.

Intuitive Intelligence and Intuition Quotient

S TEVE JOBS HAD a premonition that he would not live a long life. That was why he was driven and impatient. [57]

People are creatures of habit, and we readily adopt beliefs which we don't like to let go. For millenia, we have lived in the belief that we are strictly physical beings limited to the five basic senses (taste, sight, touch, smell, and hearing), and limited by the dimensions of space and time in which we live. Individual minds which managed to step outside of these limits are recorded in history as geniuses who lived ahead of their time. Their work was misinterpreted, obscured by other interests, and taken out of context many times. Today, centuries later in the case of many of these special individuals, we are slowly removing layers of dust and tarnish which cover their knowledge, to give names to their areas of study and scientific weight to their work. Fortunately, we have expanded our understanding of the world, perceiving that it does not always behave the same way when subjected to a number of experiments made under the same conditions. One of the basic concepts of quantum physics is that the observer is a variable in the conditions which influence the outcome of any experiment or experience. One example is the famous Double-Slit Experiement, where the fact that someone is observing the experiement can change its results.

We have entered the world beyond the five senses, the world of metaphysics. Albert Einstein has been widely quoted as saying, *"The intuitive mind is a sacred gift and the rational mind is a faithful servant. We have created a society that honors the servant and has forgotten the gift."*

If we could understand the ideas behind the work of Nikola Tesla, then today we would be living in a "better world", in a world we are so eagerly trying to define and create. But in Tesla´s day, human intelligence (or human greed) could only handle radio, AC power and other smaller inventions – "small" as seen from the point of view of hard science, not to mention from the spiritual perspective. There was no sense of human values like empathy, righteousness or tolerance, at least not on a collective level, and this is something we are still striving to reach today.

Tesla´s most revolutionary ideas, including the production of free energy for permitting the entire population to have equal access to advancing technologies, were blocked by financial and political interest groups which saw how they could make a fortune from selling services based on those ideas. The short-term personal vision of the greedy has frequently inhibited the long-term collective progress which technology based on intuition could make possible. While some groups seek what they perceive to be their own best interests, other forces seek to remove the hardships of this physical world for everyone, in order to permit us more time to look for our higher inner potentials instead of spending our energies on confronting external dificulties. One day, we may finally understand that we are all together in one great collectivity, and that anything that causes harm to another is not in anyone´s best interest.

Evolutionary development means thinking differently, leaving behind our outgrown patterns of thinking and discovering new perspectives, perceptions, values and behavior.

Globally, we are a generation that is booming with advancement and living in chaos at the same time. As we learn new ways of living and thinking, we are still wrapped in old patterns; but we are becoming more open to a new future and new views.

A new concept of human intelligence has arisen in recent decades. IQ tests formulated in the early 20th century do not measure all the qualities that humans have. Gardner's concept of multiple intelligences (MI) may be a step closer. It is composed of a variety of factors - musical-rhythmic, visual-spatial, verbal-linguistic, logical-mathematical, bodily-kinesthetic, interpersonal, intrapersonal and naturalistic intelligences. But which intelligence determines us? Which really makes us more human than the animals? Which ones makes us more human than other humans?

If we look into two personal forms of intelligence, i.e. interpersonal and intrapersonal intelligence, we enter the area of human feelings, emotions, abilities to recognize other peoples feelings and many other undefined capacities. Investigations into these two areas have given birth to the trend known as emotional intelligence. [58] The theory of emotional intelligence has finally offered answers to questions about why our logical decisions often prove to be less effective and less accurate than our emotional decisions.

Further progress in the study of how intelligence is developed has led from the concept of emotional intelligence to another aspect which is understood even less: intuitive intelligence.

Intuition has been a privileged theme of neuroscience research over the last decade, and for researchers it is the mark of our subconscious intelligence. [58] Despite considerable progress in technology and medicine, we still don't know and don't understand the functioning of much of our brain and subconscious. The unimaginable amount of information stored and the complicated and hidden operations that are carried out by our brain during each and every moment are raising new questions and arousing further interest.

> *"I began to realize that an intuitive understanding and consciousness was more significant than abstract thinking and intellectual, logical analysis."*
>
> —Steve Jobs

Intuitive intelligence is starting to attract much interest in the business world, especially in the field of management and leadership, as more and more companies realize that an intuitive approach can be very fruitfully combined with the rational one and that this combination can bring much better results. We believe that intuitive intelligence is the answer to the needs of our rapidly changing world, and can and will play a vital part in shaping people and organizations. We are definitely not limiting this view to the business world alone; we believe it can and will play a major role from the social perspective as well. As it becomes more and more evident and undeniable that intuitive intelligence plays a vital role in our lives, it is time to add another indicator to the Life Success Formula – the Intuition Quotient (InQ). We all know that such a formula is an over-simplification, as there are too many variables which influence and define success; but nonetheless, if such a thing as a Life Success Formula[33] should ever be developed, it might consist of (1) Intelligence Quotient (IQ), (2) Emotional Quotient (EQ), (3) Political Quotient (PQ) and (4) Intuition Quotient (InQ) and might be summarized as:

$$\text{Life Success (LS)} = \text{IQ} + \text{EQ} + \text{PQ} + \text{InQ}$$

In order to increase our life success, we need to build up our IQ, EQ, PQ and InQ.

The Intelligence Quotient helps you with basic problem-solving, analytical capability and rational judgment. While being *smart* is important, it is not enough to guarantee your success; nowadays, you also have to be *nice,* so you have to add the Emotional Quotient to the equation, which means improving interpersonal skills, empathy, your ability to understand people and situations, building up your charisma, working on motivation, being a team player and so on. But then again, if you look around to see who succeeds and who fails, you will find plenty of people who are both *smart* and *nice,* but who seem to be living their lives of quiet underachievement in the backwaters. Something is missing, right? It certainly helps to have a good IQ and EQ, but it looks like that is not quite enough to achieve a real breakthrough. Now we have to consider and implement the concept of Political Quotient, the ability to know how to "acquire power". You have to be able to build alliances, getting help and support and reaching out beyond your formal areas of authority. It's all about being able to make things happen. [59]

And now, look around you to see who radiates happiness, who is really satisfied with his life, both professionally and personally. Try to see who is not faking it and is genuinely satisfied with his life situation. This is the last missing piece of the puzzle. Someone might be very successful in terms of business, fame, money, etc., but is he really

---

33 The concept we are expanding on is the concept of the Management Quotient (MQ), presented by Jo Owen in his book *How to Manage*; MQ = IQ + EQ + PQ, which in our opinion very nicely depicts the key basis for "raw" business success. [59]

enjoying the journey? Is he really living a meaningful life? Does he believe in what he does or says? Does he live in alignment with his inner self? Will he have no regrets once he comes to the *end* of the journey, and will he be completely at peace with the way he lived? This is the area of Intuitive Intelligence, and this is where we believe real success lies.

We are not trying to provide you with a formula for life success that will make you just another *clone* of a supposedly successful individual; we believe you deserve better than that. You can understand our Life Success Formula to simply be a framework, within which you can search and work on your own personal and unique development and experience. Consider *Intuition and Success* as a set of tools to help you understand the long-awaited missing piece of the puzzle – the Intuition Quotient (InQ). It's not just about theory (which of course matters), but it's more about application, transforming theory into practice and growing within the process of your own experience. It is only from experience that we really learn, from both positive and negative events. We are presenting numerous examples and testimonials from highly successful people from around the world and throughout history, and each has their own success story to tell. Learn from them, but don´t feel you should try to copy them – your own experience is what counts for you.

As we said before, individual minds that were able to see outside of the limits of pure science are historically recorded as geniuses who lived before their time. One of these, to whom we can attribute a high Intuitive Intelligence, is Nikola Tesla. Let´s conclude this chapter by quoting directly from a speech of his given in 1943, during World War II, which reveals the true capacity of Intuitive Intelligence: *"Out of this war, the greatest since the beginning of history, a new world must be born, a world that would justify the sacrifices offered by humanity. This new world must be a world in which there shall be no exploitation of the weak by the strong, of the good by the evil; where there will be no humiliation of the poor by the violence of the rich; where the products of intellect, science and art will serve society for the betterment and beautification of life, and not the individuals for achieving wealth. This new world shall not be a world of the downtrodden and humiliated, but of free men and free nations, equal in dignity and respect for man."*

The Biggest Intuition Inhibitors

"I like to give my inhibitions a bath now and then."

—Oliver Reed

Noise

IN MANY WAYS, our modern lifestyle inhibits, or at least highly disturbs, our openness and accessibility to our intuition. There is so much noise in our lives that in many cases the only period in a day when we are not being bombarded with noise is during our sleep time. The habit of consuming media and being occupied with electronic devices – using the computer, tablet or cell phone, watching the television, listening to music, telephoning, playing videogames and so forth - is growing constantly and is completely taking us over. The current addiction to information about any and all subjects is considered by some to be extremely exagerated, and probably prejudicial. It is fashionable to "be informed" about whatever topic is popular for a short time, after which it is followed by another "important" topic. And people are looked down upon if they do not follow the ever-changing trends in information (which is very lucrative for those who gather and disseminate that information, but which generates a certain stress on the part of consumers to "stay in touch" with EVERYTHING). Most of this information is really just "noise" and distraction which keeps our attention focussed outside ourselves and away from that "inner voice", our intuition. We can sense this in those very rare moments of silence in between, which we just can't seem to tolerate at all, whether they last for a few minutes or even just a few seconds. So we immediately reach for more noise, something that can instantly engaged our mind and gives us a false sense of security. A study done by the research company Dscout reveals that the average users touch their phones more than 2,600 times daily, and furthermore, the same study found that extreme cell phone users (the top 10% of them) touch their phones more than 5,400 times per day. Calculating an average of three seconds for each glance, we spend from two hours up to an astounding four and a half hours a day just looking at the phone! Should we be surprised by our inner disconnection or by the feeling of a constant lack of time and, because of this, the sensation that time is speeding up? According to the Nielsen Total Audience Report, the amount of time people spend on consuming media continues to grow. For instance, in 2015, Americans spent about nine and a half hours each day consuming media while in 2016 the average had increased to 10 hours and 39 minutes [60]. This is not a healthy state of affairs. So what can we do about it?

Firstly, we must became consciously aware of this harmful obsession with consuming, and once we realize how much noise we consume, we are no longer far from the very obvious next step; to disconnect from all this non-productive noise. Despite constant pressure, we must unlearn the idea that this noise is good for us. Then we will be in a much better position to connect with our true self, with our intuition. Or, in the words of Jedi Master Yoda, from one of the most popular sci-fi movie franchises of all time, *Star Wars - The Empire Strikes Back*; when Luke argued, *"Master, moving stones around is one thing, this is totally different,"* Yoda wisely replied, *"No, no different. Only different in your mind. You must unlearn what you have learned."* There comes a time in our lives when we appear to be satisfied with what we know and consequently we stop questioning alternatives. At some point, Luke thought that it was impossible to get his ship out of the swamp, but Yoda told him that he seemed so sure of this when he really shouldn´t be.

Mind pollution prevents us from spending time with our own thoughts. We are chronically lacking silence, both in the external environment and in the mind.

The Ego

"To live in the light of a new day and an unimaginable and unpredictable future, you must become fully present to a deeper truth - not a truth from your head, but a truth from your heart; not a truth from your ego, but a truth from the highest source."

—Debbie Ford

Lisa Nichols told us a very interesting thing about ego as one of the most harmful inhibitors of intuition. She said that it is the ego that drives the mental chatter, through our need to prove, protect or hide, to defend our ego and its weaknesses, and that it will always cause us to avoid our intuition. Intuition has only one calling and that is to serve our real interests, not the false interests of our ego. That's it. So ego and intuition are opposed to each other, and diminishing one will strengthen the other.

Ego is often not only the inhibitor of intuition, but has negative effects on many other different areas of our lives - personal, love, business, etc.. "I am" and "I know" are beliefs that can be really dangerous: just think of all the violence and greed which they cause in the world, for example. Sometimes, even completely peaceful people have found themselves entrapped by the need to justify some of the negative results of ego. But please don't misunderstand our point: it's not that we are condemning the ego, as in general it really isn't a bad feature at all; it's about finding a balance. The ego helps us to survive, giving us identity, even uniqueness. Ego empowers us with will and ambition, and helps us to achieve the unimaginable. Let us emphasize again, it is the problem of balance that we need to resolve, not the existence of the ego itself.

Every time ego hurts you or someone close to you, try to stop and think why you let that happen. You should know that it is your ego that did that. You need to raise your awareness of this situation, so you can recognize it and control it in the future. By doing so over and over again, your ego will have less and less negative power over you and you will become more and more balanced in that respect.

Ego attracts benefits to itself alone, which in the long run works against the holistic-oriented activity of nature that tries to benefit the whole collectively. Compassion, love of others as part of the same whole to which we all belong, avoids the negative feedback which always appears as side-effects of egotistical behavior.

Osho, famed mystic, guru and spiritual teacher, saw the "solution for the ego" in understanding the process of the ego and accepting who we are: *"Understand the process of the ego. How does the ego live? The ego lives in the tension between what you are and what you want to be. A wants to be B — the ego is created out of this very tension. How does the ego die? The ego dies by you accepting what you are. Then you say, I am fine as I am, where I am is good. I will remain just as existence keeps me. Its will is my will."* [61]

We consider compassion to be a very effective way of balancing our ego, as with compassion we are naturally lowering our ego and vice versa, when ego is dropped, compassion arrives from all sides. It's similar to turning on the lights in a dark room.

Tip: Don't wait for the opportunity to come, be proactive and create the opportunity yourself. With a balanced ego and nurturing compassion, you naturally open yourself to intuitiveness.

Fear

> *"Fear is everything. If there was one concept that I would suggest to people to take a daily confrontation with, it's fear... God placed the best things in life on the other side of terror; on the other side of your maximum fear are all of the best things in your life."*

—Will Smith

Resentments bite you, doubts divide you, but the biggest paralyzer of all is fear, which frightens you. In the past, fear was crucial for human survival. It is a primal feeling like animal instinct, which should activate body reactions to protect and defend us against a threat. Fear triggers stress mechanisms in the body, but it is very important that at the end of danger the body reverts to its normal operation as soon as possible. Problems occur when the body is exposed to anxiety for long periods and is thus constantly working under stress (caused by various types of fear). Consequently, the level of adrenaline in the body is too high, and all that time it is negatively affecting both the function of organs and our mental abilities. This condition can lead you to develop various diseases over time.

One familiar maxim in modern society says that stress is a silent killer, and, sadly, we are living in a civilization where we are constantly subjected to different sources of fear. Fear of loss, such as the loss of your job, of a partner, of friends, of material goods; fear of failure, fear of diseases, relationships, inadequate performance, shortages of goods, animals, the future, war, death, the unknown... not to mention public speaking, which lists higher than the fear of death, for example; and the list could go on and on. Some of these fears are justified in a way, or, more specifically, in certain situations; but most of the fear we confront is simply our choice, and from that perspective, it's really ridiculous.

Will Smith, producer, rapper and, according to Newsweek, "the most powerful actor in Hollywood" [62], has been nominated several times for Golden Globe Awards and Academy Awards and is the winner of four Grammy Awards. We see him as someone who has a really deep understanding of life and its meaning, and whose advanced philosophical views are permeated with a ridiculously high level of determination, motivation and energy that drives him further and further with each step that he makes. He said one thing about fear that none of us should ever forget. *"Fear is not real. The only place that fear can exist is in our thoughts of the future. It is a product of our imagination, causing us to fear things that do not at present and may not ever exist. That is near insanity, Kitai. Do not misunderstand me, danger is very real, but fear is a choice."*[34] [63]

Some of the fears we mentioned above are part of human nature, but mostly they are forced upon us from outside, inflicted/spammed by our surrounding environment. Constant bombarding by media with information, pictures and sounds we can not process and forced reactions to them cause our unconscious learning of inadequate responses and induce feelings of fear. When you catch yourself feeling fear, think about it and remember the words of Yoda from the movie *The Phantom Menace*: *"Fear is the path to the dark side, fear leads to anger, anger leads to hate, hate leads to suffering."* You don't want to suffer, you want to live a happy and meaningful life, and in order to get that, you need to be free of fear and become more receptive to the "signals" that really matter in your life. So it is not surprising that successful people carefully select what information they let into their minds. This is a very important concept – to choose your own limits, not to accept the wide-open limits imposed by society, that lead to information overload. Instead of focusing on data and events which are unimportant for them, they consciously direct their thoughts toward the areas of their real interests. Their ability to cope with induced fear is very effective.

The first step in managing fear is awareness and recognition of it. When a person is capable of recognizing their fears and what triggers those fears, then their reactions to them can be controlled. In order to achieve a change, it is necessary to reprogram the mind to respond differently. There are many techniques that people can choose from: one of them which is very efficient is to reduce the perceived importance of situations which cause fear, meaning, for example, that we can accept the possibility of failure.

A good example of this is the fear of some important business meeting or interview. Questions start to appear about what could go wrong; after a while, you have a complete doomsday scenario in your head. There's nothing wrong with imagining future scenarios, we just need to break them down into ALL the possible scenarios

---

34 This is actually Will Smith's quote from the movie *After Earth* (story by Will Smith), where he was counseling his character's son, Kitai.

and sub-scenarios, not just the bad ones, but also the positive ones. This will prepare us for both success and failure. When we come to the failure scenarios, we should ask ourselves what will happen if we fail, what are the other possibilities, and so on. Accepting all possible outcomes reduces our fear of the situation. That is a very simple but effective technique.

The Buddhist approach to fear, for example, is based on the acceptance of it as an emotion and its subsequent transformation. Vietnamese Zen master, poet, peace activist and Buddhist monk, Thich Nhat Hanh, says that fear is energy, and if you know how to use that energy, you can produce good things. On the other hand, if you don't know how to make good use of it, it can do you more harm than good. We need to look deeply into our fear to see what it's made of. We can do that through meditation, for example. If you don't know the nature of your fear, you can not use it to do good things. The first question to ask is: What is fear? What is it made of? It is based on wrong perceptions or illusion. When looking deep into fear, we see only non-fear elements. It's like looking at a flower and seeing that the flower is only made of non-flower elements. In it, we see the sunshine, the rain, the earth, the compost, the gardener and so on. These are all non-flower elements. They have come together in order for the flower to manifest. And if we remove all non-flower elements, we see there is no flower left. It is the same thing with our fears [64]

All techniques for controlling fear require us to restore communication with ourselves in order to develop greater awareness. Being alone is one of the most powerful and inexpensive tools that can help us in this respect. It is also the point at which we make contact with our intuition. Once again you can realize for yourself how everything is so very interconnected and leading you from one thing to another. No matter where you start walking and no matter how big your steps are, you will always arrive at the desired destination. It's like a domino effect; once you flick the first domino, the wave starts till if finally reaches the last domino standing. And yes, the last one will fall also, it's just a matter of time: it's not a question of "if", but a question of "when".

One of the supporters and participant/interviewees in our *Intuition and Success* Project entrusted us with a very interesting personal experience. Due to certain classified matters, in this case we are not able to reveal who gave us this story, so let's call him George. This doesn't in any way diminish the value of the account.

George kept the majority of his assets in stocks, and one night he woke up with a strong sense that he should immediately sell all his profitable shares of a stable company. For some time, he thought that this feeling was only based on some bad dreams that he couldn't actually remember. As the morning did not bring any different feeling, he called his broker and instructed him to sell those shares. Of course his long-time broker advised him not to sell, but George wouldn't listen; his sudden and strong feeling had convinced him that he was doing the right thing. Due to the disclosure of some sensitive business information, that company's stock lost 2/3 of its value in a matter of days.

Similar situations happen to us all on a daily basis. We think to ourselves that instead of driving to work, we should go by bus today, and unknowingly we avoid a car accident. Or you may say *"I will not order my usual meal today"*, and escape food poisoning, or *"I really need to talk to this person whom I haven't seen in a long time"*, and get some important information.

To sum up, let us rephrase the following thought from Thich Nhat Hanh: *"Non-fear is the basis of true happiness. The greatest gift we can offer others is our non-fear"*. [65] Instead, we can say: *"The greatest gift we can offer our intuition is our non-fear."*

Negativity and Stress

As we are living in an imperfect world (and it seems quite obvious that it will remain this way for a long time), it is very sad that we grow up with a lack of knowledge and skills which we could use to spot and overcome negativity and stress. If the implementation of such skills were provided either by of our parents in our early childhood or later on through our educational systems, a lot of lives would be saved, both literally and in terms of people living a more meaningful life. Our thoughts often lead to a negative frame of mind, and therefore we frequently act from this perpective. Negativity brings us to a very limited space and a very narrow perspective from which it is nearly impossible to see and react properly. Being in a negative state of mind is a signal to our body to respond by producing free radicals and stress hormones[35], and thus to put our body in a bio-physiological imbalance. That makes our negativity even deeper and stronger, which also disables our perception; since our perception is one of the most common ways that our intuition communicates with us, it's very important to keep it "turned on".

Negative emotions and stress cause a number of undesirable effects on the brain, body and mind. According to research conducted by scientists from the University of California at Berkeley, chronic stress can alter how neurons connect with each other, which ultimately effects our cognitive functions, including changes in learning and memory. Even more, it also effects our emotional well-being. Maintaining this kind of state for too long can contribute to mental disorders such as anxiety, depression or post-traumatic stress disorder. A growing body of research shows the increased risk of stroke due to significant levels of stress. One study showed that those who reported experiencing chronic stress caused by problems such as health, money, and relationships are almost 60% more likely to suffer a stroke or transient ischemic attack (TIA). *"There's such a focus on traditional risk factors — cholesterol levels, blood pressure, smoking and so forth — and those are all very important, but studies like this one show that psychological character-istics are equally important,"* says study author Susan Everson-Rose, PhD, MPH. The good news is that our brain has a natural ability to recover from stress. *"Generally speaking, the brain, and especially the hippocampus, has a substantial degree of plasticity, meaning that the brain is quite malleable,"* says Sundari Chetty, PhD, a faculty member in the Department of Psychiatry and Behavioral Sciences at Stanford School of Medicine. In other words, this means that when a stressor is removed or diminished, what happens is that neural stem cells regain their capacity to generate neurons at a normal level again. [66]

"Stress is a fact of life, but being stressed out is not. We don't always have control over what happens to us," says Allen Elkin, PhD, director of the Stress Management Counseling Center in New York City. *"Yet, that doesn't mean we have to react to a difficult situation by becoming frazzled or feeling overwhelmed or distraught."* [67]

---

35 One of the commonly known stress hormones is cortisol. In "survival mode", cortisol is crucial for maintaining fluid balance and blood pressure, while controlling body functions that aren't crucial during a life-threatening situation, like digestion, immunity and growth.

Stress itself is not especially harmful. Indeed, an adequate level of stress can help you to stay focused, appropriately energetic and capable of dealing with different challenges. The problem is chronic stress and short peaks of high-level of stress. Again, the key lies in balance.

Tip: Studies show that some of the most successful ways to instantly decrease the cortisol level are running barefoot, walking, taking a nap, meditating or praying. Also, sleep is very important. But remember that resolving the source of stress is more important than just relieving the symptoms.

Firstly, we need to became aware of the stressful situation if we are in one, and secondly we need to react properly.[36] Interestingly, what we have found in our research is that, in many cases, people are perfectly aware that they are in a negative state or a stressful situation, but they usually find it hard to do anything about it, to turn things around and steer towards a positive situation. And one of the differences that separates the best from the rest is the ability to consciously shift from a negative to a positive state of mind. That skill can be learned, and it is definitely worth the effort.

> *"Failures of self-regulation are central to the vast majority of health and social problems that plague modern societies. The most important strength that the majority of people need to build is the capacity to self-regulate their emotions, attitudes and behaviors."*

> —Rollin McCraty

While it is commonly believed that we don't have a lot of control over our emotions, the research on heart-brain interactions and

---

36 You can read more about how to react and what you can do to prevent negative thoughts in the chapter *Awareness of the Present Moment.*

intuition conducted by HeartMath Institute showed that we actually can self-regulate and shift out of a state of emotional unease or stress into a "new" positive state of emotional calm and stability. They developed a set of self-regulation techniques and practices that can systematically allow you to intentionally change your emotions. Their so-called HeartMath System of techniques and technologies is widely used by individuals as well as by health professionals and companies, health-care systems, educational institutions and government agencies. *"The techniques are designed to enable people to intervene in the moment when negative and disruptive emotions are triggered."* [45]

Living in the Past – Old Regrets

"If you aren't in the moment, you are either looking forward to uncertainty, or back to pain and regret."

—Jim Carrey

We've already touched on regret a little bit, back in the *Introduction*, where we mentioned the most common regret of dying people who stated, *"I wish I'd had the courage to live a life true to myself, not the life others expected of me."* Nobody wants to have regrets, yet we all seems to have them. Because of the remorse and pain that they carry, we consider their presence in our life to be one of the biggest distractions from a blissful life, a real nightmare. What is happening is that we are relentlessly trying to turn back time, and at the same time we all know that this is impossible and that there is nothing we can do to change the past. Regrets really are a waste of time and energy, you can't build anything on them. No matter the situation you are in right now, there is actually no need for regret; why should you allow your past to dictate how you should feel now? The only reasonable thing we can do is to accept past mistakes as a part of our growing process and use them to better understand what adjustments we need to apply, not to fall into the same trap again. One way to look at it is that everything you did or didn't do is exactly what you wanted at one time in your past. Look at it this way: every regret you may have represents an amazing opportunity to grow, and maybe something happened to you in the past for that very reason – to give you the experience needed to continue your personal growth. Be at peace with your past and remember that worrying about the future is also a wasteful act.

Living in the past is one of the biggest distractions from living a blissful life. You relentlessly try to do the impossible, to turn back time, yet you know very well that this is never going to happen.

Tip: Don't let the past or the future hinder you: the only thing that matters is NOW. Bil Keane said, *"Yesterday's the past, tomorrow's the future, but today is a gift. That's why it's called the present."* By making a correct decision today, your are creating both your future and past.

In one recent interview, highly successful actor, comedian, impressionist, screenwriter and producer, Jim Carrey, said that an actor plays characters, and if he goes deep enough into those characters, he realizes that his own character is pretty thin to begin with. While there was a lot of debate about this statement, some even going so far as to say he was going crazy, this is a completely erroneous interpretation; apparently, he is just in the process of spiritual transformation. *"Suddenly, you have this separation and go, 'Who's Jim Carrey? Oh yeah, he doesn't exist. There's just a relative manifestation of consciousness appearing, and then somebody gave him a bunch of ideas; a name, a religion and a nationality, and he clustered those together into something that is supposed to be a personality."* In an article on Jim Carrey's awakening, Samuel Kronen nicely wrote that *"It is necessary to have a cultural identity, but what is perhaps unnecessary is to give all importance to that particular identity and to try and pretend that it encompasses who we are at the depths of our being. Carrey continues: 'I believe that I got famous so that I could let go of fame. It's still happening, but not with me. Dressing happens, hair happens, interviewing happens, and it happens without me. Without the idea of me. There's just what's happening, and it's not personal. The difference between money and "my money" is a gigantic chasm. It feels like things are just happening, and they are going to happen whether or not I attach myself to it or not.'"* [68]

Life is happening: if you want to live your life with no regrets at all, then listen to your heart and go for it.

Dishonesty

"There is beauty in truth, even if it's painful. Those who lie twist life so that it looks tasty to the lazy, brilliant to the ignorant, and powerful to the weak. But lies only strengthen our defects. They don't teach anything, help anything, fix anything or cure anything. Nor do they develop one's character, one's mind, one's heart or one's soul."

— José N. Harris

Scientists have proven that we learn to lie somewhere between the ages of two and five, and that we all have more or less innate tendencies to lie or to manipulate. People shade the truth, embellish the reality, cut corners or simply tell lies in order to control a situation or to manipulate things toward the outcome they desire. Dishonesty sometimes bring us some short-term gain, but when we reach the bottom line, we are most likely to pay double. Dishonesty unbalances us mentally as well as physically. From the moment we lie, we are struggling to focus on unreal events, facts or feelings, while the truth annoyingly tries to jump into our every thought, and starts coming out through all our unspoken words, our body language and our energy. A lie is an unreal mental construct we have created, and it takes up all our attention; the more we try to keep that mental construct alive, the more we remain cut off from our inner guidance, our intuition. We may be deceiving others, but we are also deceiving ourselves. Why is lying to ourselves a problem, and why should we tell ourselves the true? We can consider a tendency to lie to ourselves as being one of the major obstacles to getting a proper self-perception, and to finding our intuitive frequency. Dishonesty to ourselves is mostly about being afraid of reality, and for that reason, we find ourselves escaping from reality and avoiding pain. We are afraid of the reaction of others, we are afraid of losing our self-respect or the respect of those others. By kidding ourselves and avoiding things, we are in denial; we are definitely wasting time and a great opportunity for proper self-development at that specific moment; and finally, yet importantly, we are distancing ourselves from our intuition.

Operating through Routines

Most people have a tendency to operate within a routine; they tend to do the same thing in the same way, guided by inertia. Operating this way gives you a feeling of being on "the safe side", taking no risks, controlling the situation. But is this really so? Well, it depends on the situation, but in general we wouldn't say so. If you operate a nuclear power plant, then yes, routine can be a great ally; but for most other situations in our everyday lives, the opposite is true – by operating mechanically, through routines and habits, you are running the highest risk possible of losing all that you have or think you have. For example, if you have an innovative product or process, sooner or later, someone somewhere is going to drive by you; it's just a matter of time before it's going to happen. Operating according to any kind of routine is a big barrier that keeps us from seeing synchronicities, given that routine restrains the free flow of information, or limits access to this information to a one-way flow, which does not enable synchronicities to break through clearly and loudly enough to be noticed.

Routines make time pass you by! Once you learn how to deal with the major challenges of life, you become comfortable, you stop challenging yourself and your brain automaticaly "runs on autopilot".

"Autopilot" mode is a dangerous way to live – you don't pay attention, you lose your fascination with discovering new things, and finally you become disconnected from your life's purpose and your intuition. Years may seem to pass in a fraction of a second; it's like those years passed you by.

Tip: You are only on the safe side when you are strongly committed to constant personal or group development. The "smart changes" involved in growth will appear as you constantly overcome the natural tendency toward inertia.

When you are constantly seeking to grow in the different areas of your activity, either as an individual or as a group (e.g., family, business team, etc.), you are going to leave the door open for intuition to enlighten you and be of help as much as possible.

PART II

III. Intuition And Success

MOST PEOPLE ASSOCIATE success with what can be seen at a first glance, wealth and fame; but what they overlook is actually the most important aspect of real success - that is the success which comes from within, from what is happening inside a person, their own personal satisfaction with their life. The view of success that the world recognizes is very superficial, it's just the tip of the iceberg. The real treasure, the basis for a truly meaningful life, lies deep below the surface.

The Path to Success

WHAT IS SUCCESS? The word success is very general and can indicate many different things. Everyone understands it differently, and accordingly sets different goals. If we are to define success here, we find it more appropriate to speak about overall or total success, a Successful Life, and we would divide a Successful Life into three basic components, three separate categories or stages: (1) Financial Success, (2) Social Success and (3) Spiritual Success.

Financial Success is often associated with the material world - money, power and wealth, economic prosperity and security, while Social Success can be linked with social acceptance, publicity, fame, influence, personal persuasiveness and political power. While both financial and social success are easily spotted and stem from (and represent) the "external/outer world" of a person, true success comes from within and happens on a very different level of experience. When speaking of true success, we are referring to inner success, what we call Spiritual Success. This does not refer to religious fulfillment (although for many people this may be one aspect of this type of success), but to the achievement of inner personal goals and values not directly visible to others, which may be associated with blissfulness, fulfillment, happiness, love, compassion, honor, chivalry, integrity and resonance (being in tune with your own personal calling, your true mission in life).

We understand *Financial Success* to be the lowest level of the three; it is a stage where you create wealth, regardless of the means you use or the reasons you are lead by. *Social Success* on the other hand is not only about money or purely business-oriented anymore. In this stage, a person tends to care about his reputation as well; he has a need to be accepted by others, he wants to *lead* by example. Here, we are still in the field of *greed* and *ego*, but of a slightly different degree. These two levels represent what we define as "false success", as both are happening outside of a person and can be misleading – they change a person´s external conditions, but not their internal make-up, their level of satisfaction. And they are actually interchangeable – although people usually strive for money and stability before they seek fame and status, the order of these two stages may be inverted, may overlap, or can even occur simultaneously. Either one of these two can advance your position in the material world, without making you a better person. The highest level of the three is reserved for that part of the Successful Life which we understand as our *Spiritual Success*. When this level is reached, a person starts seeing and sensing himself and the world around him in a completely different way. Greed and money are replaced by integrity and compassion; power and fame are replaced by self-satisfaction and self-sufficiency and the word "me" changes to "we". A person is not trying to impose anything on anyone, he just IS and lives, doing things with a different kind of energy and approach, and the people around him naturally start to feel and honor that. He is not just talking the talk, he is walking the walk. *"When you trust your intuition, you act so convincingly that others subconsciously start to follow you,"* affirmed Ivo Boscarol, founder and CEO of Pipistrel, the first company in the world to bring out a fully electric twin-seater aircraft.[37]

Another aspect, worth mentioning at this point, which usually becomes more and more evident as we progress along the path of personal growth, and which slowly forces us to rethink our strategy for a Successful Life (Financial Success, Social Success and Spiritual Success), is the gradual decline of our health. The exhausting efforts and stressful tensions involved in "chasing the dream" (especially if it is the wrong one) are finally perceived, and are often seen as having been an excessive and disproportionate sacrifice. Striving for the

---

37 At the time of publishing this book, larger competitors like Airbus have only developed prototype electric planes. Pipistrel was named the most innovative company in the European Union in 2010 and is a multiple NASA Challenge winner.

misleading forms of success brings more harm than good to our body, mind and soul, and so listening to our inner voice usually becomes more important in relation to all forms of health.

"If the left hemisphere of the brain goes on dominating you, you will live a successful life — so successful that by the time you are forty you will have ulcers; by the time you are forty-five, you will have had at least one or two heart attacks. By the time you are fifty you will be almost dead — but successfully dead!" [38] explains Osho. He adds that, by following the false path to success, one may become a great scientist, but he will never become a great human being; he may accumulate plenty of wealth, but will lose all that is of worth in life; and he may conquer the whole world, like Alexander the Great, but his own inner territory will remain unconquered. [69]

In short, if the lower two levels of success are based on the "material" world and what we "see", the third level is where personal well-being reigns, which is based more on "internal experience" and what we "feel". Of course, both lower levels are important to a certain extent, as most of us can't live on thin air, unless we are living a monk´s life; again, what matters is the balance. A financially successful man is rich, a socially successful man is richer and a spiritually successful man is the richest. But contrary to most contemporary beliefs, we would like to show that it isn´t necessary to wait for our life to reach "old age" to direct us towards Spiritual Success. In fact, we think that it should be just the opposite — that by learning the path to Spiritual Success from our youth, we can open our hearts earlier, come to confide in our intuition at a younger age, and discover more pleasant and satisfying ways of achieving Financial and Social Success to sustain us when our energy begins to wane later on.

Everyone is familiar with the hourglass, the antique instrument for measuring the passage of time. The bottom compartment starts out empty, indicating that zero time has passed. As the sand (representing both the passing time and/or the amount of attention or energy) descends from the upper compartment, it fills the lower part. The fuller the lower compartment, the higher the sand, the more time has passed and the more energy/focus we have put into it, until it is

---

38 By referring to the "left hemisphere", Osho indicates the so-called brain lateralization, the idea that each of our brain hemispheres controls or is specialized in certain specific skills or behavior. The left hemisphere is logical, rational, mathematical, scientific, calculating... Check out our chapter *The First Steps Have Been Taken* for more details.

filled and the time period being measured (our lifetime, in this case), as well as the sum total of our life's energy, comes to an end. During their youth, represented by the lower part of the hourglass when it is empty and slowly beginning to fill, people usually strive for Financial and Social Success, putting the majority of their energy and focus into these; their attention is focused outwards, towards the visible things in life. Their goals can be represented by the two terms in the lower half of the hourglass – usually, Financial Success is the big thing, the base upon which they build their dreams, followed by Social Success. They usually consider the degree of happiness that they receive from achieving these two goals, the objectives they were taught to pursue, as being all the satisfaction they need from life. Later on, as we mentioned earlier, comes maturity (represented by the level of the sand reaching the middle and upper parts of the bottom chamber of the hourglass), experience and a growing contact with inner "enlightenment" (through intuition, an internal connection and a sense of fulfillment), and people find out that they have been on the wrong path. What really brings them true bliss, happiness and fulfillment is their inner well-being. From that moment of awareness on, their belief system becomes inverted - they care less for money and what other people think of them and put the majority of their efforts into increasing their personal well-being, their Spiritual Success. They tend to be much more interested in reaching a state of inner peace, achieving resonance with their intuition, and producing happiness, regardless of their circumstances and surroundings. At this stage, the earlier meaning of the word "success" disappears; instead of wishing to impress others or satisfy society's expectations, what matters is their inner experience and understanding that success comes only through proactive work on oneself; that true success comes from within, not from outer appearances and comforts. This all becomes as clear as a blue sky.

As mentioned, the process for achieving a Successful Life can be symbolically displayed by a graphic version of the hourglass, a well-known device. To illustrate more clearly this inversion of values, which can lead us to a more meaningful life and help us all to remember this essential concept, let´s do something that most books don´t suggest – turn the book upside-down (180°), just like you would turn over an hourglass to reset its function of counting time. In this way, we can symbolically start a new cycle here and now, a new life.

Welcome to the journey of becoming the best version of yourself. Now you are able to read the section of the hourglass diagram which was previously on top, and now we can gain a new and different perspective. We see a different pyramidal structure, a different motivational model, where Spiritual Success is now on the bottom, serving as the foundation for our life, on which we can build our Financial and Social Success (to the extent that we really need them) based on our true inner guidance. The triangle which can now be read from this unconventional angle shows an idea exactly the opposite of what traditional logic and social values teach us.

We see a model whose perception is normally limited to middle-age or the final years of a person's life (if it is ever perceived at all). Symbolically, we now have the opportunity to start doing the right thing in the right way and at the right time.

Another important and extremely valuable aspect of this new model is that it should be used to teach our children about the importance of concentrating their attention and efforts on perceiving their own inner being, their own inner guidance. We can provide them FROM THEIR EARLIEST YEARS with the level of wisdom which most people only achieve near the end of their lives, if at all. And with that wisdom comes a vision of reality which may be able to guide the world's development in a different, healthier direction. Guided by their more highly developed intuition, these *future adults* will acquire innovative and productive ideas while they still have the ambition (in the healthiest sense of this word) and energy to apply them throughout the rest of their lifetimes, thus achieving true success during every stage of their lives – and providing a new role model for generations to come.

This concept of "turning over a new leaf" or "turning things upside-down" in order to discover a new direction in life is also symbolically represented in the Tarot card "The Hanged Man". Tarot is the ancient art of understanding personal characteristics and life situations and determining future paths by using cards (the interpretation of which also relies heavily on intuition). The 12th card, "The Hanged Man", may seem somewhat sinister at first glance, but among other things, it represents the need for inverting your perspective, breaking old habits and limiting patterns, seeing things upside down in order to find your true direction. One may notice that even though the character on the card is hanging upside down, he does not seem to be suffering at all. Furthermore, his head is surrounded by a halo, a luminous radiance, indicating some kind of enlightenment this new point of view has brought him.

In 1971, with reference to this card, Colin Wilson wrote: *"A. E. Waite, a fellow "hermetic student" of Yeats… goes on to explain: "He who can understand that the story of his higher nature is embedded in this symbol will receive intimations concerning a great awakening that is possible."* [70]

> *"Success without fulfillment is the ultimate failure. The ultimate failure!"*
>
> —Tony Robbins

Tony Robbins, an entrepreneur, best-selling author, incredible philanthropist, and one of the world´s best life and business strategists, who has empowered more than 50 million people from 100 countries through his programs, spoke in one interview about two important skills: the science of achievement and the art of fulfillment.

Making money is based on "science" and following certain rules: *"Any age, any color, any background, any gender, if you do these things, you will have an abundance of money,"* he says. The same applies to the body: *"Everyone's biochemically different, but you and I both know there are fundamental rules, laws, there's a science of the body. You violate that science, you're gonna have a disease, you´re gonna have low energy. If you align with that, you're gonna have an abundance of energy."* Of course, inner fulfillment is not like that at all, it is not a science, it is an art. *"Most people think, 'Well, I want to get that' because they're modeling somebody else and that might work on how to achieve something."* But as he nicely continues, *"It will never work for what fulfills you. Success without fulfillment is the ultimate failure. The ultimate failure! Because if you go at something and you fail and you're an achiever, you don't* [really] *fail, you're like 'I learned something, I'll just try something else. I'm still going to get there'; but when you succeed and you are not happy… you're technically screwed."* Robbins cites a very good example, the comedian and actor Robin Williams, who was a great achiever, he even won an Academy Award for NOT being funny; he achieved everything and yet he hung himself. *"And I know someone's saying, 'You know, he had dementia, he had drug abuse, he had alcohol abuse through most of his life', because he made everybody happy but whom?"* The answer to this question is absolutely clear - himself. *"That's the ultimate failure,"* Robbins says, and continues: *"I believe our lives are controlled by one force — decisions. I certainly believe in a force greater than myself, call it God if you will, grace, whatever you want to call it, the universe. But I also believe it gives us choices."* [71]

If you never have before, maybe now is the right time to start listening to your intuition. Look deep down inside yourself and ask: "Am I really happy? Am I living a meaningful life? Do I remain in a beautiful state of mind, regardless of my circumstances and surroundings?" These are the deep waters where we believe real success lies, and when you come to this crossroads, be open for intuitive signs. They are there, and you don't even need eyes to see them. Feel them! Your body is the most advanced technological system on our planet. Experiencing inner success and fulfillment is the only way to really experience freedom and be truly successful. Again, we are not able to give a 100% infallible, working formula for a Successful Life, we are just offering you a framework within which you can search and work on your own personal and unique development and experience. Become an achiever of your own inner success by growing through the process of your own experience. It is only from experience that we really learn, from both the positive and negative episodes. We have performed extensive studies on this subject, and here we are presenting numerous examples and testimonials from highly successful people from around the world and all throughout history, each having their own success story to tell, and yes, you guessed it: at some point in their lives, they each started trusting their inner voice and letting it lead the way to their fulfillment and a meaningful life.

It's not about the money at all

> *"Following intuition is absolutely illogical, there is no sense to it, but it's exactly what will eventually make you happy."*

> —Jain 108

A very personal experience that Jain 108 confided to us shows that life is not about the money. Having a very rich father and growing up in a very wealthy family, he had or could have had everything he wanted, but he gave everything away and went hitchhiking. Why? Simply because he felt that way, he felt it so deeply that one day, he decide to follow this "illogical force" inside. *"Because it's like a magnetism, it's a force,"* he said. *"I put my thumb out and I hitchhiked for thousands of miles, I went to New Guinea and I was on my way to India, and I lived for two years in a jungle. I went from being a city boy to a jungle. I was so sick of the pollution and education that I just didn't know who I was. And I had to go live in a jungle, and there I learned the sacred geometry and I met medicine men. I met people who couldn't even speak English, but I communicated with them for years, and they were teaching me about the medicine in the roots of the trees and in the bark and the leaves, how to boil this, how to make coconut oil. So I learned from people I met in my travels about herbs and sacred geometry. Those were the best years of my life. I still look back; that was in my early twenties, it's 40 years ago, I had the best experience in my life, and that was intuition. For me to leave a rich family and go travel, I had to follow some weird internal dialog and debate that contradicted every-thing that I was doing. Something was saying, 'give everything away and go, just put your thumb in the air and just hitchhike and trust'. I lived off the trees for two years, I had no money for two years, and yet I had everything I needed, everything. So it's illogical, that's why we can't really explain intuition and I think that's the mystery: divine mystery."*

What we are trying to say is that the right criterion for measuring success is not *having more* (which is the way the world recognizes success), but rather the criterion should be *being more*. And if you ask us if a person who lives by intuition always *succeeds*, the answer may at first glance disappoint you; the answer is no (at least not by judging success in the sense that the world recognizes it), because others might be working more cunningly, more cleverly, more violently and/or more immorally. But in the sense that Buddha or Jesus might recognize the idea of success, then yes, he will succeed. Osho puts it very nicely when he says that if success is measured by happiness and bliss, then yes, he who follows his intuition will succeed. And he will remain in a blissful state of mind, whether he *succeeds* in the eyes of the world or not. On the other hand, a person that is not aligned with his intuition is almost *always* unsatisfied, whether he *succeeds* or not. [69]

There is no universal formula for success, but the framework within which each and every one of us should do his individual homework in order to achieve his individual success can be roughly defined.

Tip: *Nosce te ipsum* - know yourself. Ask questions and start listening. Get clear in your own mind what you really want and open yourself to different perspectives and ideas. Search for a deeper meaning in life and change your criterion for success accordingly. Be open to your inner guidance, regardless of the surroundings; spread your sails and become the captain of your ship.

"You should only take as much as you need, no more," says Oskar Kogoj. *"I've spent a lot of time among Indians. I was fascinated by them ever since I was a kid and read a lot about them and studied them. They told me, 'We can show you gold, we can show you the whole mountain, but you must not take it: you can take only as much as you need.' They knew that money, wealth and greed corrupt men."*

Successful People and Intuition

BEFORE THE *INTUITION and Success* project, if someone would ask us, "What are the most important things that distinguish between failure and success", we would answer with a list of five or ten such *things,* which we were sure are important for success: having clear goals, a vision, a focus, good work habits and hard discipline, surrounding yourself with the right people, being well educated and so on. You know, all the "classic tips" that you can learn about from different "success gurus". And they do work, up to a point.

But after intensive research, testing different techniques *in practice,* enormous amounts of effort put into a deeper understanding of the basic concept of human life and a giant leap in personal growth, along with the numerous interviews with highly successful people that we have done, today our answer is very different. Yes, the classic tips mentioned above are important and are part of most of the success stories recognized by the world, but the main difference is that they are not driven by inner wisdom. So what is that single most important detail that separates success from failure? We believe that the most important thing is to find your driving motivation inside yourself, to be driven from the inside out, and not the opposite. Knowing that the educational system (and in most cases "parenting" as well) is oriented to provide learning "from the outside in", we all soon come to believe that all our answers lie in the outer world. We start to believe that somebody else knows better than we do what's good for us, what we should and shouldn't do and so on. And the majority of people function exactly that way. In a decision process of any kind, they focus on others, looking for some external piece of advice and taking the risk (and accepting the consequences) of making wrong decisions, again and again. But what about the successful people? Somehow, they recognized along the way that the only one who knows what's truly best for them is nobody else but themselves, as long as they trust their own inner responses – their inner wisdom. In most cases, successful individuals are surrounded by a wide net of experts to support them with knowledge and advise them on how to deal with different procedures; but when it comes time to make decisions, they make their own choices in resonance with their intuition - which ultimately gives them complete control of their life and *destiny*.

By being in touch with many successful people, talking with them and reflecting on their ideas, we have gained an immeasurable wealth of information about what works for them. It is impossible to reflect the full value of their stories in writing, but in this book, we present some of their most significant perceptions about intuition and its relation to success. The following charts show a summary of the inter-viewees´ responses to two questions we asked in our studies, and we invite you to ask yourself these same questions:

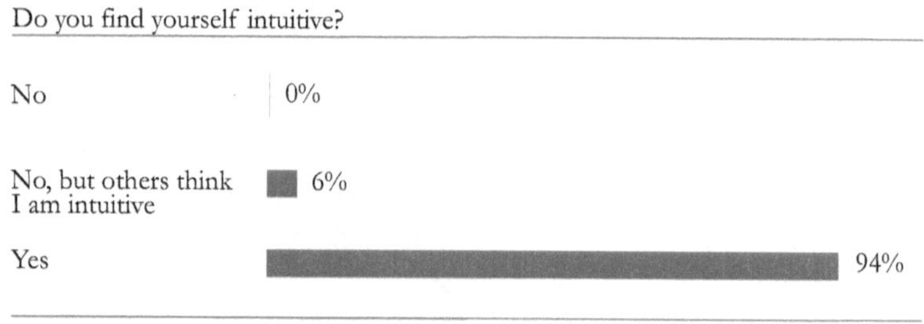

Highly successful people from around the world and from very different walks of life each have their own success story, but what we have found that they all have in common is that they all trust and use their intuition to lead the way to their success.

How would you rate (from 1 to 10) the importance of the intuition for the success?

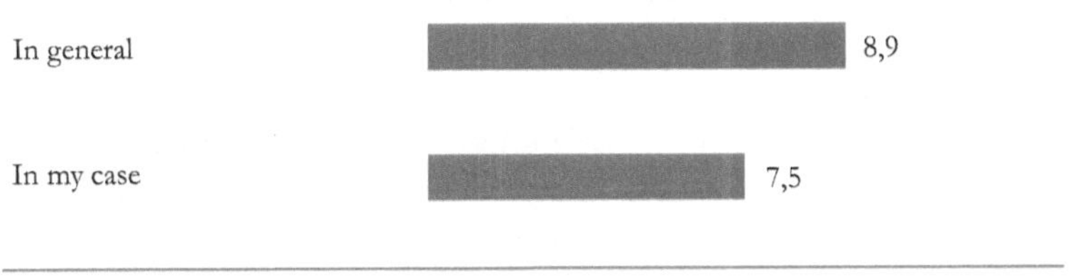

Some of the subjects of our interviews were very specific about why they consider themselves to be intuitive, while some hadn't thought about it much, but they all are certain that that they have this ability. We know that intuition is always with us, from the first day of our lives, but the question arises as to when a person "discovered" it and began to give it credit. Many of our interviewees have declared that they have been intuitive for as long as they can remember, but some of them have also described some specific event in their lives which revealed to them their number one life skill, their true calling in life. For example, let´s take four-time Grand Slam Winner, 28-time WTA Tour Winner and five-time ITF Tour Winner, Mary Pierce. *"I was pretty intuitive since my early twenties. When I won the French Open, while playing my first round, suddenly as if out of the blue I felt a message - it was like words not spoken - that I was going to win that tournament, and I did..."* As Mary went on to tell us, it was that particular event that gave her solid evidence of what she had always believed. It was from that point on that this professional tennis player began to pay more attention to her inner voice, which has helped her in her sports career as well as in all other areas of her life.

One of the most important messages we have collected through these interviews is the fact that intuition, among other things, helps us to unveil the greatness within us; it helps us to discover our true selves. Intuition helps us discover who we really are, what we should do in life or in certain situations, which are our greatest talents and how we should use them. We found these questions to be the "key" questions for becoming the best version of ourselves - to become truly successful. We all have various talents, but we can hardly see them all through our rational mind; in most cases, we need to be told about them repeatedly by someone else, or we can get that essential feedback by being tuned in to our intuition.

Most of the time, what separates those who live "more successful/ meaningful lifes" from the others is not just their ability to hear their inner voice, but also the courage to follow it. And always when we have found this to be the case, we have also found impressive stories behind this success, true success stories. The importance of intuition in this has impressed us, over and over again! Success stories are about setting and achieving goals, high motivation and hard work, but they are also the results of very interesting "coincidences", unbelievable facts and following inner guidance. Many of the participants in our project have said how intuition has helped them to discover their true potential.

Zeljko Mavrovic was the European boxing champion (EBU); he won 27 fights (22 by KO) and lost only once, in the match for the world heavyweight champion title. His life story is a clear example of what we are talking about: *'My first contact with boxing was when I was fifteen years old. I can still remember that day very clearly. A friend with whom I hung out at that time brought two pairs of old boxing gloves. I was the youngest one in the group, and the skinniest too; I was such an untypical boxer that it was almost funny. However, from the very first moment when I put those stinky old gloves on my hands, I knew deep inside me that this was it, and it was — boxing is my life. Moreover, after starting my boxing career, there were some critical moments when I started having doubts about my decision, and about myself. I started asking myself, 'Is this what I should be doing?' In those moments, my intuition helped me over and over to get through those unpleasant moments and carry on, to keep on going and succeed."*

On the other hand, we hear many stories of people who are just miserable about their lives, who feel defeated, who are disappointed with themselves and feel deep regrets for not exploring some of the unused talents which they intuitively know exist within them, because they never acted on their feelings. As Les Brown has said: *'Most of the people fail not because they aim too high and miss, but because they aim to low and hit."* What we now know is that with the help of intuition we are able to judge according to our true self, according to our true potential, and thus we are able to live life as the best version of our selves. What more can we ask for? Why should we do anything else?

Successful People Take Intuition Seriously

Despite the lack of "physical evidence" for intuition's existence and the fact that even the most successful individuals in many cases do not actually understand their intuitive promptings, they do not dismiss them, but take them extremely seriously! That is a very important finding, because it shows that they really do value intuition very highly, regardless of the fact that they do not know exactly why or how they know which decisions to make. And in many cases, due to this lack of a reasonable explanation, they don't like to talk about intuition, and won't even confess that they follow it or make decisions based on inner feelings. Like most people, experienced and successful professionals often cannot explain how they know what to do or why they know it. The only difference is that they learn to trust their hunches and simply do what they feel should be done with untroubled belief and pleasant expectations of good results.

Intuition is that most precious, outstanding and reliable force which can lead us at any moment in our lives, showing us the most direct way to reach our ultimate and permanent success. Interestingly enough, it is often the case that we are not aware of our success - it's something that we may already have achieved at some particular moment, but that we didn't consider as being success at that time; we may even believe that it is a major setback in our life. But as time passes, and we gain a deeper understanding of the complete context and allow ourselves to feel the situation, once we are able to look back and reflect on it in a completely impartial way, only then can we understand that it was actually success in disguise. For example, maybe we gave up everything to start some specific project, but despite all our efforts, the project doesn't get off the ground. We may even try again and again, and each time we fail, and this makes us feel disappointed and desperate. But after a while, when we accept the fact that this particular project is just not for us, we are able to see the true benefit for us which arose from that situation, that succeeding at that specific project would have taken us away from our true path. Looking back, we may be able to recognize numerous intuitive signs and coincidences which warned us of the wrong direction. We may even recognize that those intuitive messages went from a very gentle and silent nudge to a very loud and obvious alarm.

This is a pattern that showed up throughout our research, and we named this specific occurrence the "Inverse Success Pattern"

Successful People Pay Attention to Their Intuition

People who succeed pay serious attention to their own personal intuitive pattern, which helps them to recognize the key information they need at a particular time. It doesn't matter whether these individuals are succeeding in a business context or in some other area of activity, it doesn't matter in what environment they operate, it doesn't even matter at which stage of the developmental process they are; what is important is that they are prepared and determined to feel and to see everything that may help them to be successful – they pay attention. They are ready and receptive. And to be good at "catching" those signals, you have to know what you are looking for, you have to know what it is that you should pay attention to. You have to become familiar with your own intuitive patterns – to know what are the signs, feelings and sensations that your inner voice uses to send you messages. It's hard to hit a target when you don't know what your target is. With your intuitive pattern, it´s pretty much the same thing; if you haven't recognized and defined your own personal signals yet, you won't know what to look for, you won't have a clear target and your response to what your intuition is trying to tell you is going to be poor. In the graph below, you can see some of the feelings or signals that are directly connected to our intuitive decision-making process. Of course, we all experience them differently, but the bottom line is, at least we can define them through our own personal experiences, and then stay alert and look for ourselves to see when they appear in our lives.

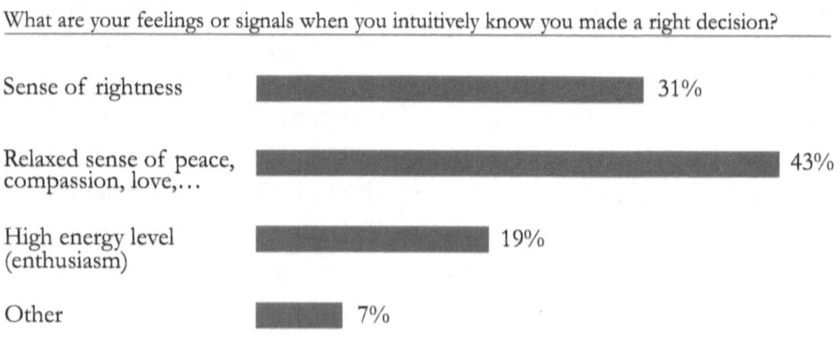

We are all individuals; we have very unique physical, psychological and mental abilities, and we are all at different spiritual and energetic levels. Thus, our forms of perceiving ourselves, of perceiving the present moment, our physical responses and our intuitive perceptions are also very unique. Therefore, it is extremely important that we constantly learn more about ourselves, because we are constantly changing and developing. Several of the successful people we interviewed have told us this, and we have pointed this out in different places in this book, as we too find it of crucial importance. Getting to know ourselves is the number one priority in life. This is especially true if we intend to be successful and a high achiever in any area of our lives.

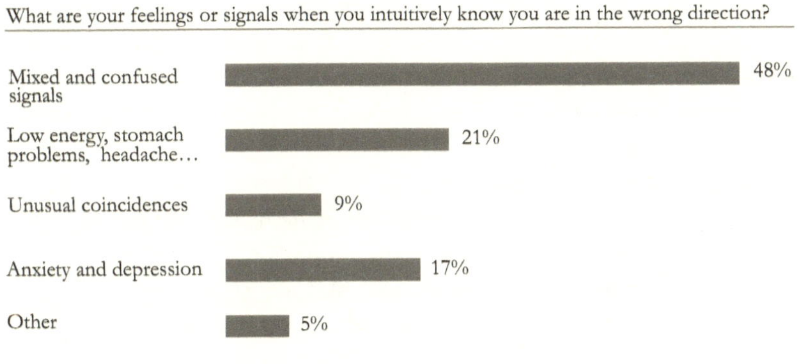

As we can see from this graph, different people sense different signals or feelings, yet there are some that stand out: and more importantly, all these signals are showing that we are going in the wrong direction, that we have not made the right choice. While these sensations are all unpleasant, they are really blessings in disguise – they help us to avoid unproductive or misdirected decisions, and help keep us on the path we should follow. So be grateful for these negative signals, just as we should be grateful for the positive signs that our intuition sends us.

According to our research, paying real attention turned out to be one of the most common characteristics of successful people. In the modern world, this ability is far more neglected and overlooked than it should be, which obviously places an important dividing line between the successful folks and everyone else.

Successful People Use Intuition to Sharpen their Focus

In trying to become successful, most people end up with a list of things they should do as a result of modeling the habits of the successful. In other words, they try to live their lives in many different ways, imitating their role models, hoping and believing that this will bring them the same success. Successful people are known to direct their attention to a very small number of activities, meaning that they develop the ability to see the whole picture, have a wide understanding of things, but when it comes to their own activities, their focus is pretty much narrow and intense. They have learned that sharpening their focus is very crucial for making any desired change, not to mention the importance of intuition in finding the right things to focus on. Intuition supports us in this way by popping up and drawing our attention, repeatedly. Among the most frequent answers to the question "What should a man or woman do to become successful?" in our research was something like this: "*In order to become successful, you have to know what you want, why you want it and what are the reasons that will support you along the way.*" What's more, the firmer your goals and reasons are, the more likely you will be to find out what are your drives, which ultimately can carry you to your own success. And partnership with your intuition will lead you to do that in a much more relaxed state and with a feeling of righteousness.

Successful People Use Intuition to Anticipate the Future

Anticipating the future and being able to properly prepare for the challenges of the future at the right time is another very important area where successful people simply dominate. The world is changing with increasing dynamics in the evolution of science and technology. Also, for this very reason, the ability to anticipate the future is more important than ever, since those who are able to better anticipate the future will have more time to prepare and thus will be ready for the changes to come. Most people usually follow new trends soon after they appear, some of them even get on board too late and thus suffer a variety of losses, but the most successful people create the changes or anticipate most of the future trends at the right time.

"I remember once when I lost my job, when I was fired out of broadcasting: September 18th, I'll never forget, 1978. I was behind on my house notes and my house was up for foreclosure. I did everything I could, I had borrowed as much money as I could borrow, I had talked to family members and friends. I did everything I could and I couldn't get enough money, being unemployed for several months, applying for job after job and I couldn't get a job. I couldn't get enough money to save the house, but I never felt, and this is very important, the feeling that I had, I never felt that I was going to lose that house. I wanted that house and so what I did was very uncanny: I relisted, I did the best that I could and at that time with the limited money that I did have, I decided to take a trip with my family to Miami, to go down and spend some time in the sun with my children and my wife. We caught a Greyhound bus from Columbus, Ohio, and we went to Florida. By the time I arrived, on the day that the bank was to foreclose on the house, 12:00 noon, I got a call from one of my former assistants who went by the house and said, 'Les, it's an emergency, call Columbus right away', and I did. She said, 'Les, you won't believe this, you have a check from the Internal Revenue Service on your income tax,' and it was enough to pay the house notes and I had money left over. I had never received a refund prior to that time or since that time, and I did not lose that house. There are thing we don't know or understand, but we do know if we do certain things, that things begin to happen that are in our favor, that show that the universe is on our side."

We believe that we all have situations, similar to Les Brown´s example above, when we are absolutely positive that everything is going to be okay, that we are on the safe side, that we just have to have faith and keep on doing what we are doing, and somehow the concern and challenge we are dealing with is about to be resolved. Let's take a look at another amazing example of how intuition can let you know that everything is going to be just fine. It is a very personal story confided to us by Dragan Djukic, who is considered to be one of the most successful handball coaches, experienced in leading various clubs and national handball teams. *"It was December 17, 1975. I was 13 years old and that morning started out like any ordinary day. I went to school, it was the second school hour, when the school headmaster entered the classroom and whispered something to my teacher. Right from the start, I knew that it was something concerning me, and it was. The teacher looked at me and said that I should go home, that something had happened. I ran, or rather I 'flew' to our apartment. After arriving there, they told me that my little brother (he was 8 years old) had fallen from a height of 12 meters, playing with a toy in the window of our apartment, and that he was in a difficult condition and had to be transported urgently to Belgrade hospital (at that time, we lived in Aleksandrovac, a small town about 230 kilometers from Belgrade). I will remember the thirty kilometers of road to Krusevac all my live! Not only because of the expression on my dad's face, in whose arms I was lying, nor the fact that the driver traveled the distance in a record 12 minutes, but because of a clear song that came to my heart from somewhere and did not stop, no matter how much I tried to push it away! It was in my subconscious. I was ashamed of my own feelings, and I was afraid that everyone would hear the sounds from my head, but the song did not stop and in some strange way made me calm and I got the incredible feeling that everything was going to be just fine. My brother had been transferred to the Belgrade Hospital by helicopter. He had a serious skull fracture and other injuries, but to our general happiness, there were no serious consequences to his health, and we just recently celebrated together the 40th anniversary of that event. Yet, to this day, I have not told anyone about that story. Whether telling it now is trust in some unknown person whose eyes will read this text, or just to support other people who need to understand the unknown parts of themselves, I do not know, and it is not my place to judge it. I felt it was time to tell it, and yes, ever since then I have followed my inner feelings, simply because they are always right."* We are honored to be entrusted with such a personal story and to act as a catalyzer so that this story will help others understand the powerful force within us which we call intuition. Djukic's experience shows that inner feelings can somehow signal us that things are going to work out well, even in the worst life situations.

Successful People Have Found Their Intuitive Channels

The majority of the successful people we have spoken with have given deliberate effort to developing their intuitive abilities by practicing some technique or method (see the graph below). Even though not all of them have done so, most successful individuals are determined and relentless in mastering the ability to hear their intuition.

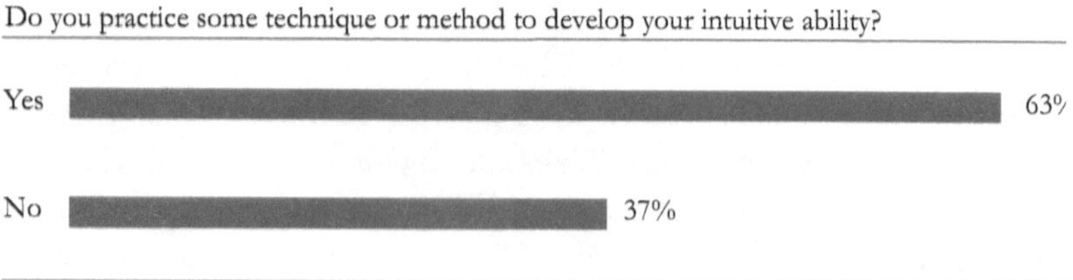

As bestselling author, entrepreneur and motivational speaker Boris Vene has told us: *"As a matter of fact, I've been mastering my ability to hear my intuitive voice since a very young age, but not through any special techniques or methods. Instead of that, I regularly practice analyzing all the most important situations in my life. For example, if something unpredictable has happened, in my mind I go back before that certain event, asking myself if there was some sign which I have overlooked, and in most cases I'm able to find it. Later on, I try to use that experience for understanding my intuition better. I find that, more often than not, in dealing with the analysis of past situations, I get to know my intuition better, and I'm more capable of perceiving its messages. To the people who would like to develop their intuition and build their relationship with their intuition, I propose imagining their intuition as a person, with whatever characteristics they might expect from their intuition. For example, imagine a wise old man with a long gray beard, who is compassionate, always in a good mood, righteous and always prepared to help you. Later on, begin to connect intuitive massages with this imaginary person and the closer you get to that person, the more you'll be able to understand your intuition and recognize even the most subtle intuitive messages - you are gonna get tuned to your intuitive channel."*

When we asked the subjects of our interviews about the specific techniques they use to develop their intuition, we found out that the majority of them either practice different physical activities, involve themselves with some kind of creative expression or practice meditation.

Which techniques or methods you practise to develop your intuitive ability?

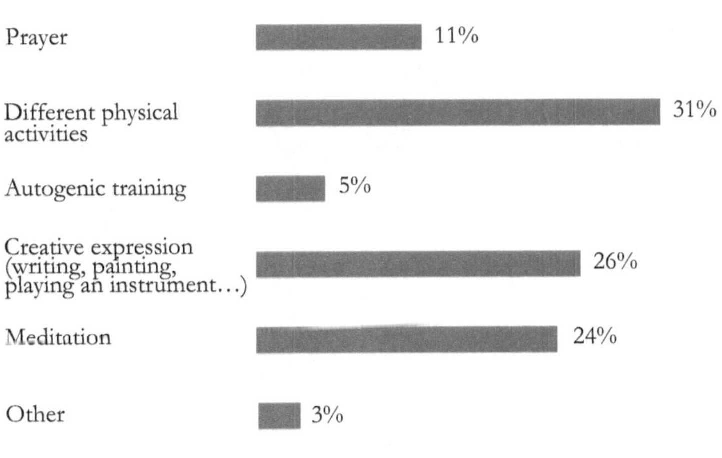

And when discussing the promoters of intuition, we find it interesting to share some statistics data on inhibitors of intuition as well. It has been shown through our research that as many as half of our interlocutors find their mind (in the way of lacking the knowledge on this phenomena) to be the biggest inhibitor, following by the ego and stress.

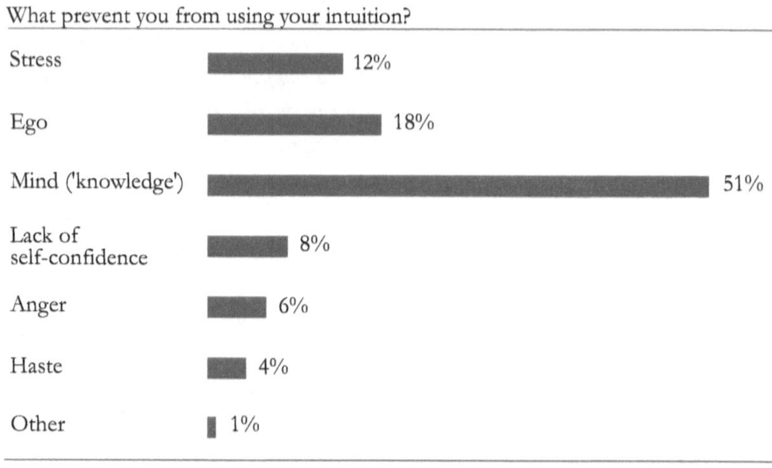

As we have seen here, there are many possible ways of developing your intuition. The more self-knowledge you acquire, through experimentation and observing your own life, the greater your chances of discovering what works for you, both in regard to strengthening what helps you find answers and avoiding emotional or psychological reactions that weaken your internal contact. The important thing is to learn the techniques that work for you and practice using them until you prove to yourself that you can trust your intuition to show you the path to success.

Intuition in Business –
A New Concept of Success

"If opportunity doesn't knock, build a door"

—Milton Berle

BUSINESSMEN USED TO do business based on a certain degree of rational decision making. Nowadays, it is more and more evident that there is something very crucial missing in the concept of business and in the process of fulfilling a company´s goals and vision – intuitive decision making. In the past, most businesses were successfully run based on predetermined processes, good analysis and more or less rational decision-making. We may say that because of the much more stable and predictable circumstances and business environment, the traditional business methods and techniques were at that time appropriate and sufficient. But through the third industrial revolution from the mid-1980s onward and the rise of telecommunications and appearance of the personal computer and internet, things began to change dramatically. It's seems like science fiction has become science fact: the world entered a period of tremendous change due to the enormous pace of technological development, which has more than obviously left its indelible imprint on the field of business management as well as in managerial capabilities. From our point of view, transition in management doctrine has separated managers into three distinct groups: (1) traditional managers (managers that stick to the step-by-step decision-making process and only trust the gathered facts and "numbers", blindly following statistics and analysis), (2) transitional managers (managers who are in the process of recognizing and supporting the value of intuition and other soft skills in management), and (3) intuitive managers (managers who are fully aware of the immense potential of intuitive capabilities, who are already widely leveraging from this inner force and have implemented intuitive decision making in their personal and business processes). They have become aware that gathering information and providing complex analyses are good for getting a perception and understanding of yesterday, but not necessarily for correctly perceiving today´s tendencies, and especially not for appropriately anticipating the future. They are justified in coming to this conclusion: many major business mistakes have been made because the manager had falsely predicted the future, relied only on the facts, which had nothing in common with the unpredictable future. That's why a manager´s capacity to predict new trends for the future has become one of the most important and sought-after skills, and companies are getting more and more interested in that potential. Digital transformation has led to the fourth industrial revolution and caused a mega-shift in all areas, with a great impact on our ways of doing business as well. The appearance of the Internet of Things, Big Data, 3D printing, automatization and robotization, artificial intelligence and many more revolutionary discoveries gives us every reason to believe that we are at the inflection point of an exponential pace of development, which is also driving the potential for fundamental change in managing businesses. This has made the intuitive way of doing business become one of the most desirable and successful ways of dealing with the uncertainty of the future. Bringing intuition into business can provide a great aid and advantage for the long term and sustainable success for any individual or organization.

Riccardo Illy, former Business Director of the famous coffee brand Illycaffè and current President of Gruppo Illy, the holding company that owns the Illycaffè company, which was founded by his grandfather in 1933 and has a presence in over 140 countries around the world, told us that he has absolutely no doubts when it comes to intuition in private and business life. Furthermore, he calculates that approximately half of his decisions are guided by his intuition. Illy, who successfully reorganized the Illycaffè company's internal business structure as well as the structures of the other firms it controlled, explains: *"Intuition is a very interesting faculty, and entrepreneurs and managers certainly need to take it into consideration more often, especially when making important decisions… I would say as a rough estimate that of all the decisions that I make, 50 percent are made by intuition and 50 percent are rationally based."*

His grandfather started the business with coffee and chocolate in 1933, but during the Second World War, he abandoned the chocolate and never returned to that line. Then in 2004, when Gruppo Illy was established and the control was passed to the third generation, it was decided to diversify, but the million-dollar question was – into which sector?

"Here is an interesting example of intuition; you have an empty sheet of paper and you have to decide where to diversify. And my intuition was that we first go back to the sector in which we had already had experience in the past, and we went back into the chocolate sector. We also went into the tea and wine sectors. We can say that the choice of the sectors that we decided to enter or re-enter was mainly related to intuition," says Illy, who also mentioned that, after intuitively choosing these sectors, they did all the required analysis and research in order to support or reject their gut feeling. As he explains, when he is looking at the business numbers, he is of course looking at them in a rational way, but in the end, it is always his feelings which determine his actions. *"If there is a bad feeling, the feeling that something is wrong, I work on the case some more, I analyze more deeply, I ask for more information, until I feel comfortable about my participation in that particular situation."*

Victoria Lynn Weston, who performs consulting services for executives, company presidents, entrepreneurs, professionals and individuals, using predictive skills to make their decision-making processes easier, told us that in the business world, there isn't a successful executive, CEO, CIO, entrepreneur or business owner who will tell you that they don't rely on intuition. *"These successful business people will tell you, they don't have time to read a stack of analysis, reviews, etc. They have to make a decision quickly and move on to the next business of the day. Of course, they compare their intuitive insights against their facts and logic."* We asked her to share with us some of her personal experience from the business world, and she gave us a few examples: we present two of them here. *"I can tell individuals what will happen, how a deal may or may not materialize and why. I focus on the key managers, express my intuitive thoughts about their strengths and weaknesses, predict upcoming events, and so on. At the beginning of my career as an intuitive business consultant, I really embraced challenges from skeptics. I'm not always right, of course, but when it's important, I'm more accurate than not. Many years ago, one of my clients was a high-profile stock broker. He consulted with me on a fluke and wanted to know about a couple of specific stocks, including the Campbell's Soup Corporation. I said Campbell's soup would drop a few points and he scoffed, saying that that stock would never drop significantly. A week later, the stock dropped and my client bought several shares."* Here´s another interesting example, when she helped a client, a fortune 100 company President with a lawsuit, to save more than $20,000: *"The man wanted to know how to best prepare for the lawsuit, and who would be the best-suited attorney. There are many details to this story, but it was about the company's private airplane lease. They were being sued for back payments. One of the more uncanny aspects was that I described how the attorney would look, 'like Albert Einstein, with wiry hair.' The attorney was able to win the case of trumped-up lease charges, saving the company $20,000 or more!"*

Vision and Strategy–See Further with Holistic Understanding

> *"Don't let the noise of others´ opinions drown out your own inner voice. Have the courage to follow your heart and intuition. They somehow already know what you truly want to become."*

> —Steve Jobs

It's hard to determine which of the elementary management functions is more important than the others, because they are all needed at some point, regardless of the type of business, and thus are all equally important. But if we look at which of the functions is the most closely related with intuition, it would certainly be vision and strategy as part of the decision-making process.

When speaking from an individual point of view, when choosing the right career, for example, it is of course unnecessary to re-em-phasize the importance of intuition and the ability to perceive valuable intuitive insights. In most cases, choosing the right career determines whether we are going to be successful in what we do or not. Well, it's pretty much the same when speaking from the organizational or business point of view. To have an adequate vision of the future is probably among the toughest challenges for any manager. Even so, many of the most successful managers and leaders claim that they get the vision for their organization directly through their intuition. And they use their intuitive ability for bridging the gap between the present situation and the future perspective of the company during the subsequent period of ten or fifteen years or more. This is a really interesting and fascinating finding that puts a new and very important perspective on managerial and leadership capabilities.

Ivo Boscarol, the founder and CEO of one of the most innovative aircraft companies, Pipistrel, told us about his experience. *"When I started developing more energy-efficient aircraft with less noise, more than twenty years ago, there was practically no one who did not at least quietly laugh at my vision and my business orientation. Often I even heard people say directly that they had never met a crazier aircraft developer and entrepreneur. Honestly, it was really painful to hear that because, when you have a very precise and clear vision in which no one believes except you, and no one except you can even see that it's possible, that's hard for anyone. So, for that reason, I didn't have any support from the outside world at that time, even though I needed it very much. All I had was my intuitive vision and a very strong conviction that "this is it" and that I should keep on going, keep on going and not let the opinion of others distract me on my way. Therefore, I can say with a great deal of certainty that the whole philosophy, vision and strategy of Pipistrel is based on pure intuition. I was intuitively aware that the future of aviation would be in electric aircraft, and as you know, we have developed the first two-seater and then even a four-seater electric plane, which is still the only aircraft of its kind. The hybrid plane, which we also have developed and presented to the public, is also based on intuition. Therefore, an executive must trust his inner language, be absolutely sure of it, and go ahead, regardless of what is happening around him, because those around him do not know what is happening inside him individually, and that is all that is important."*

Living in an age of exponential change and uncertainty means that operating based on the facts from yesterday and today just will not be enough to prepare us for the future. Yes, we have continuously more sophisticated computers and other technology to support our business, the Big Data concept and others, but as responsible managers or leaders, we have to know the road we are about to take.

> *"A leader is one who knows the way, goes the way, and shows the way."*
>
> — John C. Maxwell

We have to believe in what we do and in why we do it or strive to do it. This way, we will act convincingly and we will be followed. Simply adapting to the digital age and leaving control of the steering wheel to technology is not the move a true leader would make. Organizational survival requires a clear business vision, explorative business strategies, full of out-of-the-box solutions which will appropriately fit into the future. To attain sustainable success, you must have a clear vision of your business, and that is all right as long as you accept that vision in a correct and constructive way, which we believe must include the use of intuitive insight.

Intuitive Business Leadership Will Take You to Another Level

> *"Very often, people will do a brilliant job through the middle management levels, where it's very heavily quantitative in terms of the decision making. But then they reach senior management, where the problems get more complex and ambiguous, and we discover that their judgment or intuition is not what it should be. And when that happens, it's a problem; it's a big problem."*

> *—Hayashi A. M. [32]*

Intuitive business leadership? What is that? Well, we believe if you've read this far into the book, you probably know the answer already. Nevertheless, let's look at some of the situations which in a way illustrate what intuitive leadership is. All three examples below were gathered during our research.

Let's say you are an executive director, responsible for production in a large parts factory in the automotive industry. Being in the business for quite a long time, you have gained different kinds of experience; we can say that you are very experienced and competent in your position. Over the years, you have learned that being physically present in the production area from time to time gives you a very clear inner feeling of how well things are going or if something has to be corrected. One day you go on your routine "walk" through the facilities that you are responsible for, like on any other day, but something just doesn't feel right; something is bothering you, but you don't know what it is. Knowing that you must find out what's wrong, you immediately call an urgent meeting with all the leaders of the production departments. Together, you decided to make a quick audit, and soon enough, it turns out that a big part of the stock of one material is significantly out of the tolerances. If you hadn't managed to discover it so quickly, your production line would have stopped for sure, as well as the production line of one or more of your car assembly customers.

Imagine being a chief executive officer of a large, growing retail company. You are involved in the monthly hiring process. According to the predetermined procedure, you are informed of the names of newly selected employees once a month via email, and you are about to give your confirmation of the suggested list for new collaborators. Your hiring process is well defined, and you have never had a major problem with the new employees. Being aware of this, you usually give an instant confirmation on the suggested list, but this time you instantly open the attached list and scan the names. Because one of the names draws your attention, you decide to ask for more information about that person. After digging for some additional information on him, it turns out that that particular candidate has several lawsuits with his past employers.

Or, for example, you may work as a project leader in a marketing agency. Your first project went extremely well; you met all the goals and deadlines. The client has openly showed his satisfaction, that's why your boss decided that you will take charge of the biggest marketing project in the company. Because of the complexity and the short deadlines of the project, two of the previous project leaders had to admit that they had bitten off more than they could chew. Aware of the great opportunity on the one hand, and the high risk on the other, you sit down at a presentation meeting with the members of the project, your boss and the client. In the very first moment of the presentation of the project goals, you get a tremendous insight about the outcome, and therefore you hardly follow the rest of the presentation. Your focus from that moment on is just on hearing the voice of the client – you are looking for an omen to confirm your vision. After a few minutes, your expectations are fulfilled. Now you know what your goal is, and you immediately start to get operational. You feel that your next step is to get your team to "buy" your idea, to give them a reason to trust your insight, and you know you need help with that. By carefully observing the members of the project, you try to figure out which of them you need to attract to your idea: you are aware that the other members of the team will join in after that key figure gets interested. After you convince this key figure, the rest is routine for this professional team, and soon you meet all the expectations for that project.

Our next example will show how intuitive business leadership can successfully deal with the setbacks and unpleasant situations faced by any manager and leader. It's another example that Boscarol confided to us. *"Over the last two decades, our company has gotten used to growing according to all the key business performance indicators, along with the turnover and profit of the company. Year after year, we have continuously improved. The management had gotten used to that, the employees had gotten used to that, and I got to used to it as well. And then, out of the blue, we found ourselves in the middle of the biggest global financial crisis ever. As a company that develops and produces high-end products, we knew that we would have a really hard time surviving. By the end of the year, before Christmas, as always, we had prepared a small party to close the year, and I was about to give a speech. For obvious reasons, I had more or less bad news to tell everyone. I had to talk about the possibility of downsizing. As soon as I touched on that subject, that very same instant, I could feel a tsunami of emotions from everyone, predominated by fear. The atmosphere was really heavy and depressed. At that moment, all of a sudden, I got an intuitive flash that during the next year we would win a NASA aircraft contest, and that I should tell the people right now. We had already intended to take part in that contest, but to make such a prediction of winning was close to insane. But I had such a tremendous inner certainty about that, and something inside of me was literally pushing me to tell them, right away, and so I did! The atmosphere instantly improved, and we had a great time at the party: but what's more important is that ten months later, we actually won that contest. Winning that contest brought us 1.3 million dollars; we entered the world's top league of aircraft companies, which on the bottom line resulted in increasing sales, and we have managed to overcome the hard times."*

There are many other examples of intuitive business leadership in all kinds of different business fields. For example, Walter Isaacson pointed out in the authorized biography of Steve Jobs that he was one of the best examples of an intuitive business leader, a highly successful executive and a man considered to be one of the great product visionaries of our time, who spoke openly several times about the value of intuition in business. Among other things, Jobs said, *"Intuition is a very powerful thing, more powerful than intellect, in my opinion. That's had a big impact on my work."* Another important message of his, in which he put intuition before intellect, was this one: *"I began to realize that an intuitive understanding and consciousness was more significant than abstract thinking and intellectual logical analysis."*

By analyzing these and many other examples of intuitive business leadership, we have been able to compile the following list of what we are convinced to be the main characteristics that are most common among people who have successfully applied their intuition to business leadership. Successful business leaders are:

- *Inside-to-outside oriented*: intuitive business leaders are, first and foremost, oriented to guidance from within. After getting their own inner conviction, inner vision and internal GPS direction, only then do they look outwards to operate in the external world.

- *Driven by inner motives:* intuitive business leaders are driven by their own inner reasons; external motivation is of secondary importance for them. They place their reasons even before their goals – they are very well aware of the fact that the goals may change or even vanish, but the reasons why they are doing something are there to stay and to support them all the way.

- *Deeply enthusiastic:* their personal motivation and level of engagement is highly above average, which is based fundamentally on their reasons and determination to repeatedly achieve success. Their way of involving others to contribute and participate is unique, and brings out the very best from any member of the team.

- *Highly sensitive*: intuitive business leaders have highly developed levels of empathy, compassion, emotional and social intelligence, which help them to more easily understand different behavioral patterns and to find the essential key in the majority of different situations.

- *Totally original:* intuitive business leaders have a transformative approach, creating innovative changes and generating new trends, rather than following the old ways of doing things. Being original is their passion, and their key advantage as well.

- *Honestly interested:* intuitive business leaders ask the right questions at the right time, and are able to see the real truth in the answers. They challenge collective intuition in order to bring perfect team results.

⊃ *Open to using situational assessments:* situational assessments (along with the power of their first impressions) are among the techniques that are most widely used by intuitive business leaders, and are absolutely indispensable in any kind of crisis management. These are used for determining the pure essence of any new situation or any new step during operations.

⊃ *Living examples*: they know that "walking the walk" is the best way to win the crowd, they attract followers just by being authentic.

⊃ *Never swayed:* intuitive business leaders are aware that perception of the current situation, influenced by old patterns, past results, data, statistics, analysis, individual perceptions, etc., can be highly distorted. They exploit their own powerful state of mind, of being in the present moment, of being tied to the energy which connects everybody with everything, and rely less on the fears and pressures of others.

It is our ability to resonate with these vital indicators of intuitive business leadership that can give us the needed boost to become true intuitive business leaders. By experimenting with the use of these indicators, we can significantly improve our personal and business performance. The most common answer to the question *"How can intuitive business leadership be developed?"* given to us by the people we interviewed was that you have to gain experience by applying your intuition in different areas of business, and that you need to reflect regularly on important business situations from the past to perceive how your intuition has already helped you, followed by applying the necessary self-corrections in practice.

Being involved in intuitive business leadership is not easy at all, as you are actually the only person who is able to "hear" what your intuition is whispering to you. But as a manager or leader, it is your mission to activate your co-workers to strive for your vision and strategy. So it's crucial that your co-workers also start to sense the guidance you receive, and start to follow you.

Being an intuitive business leader and following your inner knowing is not easy: it constantly requires that you change and adapt, to forget who you are in your mind, and to remind yourself who you are in your heart.

Tip: Start working on your inner feelings from the very first moment that they appear, and always expect good things to happen — stay positive, no matter what. Your heart always knows the answer, and with your full dedication, persistence and unwavering belief, your co-workers will start to sense it too and will start to follow you.

Intuitive Skills Assure Long-Term Efficiency and Success

Appropriate skills play a particularly important role in the development of qualified management personnel in any organization. Standard competencies acquired with standard education are usually not enough to enable anyone to adapt efficiently to the fast changes and rapidly growing need for an innovative and creative organization. This is why the need for identifying the key characteristics of successful individuals is becoming more and more obvious. The recent world financial and economic crisis can be understood as a kind of warning concerning the increasing importance of finding capable managers whose knowledge, skills, personal traits and willingness to act in a time of uncertain conditions secure the organization against harmful external and internal influences, which may even be fatal in extreme cases. [72]

Intuitive skills are one of the most powerful tools for assuring the long-term efficiency and success of any organization, especially in these times of quickly changing and uncertain business conditions. Intuitive competencies, as the most complex and integrated of all human abilities, are thus related to the physical (instinctive), emotional, mental, spiritual and energetic conditions of any human being. They assure us the capacity for gaining a holistic understanding of the specific situation by stepping outside of the traditional ways of doing business.

- ⊃ *Intuitive information gathering:* on one level, this is about paying incredible attention to the very small details of any situation, but it also includes observing the larger circumstances and broader perspective by noticing what else is going on around you. Intuitive data collecting is a faculty which is the foundation of human nature, and occurs primarily at the subconscious level. It covers all the aspects of human existence, physical, emotional, mental, spiritual and energetic, and is very closely connected with intuitive communication. The most important thing to remember about intuitive information gathering is that thinking about how to acquire all the information needed, bringing the process to the conscious level, will actually reduce our ability to collect data.

- ⊃ *Intuitive problem solving:* the most important advantage of intuitive problem solving is its speed. Intuition is typically viewed as occurring very fast, and that's very appropriate when dealing with a problem which needs an urgent solution. Intuitive problem solving is considered to be very closely connected with intuitive decision making, since by making the right decision we are able to successfully resolve the problem (see below).

- ⊃ *Intuitive creation and development:* intuitive creation and development is a tangible skill, sourcing for its creativity and new ideas from diverse fields such as art, music, nature, history, technology, dreams, meditation, prayer and all others.

- ⊃ *Intuitive decision making:* one of the most important tasks in business as well as in our day-to-day lives is decision making. Decision making is usually seen as a systematic cognitive process of choosing among the alternatives, and it's considered to be the most important skill of any successful manager or leader, especially in handling changes and dealing with conflict or crisis situations. Professor John Mihalasky of the New Jersey Institute of Technology is convinced that effective, superior decision making is highly related to intuitive ability. During his research, Mihalasky tested hundreds of business managers for intuitive ability. One of his studies included 25 managers who had held top decision-making jobs for five years or more. He selected all of them from small manufacturing enterprises to ensure that collective groups within larger companies had not diffused their individual decision making. The results were notable; of those 25 men selected, 12 decision makers had helped their firms to double profits in five years. Eleven of those 12 decision makers scored high on the intuitive test. This positive correlation between intuition and business performance has also been discovered by many others management scholars. Weston Agor, author of *Intuitive Management: Integrating Left and Right Brain Management Skills*, studied thousands of managers from numerous industries and companies. Agor found that thriving managers made effective use of intuitive decision making. Henry Mintzberg has also found that, particularly in unpredictable, unstructured and ambiguous situations, top managers rely on intuitive hunches to deal with problems that are "too complex for rational analysis". [73]

⊃ *Reconciling the intuitive and logical perceptions:* at some point in the process of making choices, intuition, as an unconscious function, has to be connected to our conscious or logical perceptions. This allows us to be able to work on a certain intuitive idea, insight, hunch. Until that integrative moment arrives, we may lose a lot of time by not taking action, because we were unable to reach the "aha moment" of reconciling the intuitive and logical data, and to give our brain a "green light" to start the action. In order to accelerate this process, we should regularly perform some of the methods and techniques presented in this book, so that the two halves of our thinking process will already be "introduced" and used to working together by the time we have an urgent need of them.

⊃ *Intuitive communication:* intuitive communication is far more than just talking and listening to the words in the conversation. It is about being fully aware of all the channels which actively interact within ourselves. To master intuitive communication, we have to be aware of our physical, emotional, mental, spiritual and energetic aspects. This highly complex, multi-channel communication brings out the underlying messages for the course of action, helping us to "read between the lines" when the message is not clear on one level or another.

⊃ *Intuitive leadership:* the pace of action in today´s business world is arguably much too fast to keep up with if we only rely on the traditional way of doing things. This makes the intuitive way of doing business an absolute "must". Fast interpreting, adapting to new circumstances in a split second and taking the next step are some of the features of intuitive leadership. Intuitive leadership is a capacity which gathers all the intuitive skills into one complex whole. By mastering the intuitive leadership competencies, you will develop that so-called "Midas touch" - everything you touch will turn to gold. While this expression should not be taken literally, it´s really not so far from the truth either.

After getting an idea of some of the intuitive skills that can be applied to business, you should try to recognize which of these intuitive competencies[39] you have already developed, and to what point; which of them you have already recognized and which are completely new for you; and which work for you already and which you feel you should work on. This section of the book is a quick overview of the key elements of intuition in business, to help you explore and encounter some other perspectives and to help you reflect on your own degree of intuitive preparation in order to become a truly intuitive leader.

Collective Intuition—Teamwork Applied to Intuitive Guidance

Kathleen Eisenhardt, a well-known strategy researcher, argued that collective intuition among members of a management team contributes to the group's ability to quickly recognize strategic issues such as evolving environmental opportunities and threats. [74] The same opinion was shared with us by the author and former director of the Düsseldorf office of McKinsey & Company, Inc., Dr. Peter

---

39 Intuitive competencies, like any other skills, are not considered to be of an inherent character in a person´s nature; they are learned skills which we all have the basic ability to acquire and the faculties to develop (we discuss more about growing your intuitive abilities in the chapter "Developing Intuition").

Kraljic[40]: *"As a leading manager or decision maker, you have to discuss within your team every important issue that you can. By doing so, you raise the level of trust of certain decisions, especially if you manage to tap into your team's intuition, which is superior to that of the individuals. The leader must be aware that, in the case of a coherent performance by his whole team, besides the individual intuitions of each member of the team, the collective intuition or team intuition is formed, and represents one of the most powerful tools for any leading manager. The leader must have this in mind, and keep a goal-oriented focus to achieve that coherent state of mind within the team. Any teamwork technique, if it's guided appropriately, should result in the collective intuition of the team, and should bring tremendous breakthrough results, which none of the members of the team could achieve if they were working on their own."*

Slovenia is a special country, known for the quantity and diversity of its blessings, including the genius of its population, and one example of this is 88-year-old Ales Mizigoj, who is considered to be the oldest active business manager in Slovenia. He was the CEO of the Medex company for 40 years, and for the last 15 years he has been working as a consultant for the Board of Directors of the same company. Winner of the award for Manager of the Year and numerous other awards in various fields, he told us about his experience with collective intuition: *"Intuition is a secret faculty which I have used quite a lot during my managerial career. At that time, when I was named CEO of the company, we were deep in debt and on the verge of bankruptcy. We somehow managed to keep the company from closing. We succeeded in part because of the effort and work we put in, and in part because of the creativity we managed to apply, even though we were in a very unenviable position. But the key factor, more than anything else, and which we must credit with that success, was strong intuition. I always had that inner feeling of what we should do, when and how we should start some new project and from which side we should expect some serious danger for the company. As a manager, the first thing you must do is to pay attention to your intuition, what it is telling you (sometimes intuition is just whispering, and sometimes it's screaming). The second thing is to follow your intuition as soon as you sense it, and the third thing is to have the ability to actively involve all of the key people in the company to be part of the collective intuition. Not many managers are consciously aware that they actually conduct the process of forming collective intuition, yet they do it each day, if they are successful in their business."*

---

40 Dr. Peter Kraljic is also known for having created a powerful purchasing tool, a matrix called the Kraljic Portfolio Purchasing Model, used for analyzing the purchasing portfolio of a company.

Dr. Federico Capasso, Harvard University professor and a prominent researcher in applied physics, shared his views on collective intuition with us: *"Over the years, I have learned that intuition and creativity can be learned or achieved. I can often see that ideas, fascinating ideas, intuitive insights, can emerge from the collective discussion between people, especially through open-ended discussion or 'brain storming'. And, fascinatingly enough, sometimes it's even hard to say at the end of the discussion whose idea it was. It came by combining lots of little things, and then the right way of thinking intuitively emerged. So I think intuition should not be attributed only to a single individual but also to a group of people that interact creatively. That is not easy because of human nature, and in general lots of people, particularly young people, are very possessive of their ideas. I also went through this phase, but if you can overcome it, your intuitive and creative abilities increase enormously. Intuition is an evolutionary process: it relies a lot on the evolution of our brain, and with the right stimulation in a group, every scientist can develop a good dose of intuition and be able to make a really important leap forward."*

As these cases show, intuition works not only on an individual level, but also on a group level. When the members of a group or team are tightly united, with similar levels of dedication to a common objective, they can access a collective intuition through discussions, brainstorming and other group techniques, where one person receives part of an idea and other members receive other parts, until together they arrive at a complete solution. The best managers learn how to help their collaborators and associates harness their contact with their individual types of intuition in order for each of them to contribute to the collective goal.

The Role of Intuition in Decision Making

One of the most important tasks in business as well as in personal life is decision making. Decision making is mostly a systematic cognitive process for choosing between the alternatives available, and it's considered to be the most important skill of any successful manager or leader, especially for handling changes and dealing with conflicts or crisis situations.

There are many different barriers to the cognitive decision-making process, such as lack of reliable information (too much or not enough information), lack of time, difficulties with defining the real problem, developing and selecting potential alternatives and many others.

"Many scientific models do mimic your decision processes; but which are similar enough to be redundant and which offer something you cannot do?" [75]

One may easily ask, "How reliable is our intuition? How much should we depend on gut-level instinct rather than rational analysis?" In a society where intuition is traditionally looked down upon, these questions not only have to do with the level of success we should expect from decisions made based on intuition, but also with the level of acceptability or criticism which we (and our decisions) will receive from those around us.

Dr. Gerg Gigerenzer stated that he found about 50% of all decisions made by decision makers in large international companies to be decided on the basis of pure gut feeling. These managers would never publicly admit this fact, because they are afraid of being held responsible if something goes wrong [or of being laughed at]. They are smart enough to find ways of disguising their methods for choosing options, and strategies for "reasonably" implementing their gut-feeling decisions. For example, a top manager may ask employees to find facts that support his decision, and then his initially intuitive decision is presented to the company as being based on facts or Big Data. That's a huge waste of time, intelligence and money. Aside from the responsability issue, the financial aspect, the cost of covering up their "embarrassing" use of gut feelings, should not be overlooked. In same cases, managers may even hire a consulting company to provide a 200-page document to justify their intuitive insight. But the most expensive strategy for hiding intuitive decisions is so-called "defensive decision making". *"Here, a manager feels he should go with option A, but if something goes wrong, he can't explain it, so that's not good. So he recommends option B, something of a secondary or third-class choice. Defensive decision-making hurts the company and protects the decision maker."* In the studies made by Dr. Gigerenzen, this happens in about a third to half of all important decisions. It's not hard to imagine how many opportunities, and consequently how much money, these companies lose. [18]

Intuition can help us in our everyday decision-making, but it is of even greater importance when it comes to crucial milestones in our lives, regardless of whether we're speaking of business or personal matters. Either one of these areas influences the other immensely, and our life is usually formed by a combination of the two. Therefore, the best possible results are achieved when we find the right way to combine and balance our personal and professional lives. This of course can be very hard to do sometimes, but if done according to our inner guidance, it can lead to the most rewarding lifestyle. When we do that, we can experience the best possible version of our future. After a while, we become more confident in our decision-making process and intuitive decision making becomes very natural to us. Stjepan Mesic, the 2nd president of Croatia, revealed his own very personal experience to us regarding this matter: *"When I ran for the Parliament, I felt a strong force driving me to do so. It was very encouraging, and was built on a sense of responsibility, that I had to do something for my nation. My grandparents and my uncles were killed in World War II. Luckily, my father survived the war, but he died when I was 19 and my mom had died when I was 16 months old. So in some ways, I was completely alone. But I had a strong feeling that I had to do something, and it was that strong inner feeling that led me to run for the Parliament. Everyone, the whole system, was against it, even my wife and my friends were against it. But there was this force inside of me that was driving me forward, pushing me to accomplish my goal. It was very hard and in some ways it seemed impossible, yet I don´t regret it at all."*

Intuition as a Determining Factor in Employee Selection

"The most important thing in communication is hearing what isn't said."

—Peter Drucker

Knowing more than what was spoken is one of the advantages to intuitive communication, as we've already seen. Openly listening with full understanding and empathy, without judgment or any other negative thoughts in our mind, brings us much vaster knowledge than logic can. Emotional intelligence, a relatively new field of study, is based on both the correct understanding of emotions (those of ourselves and others) and the application of those emotions to reinforce our thought processes. We must say that emotional intelligence, along with social and intuitive intelligence, composes just about all that any business-person needs, especially when dealing with unknown people, as in the case of employee selection. And one of the most important tools for developing our emotional intelligence, not only for perceiving the emotions themselves but for discovering how to use them to improve the results of our efforts, is intuition.

Intuition has an extremely important role in employee selection, and in meeting new people in general. During our research, one very interesting fact was that none of the interviewees responded negatively to the question: *"Do you find intuition important in meeting new people?"* – they were unanimous in declaring that intuition is important when meeting someone for the first time. In conversation with Debra Cafaro, Chairman of the Board and Chief Executive Officer of Ventas, Inc., included by the Harvard Business Review on its list of the top 50 "Best Performing CEOs" in the world since 2014, she revealed to us her personal insight into this matter. *"From my point of view, intuition is very important in deciding about people, especially during job interviews or when meeting new people. Sometimes I have a bad feeling about some people, and usually it turns out that it was a good decision to stay away from them, or not to get into any kind of relationship with them."*

A very interesting and similar view on the interconnection between intuition and employee selection was presented to us by Ivo Boscarol from Pipistrel: *"Intuition is extremely important in identifying and selecting people. I can say that a large variety of people appear for job interviews at our company, with very diverse profiles and different personalities, some more appropriate, some less, but everyone with a story that sounds very reasonable at first glance. But things are not always the way they look, and you recognize the truth with the help of intuition."*

If you wonder why Boscarol's insight is so important, let us share an amazing fact about his company – in the last 27 years, only 7 people have left the company. *"We practically have no fluctuations,"* says Boscarol. [76]

Closely related to these cases was another experience that Riccardo Illy shared with us, where he pointed out the importance of the intuitive approach in selecting people for the most responsible jobs, like CEOs or the members of the board. *"In those situations, you have to be rational, but again, in my opinion, intuition is vital. And I can say that each time I didn't follow my intuition, I made a mistake. One time, I remember it very well, when we were selecting a sales and marketing manager, I met a candidate who was a finalist for the job. Looking from the rational side, he was the perfect person, his curriculum vitae and everything was just perfect, but something about him was bothering me. Since I just couldn't define what was wrong, we eventually hired him. In a few weeks, my bad feeling about him turned out to be right: he was very different from what we expected him to be and we realized that we had made a huge mistake, despite the very obvious intuitive message."*

Smiljan Mori, motivational speaker, author and successful entrepreneur, told us how, with intuition, you don't need even Richard Branson´s 60 seconds to figure out who is standing in front of you, what kind of person they are, what are their beliefs, whether they have good or bad intentions and how to act and behave in relation to them. *"With the help of intuition, all of this is somehow already known to you in a fraction of a second. If you are not immediately sure of what you feel, you still can get confirmation for your intuitive signal through the observation of the person's gestures, body language, tone of voice, and so on. As an entrepreneur, a motivational speaker and a man who also encounters a large number of people, I give immense importance to intuition when meeting new people. Nevertheless, I also make mistakes: for example, when I feel a strange feeling of anxiety in my stomach and chest at a first meeting, but even so I rely on facts and reasoning: I decide to give this person an opportunity for cooperation, but in the vast majority of such cases, I come to regret it, because it quickly becomes apparent that my intuition was correct."*

In his first autobiography[41], Virgin Group founder Sir Richard Branson says, *"I normally make up my mind about whether I can trust somebody within sixty seconds of meeting them."* And in Phil Dorado´s 2009 book[42], Branson explains further: *"I can make up my mind about people and ideas in 60 seconds. I rely more on gut instinct than thick reports."* [77] [78]

We must not forget to look at the other side of the coin as well. It is of crucial importance for the process of employee selection that Human Resource personnel intuitively feel or detect who is the right person to join the organization, but on the other hand, it is also very important to detect job candidate's intuitive skills. This is especially true when speaking about managerial and executive positions, as they will be the captains of our ship and we want them to be able to navigate even when there´s rough sailing. And as we already pointed out, traditional managers/leaders are no longer adequately "equipped" for today's business world, therefore Human Resource personnel must remember to search for the faculty of intuition in candidates if they want them to have high performance.

------

41 Losing My Virginity: How I Survived, Had Fun and Made a Fortune Doing Business My Way
42 The 60-Second Leader: Everything You Need to Know About Leadership, in One-Minute Bites

IV. Intuition in Practice

Intuition And Creativity

"Doing a new thing in the old way doesn't bring much success. You have to literally give free reign to your intuition and creativity, to bring you new ideas and new outcomes: that's the only way for you to achieve constant growth and above-average results".

—Edward Clug

ALONG WITH PROBLEM-SOLVING and moral and social judgment, creativity is considered to be one of the main domains of the intuitive process. Exactly how intuition is linked to creativity has not yet been scientifically established, but that's not something that people worry about too much, as long as it works in practice. Thus, many successful entrepreneurs, scientists, artists and others often credit the role of intuition as part of the creative process that has produced the best creations in their specific fields of work.

Let's take a look at the thoughts of a successful former ballet dancer who is now working as a masterful choreographer, Edward Clug. This is what he told us in regard to the link between intuition and creativity: *"For me, intuition has always meant an initiation, an inspiration, creativity and silent guidelines in everything I was doing. When I look back, to my great surprise, I can say that my knowledge and my experience has often been my biggest enemy, when I was facing new challenges.*" As he explains further, knowledge and experience somehow always tried to silence his intuition and creativity, to guide him in a known way, to follow the old familiar trail that had already brought him some good results, but *"doing a new thing in the old way doesn't bring much success,"* he explains, and continues: *"Just recently, I had a ballet performance in Zürich, and in interviews afterwards, they asked me where my inspiration came from. And I said that it came from music, literary themes, from experiences, from past events and so on. Well, that´s not exactly correct. All great creations come from something that doesn't exist yet, otherwise it's just partly creation, it's something that we already know in some other form. Knowledge and experience come into the process later on, to shape the intuitive idea into a new creation, but before that, in the process of initiating the idea, knowledge and experience are troublemakers in your head, they constantly try to trigger old patterns instead of being open to the true spark of originality."* Clug sees intuition as a kind of mechanism for discovering our creativity. *"Someone asked me if I could describe creativity with some formula or equation, what would that formula or equation be? And I said that for me, creation is equal to expectation of something extraordinary about to happen, which means that you have to expect it and you have to believe that you are going to receive it: the stronger your faith is, the sooner you are going to meet your creation, and the mechanism for that is your intuition. In the creative process, you have to start with very small steps, all the time believing that you are about to meet your inspiration, and forget all you know, all you have done before, all you have experienced before, even forget about what you wish to accomplish and just quietly nourish that pure feeling that it will happen, and be grateful for the things that happen to you."*

Hollywood film producer and two-time Oscar award winner, Branko Lustig, shared his personal experience with us about how intuition helped him when creating the spectacular epic historical drama "Gladiator", which won five Academy Awards and was nominated for an additional seven. Lustig told us how, together with Sir Ridley Scott, he had a strong feeling that they needed to add certain scenes which, as time has shown, really made a difference: *"A good film producer intuitively knows what needs to be changed to make a better movie. 'Gladiator' is a perfect example of how a screenplay that was originally nothing special can result in a hit movie. We made the movie good by following our inner feelings, which suggested to us that some things were just not right. Then, every night, director Ridley Scott and I would have meetings where we would be writing and corresponding, and we also invited the author. In the original screenplay, there was no love story behind it, and we intuitively knew it had to be there. Ridley and I added all these scenes into the movie, because we felt it had to be that way."*

Another field that we had the opportunity to dig into and find the influence of intuition is the world of music. Music is deeply connected to creativity and a certain state of mind where intuition often happens. A well-known and highly sought-after conductor, pedagogue and composer, Simon Robinson says that intuition is a process of "inner tuition"; most of the time, it is something we know, but we don't know that we know it. *"The association that first comes to my mind when I think of intuition is "luck", the inborn tool for survival, a tool for success."* Robinson is conductor of the Opera and Ballet of SNG Maribor, and actively works as a guest conductor with many renowned music organizations, like the Royal Academy of Music of London and Cambridge and the Royal Liverpool Philharmonic Orchestra (which is the UK's oldest continuing professional symphony orchestra). Among the many honors he has received for his achievements, Queen Elizabeth II awarded him with The Most Excellent Order of the British Empire. *"As a conductor, as a musician, you have to be both a "transmitter" and a "receiver": you have to feel the energy around you, from three to up to ten meters around you, and in doing so, your well-developed intuition can be of great help. A lot lies in hard work, relying on preparations, on knowledge, but for one to achieve real added value and creation, you need a combination of both. When you have the technique 'already in your pocket' and you are in touch with your intuition, it's just something the audience feels at concerts. These moments are magical, because it is not just what people hear, it is also about how they hear it, what they feel, how they perceive and here the role of intuition is inevitable."*

Everyone can use the leverage of intuition to boost their creative side and benefit from it at its best. If you wonder how you can do that, the following tips from some of the most successful people may be of great help.

Tips:
- establish an inspiring environment
- set a clear intention for creation
- when being creative, have some greater purpose in mind
- calm all of your five senses
- expect the creation to happen without any doubts
- don't think, just observe
- don't suppress newborn ideas that come into your mind
- start intuitively connecting the most ordinary things
- express your ideas by using metaphors or visual imagery

Britten C. Anthony is a painter who believes that painting is a medium for universal communication, directly from the source which "lives" in all of us. She has a lot of trust in her intuition and believes it is the most important thing for a successful life. She sees intuition as simply a guide that makes her choices easier: *"Intuition is just knowing myself and listening to the real me. I rate this as number one for any kind of success. Intuition is simply the real me - authentic and true - present in the moment and part of something much larger than I will ever logically understand."* As she told us, when painting, most of the time she can tap into her intuition when she is not thinking but just allowing herself to be present in the moment. *"Intuition urges me to move toward a color or move my brush a certain way. Intuition guides me from beyond my mind. I feel calm and relaxed, without questions."* For her, intuition is not something that can be called upon or forced, it is already there, so she just needs to notice it. How does she manage to do that? Well, she puts a lot of effort into practicing awareness: *"When I have a problem, I do something to release my mind from it, like exercise or meditation or painting... I just paint, intuition guiding me, and the painting is, 99% of the time, exactly what the client wants."*

Intuition in Design

*"I believe very strongly that you have to follow your intuition
– that's the crucial thing that separates leaders, inventors, and
other creators from average people."*

—Pontus Fontaeus

"Retired" car designer, Goerg Gedl, started his career at Audi and later worked in the design department at BMW, where among other things, he also took part in the creation of the legendary M1. Regardless of his age, he is still very active in designing: in the last two decades prior to his "retirement", he has been actively cooperating with the Adria Mobil. He never lacks ideas and creativity. On one hand, there is the exceptionally rich experience from which he draws his designs, but on the other hand, as he explains, is creativity, an idea, which often originates in intuition. *"Talent is not enough: you must also have incredible perseverance, stubbornness and of course intuition, which in my opinion shows in the creativity and ideas that a designer has,"* Gedl told us. He was also the mentor of Robert Lesnik, Director of Exterior Design at Mercedes-Benz Passenger Cars. Gedl believed in Lesnik from the very first moment on. When speaking about personal experience with intuition, Gedl shared a very interesting story with us from the time when he was at BMW and working on some models there. One day, Bob Lutz, former Vice Chairman of General Motors and at the time Executive Vice President of sales at BMW, came to the office and with no further explanations said: *"I cannot sell this, this is no good. I will come back in two weeks."* Gedl felt disappointed and tried to figure out what exactly was wrong with the design, but without real success. After a few days of struggle, a solution "popped-up" all of a sudden: he did some modifications to the design and it was much better than before.

"I use my intuition in my profession a lot, especially in the earliest stages of the design process, when it is absolutely necessary to raise your level of creativity by listening to your inner voice, and later on in the process to cut the process time and to do the right thing at the right time," explains internationally recognized car designer, Pontus Fontaeus, Director of Interior Design at Faraday Future at the time of the interview and now holding the position of Executive Design Director for GAC Advanced Design Center Los Angeles. In his opinion, intuition is what makes the difference between

creative people and the rest of the world. "*In each design project, you have to take into account many facts, circumstances, and experiences, but when you come to the point of inventing something completely new, I believe very strongly that you have to follow your intuition – that's the crucial thing that separates leaders, inventors, and other creators from average people,*" says Fontaeus, and adds that when he looks back, it seems that he has always relied on his gut feeling. He shared an interesting personal experience with us: "*For instance, before I went to Faraday Future, it was the day before Christmas in 2014, and at that time I had the privilege of consulting for both Jaguar Land Rover and a company in London doing aircraft design. And I just had a feeling, as I said, on the day before Christmas, that I needed to think about moving to America, especially to California, like a feeling that something important for me was happening in California. And later on, one thing led to another and it just happened, I moved to California. But if I hadn't have had this really strong sensation which had actually showed me the direction for my future, I would not have acted as determined as I did and it wouldn't have happened for me. I still remembering that really strong impression, how much I felt that I had to take action on my intuition.*"

Intuition doesn't offer a logical explanation, but usually, when looking back at things, you can see a much clearer picture and in most cases, according to our research, you can confirm the right choices you made based on your gut feeling.

"*We are much more than just the body, much more than official science can explain: we are far more than we can even imagine,*" says Oskar Kogoj, world-renowned industrial designer, academic and artist, who is skillfully intertwining spiritual insights, extensive knowledge, rich experience and his intuition, which helps him in the role of a spiritual artist who is materializing a variety of unique masterpieces. He shared his personal belief with us: "*As far as design is concerned, intuition is of essential importance because it brings us the revelation of elements of knowledge and cognition. If we succeed in joining these revelations into a creation, and if we do that with the purest heart, then we are most certainly rewarded, as we have contributed to the development of humanity, to the development of the Universe.*" For Oskar, it is perfectly clear that intuition is something we all possess, we are all born with and have access to. And as he told us, the more we grow spiritually, the more developed our intuition becomes. "*We all have premonitions, we all have intuition that we can use in our everyday lives, either for personal or professional purposes, for creating or destroying: but the problem is that it is still very hard to prove it, therefor intuition still doesn't receive the attention it deserves. I feel sad because of that, because many people would be much more satisfied with their lives and would be living much more meaningfully. Nevertheless, if more people would rely more on their inner voice and not blindly follow "false" external goals, all of humanity could make a giant leap forward in our evolutionary process,"* said Kogoj, who remembered the words of the great architect, Joze Plecnik[43]: *"Plecnik said: 'Inside of me there is a dragon: once I managed to tame him, he started to serve me.' That's what he said, and he knew exactly what it is all about; a great spiritual man, even today we cannot fully understand the great impact he had."*

Alessandro Camorali, founder and CEO of the Camal Studio, which deals with virtual modelling and design, is another successful designer that shared his insights with us. Camorali, who previously worked for Stile Bertone, Fiat and Ferrari, believes that, on the one hand, intuition can be used to avoid negative experiences, and on the other, it helps push you beyond "traditional" thinking, which is especially important in design. *"The role of the designer is not only to decide how to draw an object, but first of all what to draw. So the intuition comes first, the drawing itself comes second. When you think of a new project, the first thing to do is not to look around, but to look ahead."* Camorali says that intuition communicates best when our mind and body are in a relaxed state, and he believes that every experience that we have carries hidden intuitive messages, we just need to grasp them.

As these testimonies show us, while the creativity of design also depends on technical knowledge and artistic abilities, the real drive for developing new and exciting forms in our lives comes from that magical place within us, our intuition.

Intuition And Sports

> *"Intuition is very important in sports, as in life in general, because a lot of our decisions are actually based on our gut feeling, without our even being aware of it… I mean, there are a lot of things you need to be successful, but obviously intuition is a deeper force that really guides you and directs you toward your success."*
>
> —Mary Pierce

---

43 Joze Plecnik was a major influence on the modern architectural identity of Vienna, Prague and Ljubljana.

Intuition as an unconscious but lightning-fast and accurate process which also has its special value in sports. Sports history is literally full of breath-taking and spectacular intuitive reactions from expert athletes in all possible athletic disciplines. Athletes are often as amazed by their past intuitive reactions as their audience is, and in most cases, they are completely unable to logically understand and explain why and how they managed to consider the specific situation and react in the best possible way in just a fraction of a second. Just try to imagine how fast the reaction of a tennis player must be when returning a serve with the ball coming at a speed of over 260 km/h[44], or the speed of a badminton smash, which can reach over an astounding 400 km/h[45]! How many fast and *inaccurate* decisions can a Formula 1 driver, a boxer in the ring or an alpinist in the Himalayas make and still survive?

When the ice hockey player, Wayne Gretzky, was asked for the secret of his success, he replied: *"I don't know; I just go to where the puck is going to be."* Now, you can believe that one of the world's greatest ice hockey players had some sort of clairvoyant talent, or you can look for other answers. Researchers in a recent journal article preferred the latter and pointed to years of experience, thousands of hours of deliberate practice and the appropriate use of mental processes – one of which is intuition. They argued that Gretzky was subconsciously making very fast decisions based on knowledge, stored memories and a holistic view of his surroundings. [79]

A study done by the University of Chicago showed that beginner golf players play better when they think rationally about what they're doing. But expert golf players are quite the opposite – the more they rationalize things, the worse are their results. [80] These and many others facts point directly to the very great importance of intuition in sports: but the question is, why? Why is it so necessary for athletes to be connected to this source of instant knowledge? The first reason would be the very high dynamics of action, especially in professional sports, which leaves very little or even no room for considering the

---

44 On 9 May, 2012, Samuel Groth (Australia) served an ace recorded at 263 km/h (163.4 mph) during an ATP Challenger event in Busan, South Korea. The serve came during Groth's second-round match against Uladzimir Ignatik (Belarus). In that match, Groth also hit serves recorded at 255.7 km/h (158.9 mph) and 253.5 km/h (157.5 mph), both of which surpassed Ivo Karlovic's (Croatia) previous record of 251 km/h (156 mph). [144]

45 The fastest badminton hit in competition (male) is 408 km/h (253.55 mph) achieved by Lee Chong Wei (Malaysia), during the 2015 Hong Kong Open. [145]

facts and reacting logically. Sports like ice hockey, soccer, basketball, racket sports, boxing, martial arts sports and motor sports are some examples, which require incredibly fast reaction times. The second reason would be that, in sports, there are always new situations, there are not even two identical situations in the entire history of any sport. There are billions and billions factors which make every situation completely unique in many ways. The next reason would be the true need for excellence in anticipating the next situation, the next move of the opponent and so on. The last but very important reason would be their expertise – athletes, especially professionals, have gone through thousands and thousands of training sessions, and have gained a massive amount of experience, knowledge and subconsciously stored information, which finally lead them to master their discipline and connect their expertise and their intuition into one integrated guidance system.

In support of the inextricable link between expertise and intuition, let us take a look at the example of boxer Dejan Zavec[46], 4-time IBF World Welterweight Champion and WBF Super Welterweight World Champion. *'Intuition is usually a hidden ability of ours, which can help us a great deal in many ways, if we managed to discover it. I can't tell you when I first recognized and started to respect my intuition, because I think I was following it literally forever. Maybe because I had a very difficult childhood, and also a later period during adolescence, and I was kind of forced to use it already as a very young child. But in my sports career, I'm convinced that I gained a respectable level of sports intuition soon after I start mastering the boxing techniques. After that, I didn't need to be focused so much on learning the techniques, but more on catching the right flow of the energy and feeling of the moment, and everything was coming to me through my intuition – the tactics for the fight, specific combinations, everything!'* Zavec also told us how easy everything becomes when you manage to reach the point where your knowledge and your inner feelings join together as one. He refers to this meeting point as an incredible advantage one can have or acquire: *"You get an incredible advantage; you start to master yourself and the situation you are in! Knowledge is vital, but nothing can compare with that special feeling of total truth, which completely overtakes you, and you simply know what you should do next."*

We could not agree more with this boxing champion – yes, knowledge is the essence, the foundation for anything that you build, but after that it just takes practice and self-work, becoming more

---

46 In the boxing world, known as Jan Zaveck.

conscious of our own inner reactions and signs, to reach the highest level and to deal with the challenges in an intuitive manner. So, if you were just beginning to practice some sport, play some instrument, or anything else, you wouldn't expect yourself to be an expert right away: you should take a series of small steps first, learn the theory and gain experience through practice.

Sticking to the boxing ring for a while, which by the way may symbolize our fight for life in many ways, let us take a look at the nature of intuitive functioning, which guides us most of the time on a subconscious level to successfully avoid logical thinking and its obstacles. We have already mentioned the European heavyweight champion, Zeljko Mavrovic, who among other things also told us about two ways in which he experienced his intuition in boxing: *"Intuition is part of the human subconscious. We can tap into it when the channel that connects our subconscious with our conscious mind is completely empty of thought. I have experienced it in many ways, especially in the most difficult boxing matches. For me, there were two general types of matches; the matches where you stick to the tactics laid out by your trainer's team and that's enough for you to win, or the matches where your tactics are not working like they should for some reason, despite the corrections and suggestions from your corner. That's the moment when you had better be aware that you are 'on your own', and you have to literally 'forget' all your thoughts, drop your plans and tap into your intuition as soon as you can."* And if you succeed in that, Mavrovic explains: *"Your body rhythm changes, you start to feel your opponent more clearly, you are even able to reach his weak points, and the match slowly comes under your control. I actually won the great majority of those fights, but I wasn't aware of how I did it. Which combinations, which punches I had used, I actually couldn't remember at all. Later on, when we reviewed the recordings, in many cases we could see the unusual technical combinations that sometimes were completely new: who knows where they came from."* But not only "in the ring", also out of the ring, in sports in general, intuition can be of great help for a sportsman. Mavrovic gave us the following example: *"Inside himself, an athlete can feel certain details of his physical condition long before they actually appear on the physical level, and if you respect that valuable intuitive information, you can avoid some serious injuries and accidents."*

Mary Pierce, 4-time Grand Slam Winner in tennis, has revealed to us her experience with intuition in sports: *"Speaking of intuition in sports, I think that anything that an athlete does is somehow related to intuition, it's just a question of whether or not you are following your gut feeling. With regard to tennis, when you go on the court and you play, things are happening so quickly that you really don't have time to stop and think and analyze. I mean, you just have to play - so it's like you are operating by relying on your instincts and intuition."* The same thing we found in boxing is also confirmed in tennis: things are happening with lightning speed and you have to react with the same lightning speed and in some way "predict" the future. You don't have time for second-guessing, you must trust your intuition, and the greatest athletes do have this capability. As Pierce explains: *"You just have to know where to go and what to do, and you don't hesitate or second-guess yourself. I have noticed with myself and other tennis players that when you are playing your best, you don't hesitate and you don't wonder about what to do. You just go for what naturally comes to you through your intuition, because as soon as you start to think and hesitate, you start to make mistakes, and you slowly start losing your match."* Pierce also told us about the hunches and premonitions that athletes have sometimes, in relation to the positive or negative outcome, and recounted the following personal experience: *"Sometimes, when I was in a tournament, I would wake up in the morning with the feeling that I was gonna lose that day. You don't want to lose, you want to win, but sometimes you just have a feeling like you are gonna lose that day. Of course, you try to ignore that feeling and say 'OK, whatever', and just go back to your day and do whatever you normally do, do your routine, warm up and practice, and then compete and give 100 percent in play: but then in the end, you don't win."* But, interestingly enough, the exact opposite can also happen. Mary told us about winning her second Grand Slam singles title at the 2000 French Open: *"When I went to play, during my first match, I had a strong feeling, like deep inside of me I could feel that this was my time and that I was gonna win this tournament. Winning the French Open was my dream, and because of that, it was even more difficult for me to play and to compete at that tournament: but what I felt at that moment was something really special and convincing, that is really hard to explain. And I never told anyone about my feeling, my intuition, I just kept it to myself for the whole tournament."*

Sometimes, intuition in sports can also mean the ability to survive, like in mountain climbing or alpinism. Alpinism is a wonderful sport in many different ways, which demands proper psychophysical abilities, knowledge, experience and intuition to maintain safety in uncertain mountain conditions. Marko Prezelj is a renowned mountain climber, famous for being the only mountain climber in the world to have received four *"Piolets d'Or"*[47], the highest award in the mountain

---

47 The *Piolet d'Or* or Golden Ice Axe is an annual mountaineering award given by the French magazine *Montagnes* and *The Groupe de Haute Montagne*.

climbing sport. This is his view on intuition in alpinism: *"The alpinist who is seriously engaged with this sport has to pay real attention to his intuition, literally in order to survive in the mountains. Intuition in alpinism is often unduly neglected, although it is at least as important as the psychic stability of the climber or his physical preparation and technical knowledge."* For Prezelj, there are two essential factors which define successful professional climbing, and which can also be understood as real "lifesavers", as he explains in his own words: *"In my opinion, the two most important factors for professional climbing are the psychic stability of the climber and his awareness of his sixth sense or intuition. These two factors complement each other and enable the climber to make the right decisions, even in the most difficult moments. In my career, I have faced many situations in which I made an intuitive decision that turned out to not only be the right one in terms of a successful climb, but also in terms of my safety or the safety of my colleagues. For example, you are thinking of climbing one line, but because of some strange inner feeling, you decide to change your plan, and later on you see the avalanche on the route you were supposed to take. Strange, but those kind of situations do happen: I'm not saying that they always save lives, but on many occasions they actually have."*

Viki Groselj is another world-renowned and award-winning climber who has scaled 10 of the world´s 14 "eight-thosanders", mountains with an altitude of over 8,000-meters. Viki lost his brother in the French Alps and seven members of his expeditions in the Himalayas, and more than fifty of his climber friends died on other mountains. Therefor, he is more than aware of the constant risk of death in mountain climbing and of how to survive in the toughest mountain conditions. He has entrusted us with an incredible near-death story from one of his recent expeditions in the Himalayas: *"I have had many frightening situations in my forty-year climbing career, during a number of mountain expeditions, but the one that I'm about to tell you, I shall remember all my life. Maybe because I'm still not sure what saved us that day, and certainly because of the frightening consequences of that event – the April 2015 Nepal earthquake*[48]*. That morning, we drove to the starting point from which we planned to explore some new, untried mountain directions. We start to move toward the bridge which we should cross to enter the steep and rocky slopes. After walking a*

---

48 The Nepal earthquake of 2015, also called the Gorkha earthquake, a severe earthquake [7.8 on the Richter scale -https://www.mercycorps.org/articles/nepal/quick-facts-what-you-need-know-about-nepal-earthquake] that struck near the city of Kathmandu in central Nepal on April 25, 2015. About 9,000 people were killed, many thousands more were injured, and more than 600,000 structures in Kathmandu and other nearby towns were either damaged or destroyed. [146]

while, I got the sudden idea that we should return to the exact place where we had stepped out of the Jeep that drove us to the place. So we returned to exactly that place to take some photos, which took us maybe ten minutes. As soon as we did that, the earth started to shake with tremendous force, and we could see how the huge rocks fell like a waterfall from the slope which we would have already been walking on if we hadn't turned back to take those photos. When I think back, I really wanted us to return to our starting point, I actually insisted, despite the fact that I'm usually not so strict about such thing, which makes me ask: 'Were we just extremely lucky, or was it something else?' That is still my question, but I have noticed that, whenever I think about intuition, I unconsciously think back to that shocking event."

As we have seen, becoming a more intuitive athlete can result in preventing different sporting accidents and injuries, as well as increasing the effectiveness of training and improving the level of achievement in competitions. That being said, intuition can also help athletes to enhance and perfect their sports performance abilities, especially through accelerating their reaction time by intuitively processing vital information, correctly responding to new situations and properly anticipating imminent future situations. Therefor, athletic training should also include the systematic and constant recognition and development of intuitive abilities in each professional athlete, when they are still students or amateurs, or even as children. Because of the fact that athletes are prone to high physical and mental stress, which in many cases leads to anxiety, learning intuitive techniques is vital for the athletes to avoid some major psychological problems too. Learning the concept of an intuitive lifestyle is also very important for their lives outside of and after their professional career, especially in the period of actively adapting to new ways of life after their athletic career.

Now let's shift gears and look at the value of intuition in the realm of sports coaching. Recently, there has been a growing interest in using intuition as a successful tool in sports coaching, and as a skill belonging to the top-performance coaches in practically all sports disciplines. Enhanced awareness, better anticipation of key information concerning present and future situations, and decision making in time-limited situations are all part of the wide spectrum of benefits for intuitive athletic coaches.

Zmago Sagadin is one of the most successful and recognized European basketball coaches, with 25 national and international laurels. He has developed eleven NBA players, more than any other

European trainer. All told, he has developed more than fifty players who have gone on to the highest European levels or NBA league. [81] His coaching approach was very systematic (rational), but in the toughest moments, he leaned on his intuition and worked on developing it. *"I was the type of coach who mainly built on serious and systematic work, who would think over a question a hundred times before making a decision, so no doubt, I was very rational and I was a hard-working coach. But I must say that in the hardest moments, and in professional sports that means when 'the best confront the best', you need to have something more, you have to add something beyond rational thinking, and here we come to the area of intuition. Of course, I had to use it on many occasions, especially, as I said, in the toughest situations."*

Recognizing both his own natural tendency for logical and methodic choices and the added benefits which intuition can bring to the coaching profession, Zmago began to systematically develop more intuitive techniques. *"I must say I highly honored my inner voice, because on many occasions, it brought me a great deal of help and I believe that intuitive operating is one of the vital parts of top coaching performance. Since I was very analytical, I was following every small detail of the game, and I was constantly analyzing the facts of the game in my head. So during the time-outs, I had a very clear picture of where we were in the game as a team, as well as what was the situation with every individual player; and when my analytical perspective was upgraded with my intuition, I was able to give my team the best guidance and we would usually meet with success."* And he continues, *"Intuition has helped me many times when I couldn't resolve a problem on the analytical level, especially when I was highly involved in resolving the problem and I already had a strong desire to find the solution. When all this would come together, I would find my intuitive guidance very easily, and all that I had to do then was apply it in action without hesitating."*

Sagadin confesses that he only started to respect his intuition after a few serious regrets, when he had intuitive hints but did not apply them: *"That's why I think it's not so important to constantly seek your intuition, but more to respect it when you receive it, because when you really need your intuition, you will get it; the only question is, will you apply it or will you get scared and disregard it."* He sees great potential for using intuition in both team selection and coaching: first, which players should be invited to the team you run, and secondly, which players should play in which game, or more specifically, which player should play in which part of a game. *"In my career, I had to produce at least two prospective new players each season. Literally, I had to produce them from scratch, from a no-name to a prospective young player, and to do that, I had to combine the analytical work with my intuition. There were a few cases when the rest of the professional team and the club management didn't agree with my pick for new player, but I knew we should hired them and I was nearly always right."* As far as decision-making during the game goes, deciding in a split second what combinations to play and with which players, Sagadin says that that is pure intuition. *"In addition, intuition in coaching is of great help in communicating with your team, since no two players are alike. And because of these differences, your communication with each of them must also be different. Many situations force a professional coach to communicate intuitively, because one wrong word can do enormous damage to relationships within your team, especially if it's comes out under high-pressure circumstances,"* he adds.

Paul Gardner is a former NHL player and professional scout. Now he is a professional ice hockey coach, with experience in numerous hockey leagues including the OHL, AHL, NHL, KHL, CHL and DEL[49]. No doubt his experience as a professional athlete and coach gave him a deeper understanding of intuition. *"As a coach in professional sports, I believe I use intuition a great deal in my decision making, from game to game or as often as day to day. I also believe that the older you get, the more confidence you have in your decision-making and in your intuition. Intuition and confidence go hand in hand. I use intuition a great deal in choosing a lineup or in deciding which person to use at a critical moment. The more important the decision, the more intuition comes into play. My intuition communicates with me through constantly being in my mind: it takes over your thoughts until you know it is the right decision. Once you feel it is the right decision, it goes away until the next time it is put to use."* Gardner confirms something that all the people we interviewed agree on: *"I definitely believe that successful people use intuition a great deal more than unsuccessful people. Successful people have great intuition and the confidence to use it. I believe they go hand in hand* [intuition and success] *and grow stronger the more you use them."*

A great sports educator and successful professional tennis coach, Zoran Krajnc, who has received several national awards for best Slovenian tennis coach, spoke to us about intuition in his career: *"Intuition is actually much more important for the athletes than it is for the coaches, but even so, the coaches are the first ones who should meet intuition on the conscious level and then plan how to constantly encourage the athletes to feel their intuition subconsciously. Any successful coach has to do the majority of his work before*

---

49 OHL - Ontario Hockey League, AHL - American Hockey League, NHL - National Hockey League, KHL - Kontinental Hockey League, CHL - Central Hockey League, DEL - Deutsche Eishockey Liga

he even steps onto the court, and by that, I mean that he must plan the coaching process, understanding the key factors of each player, his background, personal characteristics and much more. Planning is also of the greatest importance because it allows the trainer to achieve inner peace, which is a precondition for leaving key decisions to our intuition." After the coach makes his initial plans, deciding who to use in which situations, he has to adjust them to the realities of each moment during the game. *"Many times, I rely on intuition for deciding the right move at the right moment. This is the point where the coach should use the phenomena of intuition in the fullest sense. In conversations with the athletes that I work with, they just confirm my intuitive instructions on the court. There have been countless times when they say that they also could feel that a certain decision at a given moment would be successful. It is a kind of 'intuitive link', which results in a certain playing strategy, which was then successfully implemented."* Krajnc also uses his intuition when selecting the players for his team. *"Many players have the necessary physical abilities, knowledge and technique, but the successful players will be those with 'something more'. I am not talking about perseverance, the desire for success, the perfectly executed technique or position on the ranking list: I am talking about that special intuitive message which gives a coach confidence in that player, which eventually makes all the difference. It is about the kind of 'added value' which a coach intuitively feels that the player will be able to demonstrate at the most crucial moments of a match, and this is actually far more important for the coach than the player's current performance or abilities.*

The example of French coach Patrick Mouratoglu, who currently coaches Serena Williams, is very well known. Many years ago at one of the Tennis Europe tournaments for players under 14, Mouratoglu had decided to support the athlete who had lost the 1st round of that tournament. Back then, he was able to see the potential that is needed for the top world players. Besides that, that boy came from a country that until then had never had a serious tennis player in it's entire history, or any tennis tradition at all (Cyprus). Sure enough, that boy was promoted with his trainer's help and developed into one of the more successful tennis players in history. I'm talking about Marcos Baghdadis, winner of four ATP[50] tournaments and ranked among the top ten tennis players in the world."

Krajnc has yet another excellent example of coaches using their intuition in the selection of which athletes to work with. *"This story is well known among tennis connoisseurs. During the war in Bosnia, an Italian tennis coach, Richardo Piatti, was looking for a boy who he used to see at all the international tournaments, but all of a sudden, he wasn't present at the tournaments anymore. This boy wasn't among the best in the tournaments, but Piatti intuitively*

---

50 Association of Tennis Professionals

knew that that boy had something more, so he decided to search for him. After a while, he found him with his parents in a small apartment in Rijeka, in Croatia. They started to work together, and that boy won 10 ATP tournaments and became number 3 in the ATP ranking. You guessed it; I'm talking about Ivan Ljubicic, also a very successful tennis coach, who is at the moment coaching the great Roger Federer."

While the list of benefits that intuition brings to sports and coaching is very long, one of the most important of these, according to Zoran Krajnc, is the role of intuition in protecting the athletes from injuries. *"There is a huge number of examples of this in top-class sports, so mentioning each one would not be interesting, but there is one thing which must be told. The higher the awareness that athletes and their coaches have of their inner knowing, their intuition, the higher are their chances of avoiding injuries, and thus of becoming the best in their discipline. As a rule, the biggest sport champions are rarely injured seriously and they usually finish their sports careers well. To name just a few of them: Roger Federer, Lionel Messi, Usain Bolt, Cristiano Ronaldo, Michael Jordan, LeBron James, Marcel Hirscher, Martin Fourcade, Noriaki Kasai, Tina Maze, Ingemar Stenmark and many others."*

We talked to another amazing name, which every tennis enthusiast know - Nikola Pilic. Niki, as he is nicknamed, is a former professional tennis player, professional tennis coach, founding member of the ATP Tour and much more. He is the only person to have won the Davis Cup[51] with players from three different nations, and to have a total of five wins. Over his 40-year coaching career, he produced over 40 players that ranked in the top 100 on the ATP list. Boris Becker, Goran Ivanisevic, Michael Stich, Novak Djokovic, Ivo Karlovic and Ernests Gulbis are just some of the successful names that Nikola has coached individually during the course of his professional coaching career. Let's see what thoughts he shared with us in terms of intuition and success:

"On the way here, I was talking to my wife Mia, who is a former actress, and she told me that everything that she did intuitively met with success, and I couldn't agree more! Experience and know-how is very important for any coach, but the most important thing is to feel who to work with and how to work with that person. And that is something you just can't learn, it's something you have to know within

---

51 The premier international team event in men's tennis. It is run by the International Tennis Federation (ITF) and is contested annually between teams from competing countries in a knock-out format. It is described by the organizers as the "World Cup of Tennis", and the winners are referred to as the World Champion team. [147]

you instantly; you have to feel it or you will not be successful. It sounds complicated and it seems strange, but only if you start to get dramatic about it: otherwise, it's the most natural thing in the world. Everyone has that ability, and we may develop it or not, we may use it or not, it's our free choice."

Pilic has found that, while logic has its place, intuition is usually the determining factor in many major decisions. *"Many times, I have discussed some decision I made and which was successful, how did I come to think of it, how did I know, why did I make that choice, and very rarely could I find some logical explanation for the unusual decisions which brought me the greatest success. In my coaching career, I often faced the question, who among the players I was working with could reach for something more. And that wasn't a matter of analyzing and comparing their strengths and weaknesses, but going a step beyond that, looking into their future; and in such cases you have to rely on your inner voice, your gut feeling."* And he gives an example: *"I can remember the 1988 Munster Open. Before that tournament, I was working for two or three weeks with Michael Stich, who was at that time 102th on the ATP ranking list. I was in charge of inviting the players to the tournament, and I gave a wild card[52] for the main draw to Michael Stich. That day I received over twenty telephone calls asking why I gave a card to him and not to some other better-ranked players and so on. No doubt, I could have chosen at least five better players according to the statistics at that time, and with my decision, I definitely surprised not only the players who were candidates for the tournament, but others who didn't understand my choice. But that surprise was nothing compared to when Michael performed, because he actually won that tournament. So when a coach observes a player, he doesn't just observe his forehand, backhand or serve, but he must go deeper, he must see what is in his heart and soul, and then comes the intuition which says, 'this one is right and this one is an "empty bottle"', a 'flasche leer' as Giovanni Trapattoni says. And this is just one of the many examples which helped me to believe in my inner voice and to expand my desire for developing my intuition."*

Nikola Pilic offers another relevant story: *"I believe that with intuition, we can know or guess many things. In that area, I may say, I am literally like a psychic or mindreader. It's all about a special feeling, which I think you either have or you don't have. To support this idea with an example, it was in the year 2010 and at that time, I was captain of the Serbian Davis Cup team. The French team was playing with Gilles Simon and Gaël Monfils, while Serbia played with*

---

52 Wild cards are usually offered to the lowest level of players in any tournament draw. They don't qualify technically; rather, these invitations are handed out on the basis of potential or emotional appeal, because, simply put, their current rankings are not good enough to earn them a direct entry into the tournament. [148]

Novak Djokovic and Janko Tipsarevic. There I was standing with two Croatian journalists, it was on a Thursday and it was a draw, but I said to them: 'You have to promise me to keep this to yourselves until Monday, OK? With 2:2, there is going to be a match with Michaël Llodra against Viktor Troicki, and Serbia is gonna win the Cup.' A strange prediction, since neither of those two players were even scheduled to play. But as you know, it happened just like I said, those two played, and in a dramatic final, Serbia defeated France 3:2 to win their first Davis Cup title. Some may comment that it was just a lucky guess, but for me it was obviously one of the intuitive hints which I managed to catch."

In all the cases cited by these athletes and coaches, we have seen how intuition can guide not only their instantaneous reactions to the changing circumstances of the moment, but also their long-range decisions concerning how to play or who to work with. And you can have the same results in your life.

Intuition in Chess and Go

"There are actually not many things in chess that I am absolutely certain about. On the most difficult decisions, for sure you have to calculate, but intuition is just as important to me."

—Magnus Carlsen

Another activity which wasn´t mentioned in the previous chapter, but which many people classify as a sport because of its competitive aspect, is chess. According to America's Foundation for Chess, there are 169,518,829,100,544,000,000,000,000,000 ways to play the first 10 moves in a game of chess. There are 400 possible setups after one move by each player. There are 72,084 possible setups after two moves each. There are over 9 million possible setups after three moves each. There are over 318 billion possible setups after four moves each. The number of distinct 40-move games in chess is far greater than the number of electrons in the observable universe. The number of electrons is approximately 10^{79}, while the number of unique chess games is 10^{120}. [82] According to Jonathan Schaeffer, a computer scientist at the University of Alberta who demonstrates A.I. (Artificial Intelligence) using games, "*The possible number of chess games is so huge that no one will invest the effort to calculate the exact number.*" [83]

As we begin to understand these illustrations of the complexity of this strategic game, we can see that it's really about the enormous number of combinations of possible moves. So the question is, how to analyze all the possible moves in the given time and how to find the best move when under pressure from the clock. Every chess player knows about silent inner talk when calculating the next move: *If I take his pawn, then he takes my bishop and he attacks my rook, if I…* Deducing an opponent´s next move sounds like the perfect job for a computer algorithm, but for a human, you can be sure that the more deeply we analyze, the more time we need for checking all possible combinations after three, four, or five moves, and the more chances we have of making some serious mistake in our calculations, or of finding ourselves running out of time. So, if we are in the middle of a game, after each move we have exponentially more possible situations and need more and more time to calculate. From minute to minute, we grow more tired; different emotions start to appear; we have already made some mistakes, or at least we have some doubts about our past moves; maybe we are thinking about our opponent´s attitude: why did he make this or that move; fears may appear: and how can we possibly calculate in the midst of all that? At that point, when we are forced to stop rationalizing the next move, for any of these or other reasons, in order to avoid playing Russian roulette – we must switch over to "intuitive mode" right away! And as soon as we do that, the moves become faster, tactics start to follow an instantaneous strategy and we win the battle against time for each move. The calculations are now there just to verify our intuition (we are able to do them in time, while waiting for the opponent´s next move) and the emotions and time pressure suddenly transfer to the opponent. The inner feelings bring the first scent of victory, the opponent notices that and now we are actually only a small step away from winning. The question is what is it that distinguishes between the quality of different chess players? That question has been posed to many of the world´s top chess players throughout the course of history, as well to two players who are considered to be among the greatest in the history of modern chess: Garry Kasparov, who was ranked No. 1 in the world from 1986 to his retirement in 2005 [84], and Magnus Carlsen, who became World Champion in 2013 and still holds the title as this book goes to press in early 2018. [85] Beim, Botvinnik, Kramnik, Capablanca, Fischer, Kasparov, Tal, Anand, Carlsen, and other chess greats have answered that question, and the answer was always the same - intuition.

This is what Garry Kasparov says about intuition: *"We should learn how to trust our gut; intuition. In most of the stories I looked at and in most of the quotes I collected, I didn't see people picking up intuition as a crucial element of success. While in my profession, in chess, intuition is virtually everything, because chess, while some people don't recognize it, is a mathematically infinite game. The number of moves in the game of chess, all the moves, contains 120 zeros, which is more than the number of seconds since the moment the Big Bang created the universe.*

"How can you find your way in this ocean of possibilities? And of course, how [can] a man fight a machine that could calculate tens of millions of positions per second? [Through] intuition, because it is all about [the] decision-making process. We never employ calculation as the main tool. It's one percent of calculation or less, and 99 percent of our understanding, of our ability to find intuitive ways of comparing compatibles, material versus quality, time versus material; intuition plays a key role.

"We have to trust our intuition; our instinct. Because in life, also, we have many opportunities where we cannot foresee all of the consequences. There is only one choice. To trust your gut." [86]

Intuition is central to all chess decision-making, and an understanding of its role is vital in improving one's game. In chess, at the highest level, intuition usually comes first in deciding a move, then calculation. Bill Wall quotes former world champion Garry Kasparov as saying that first, intuition gives the player a candidate move, and then the calculations are used to verify the soundness of that intuition. The intuitions themselves also arise from experience. Intuition is the result and response to an instructive form of learned strategic calculation. The rational brain further analyzes those results to look for flaws. An intuitive move is one made not because of calculation, but because the player recognized that it will produce a position of a type in which a familiar strategy usually worked in the past. [87]

As you will see, other great chess players have had pretty much the same experience: they all say that intuition is a key component of their chess game.

"In chess, intuition manifests itself first and foremost in the ability, in a somewhat unconscious way, and with a high degree of accuracy, to choose between different lines of play." [88], says Valeri Beim.

"Intuition is the first move I see in the position," says Viswanathan Anand. Helmuth Pfleger also finds intuition to be the tool responsible for reaching a solution which you later find hard to explain: *"Intuition in chess (but not only in chess) is either a conscious or subconscious process, as a result of which an individual, without prolonged deliberation, reaches a conclusion, which he himself is unable to explain."* And what does Vasily Smyslov have to say about intuition in chess? *"In my games, I depend not only on my experience, knowledge and analytical ability, but most of all on my intuition, for it is this 'feeling' for the position that enables us to evaluate accurately and profoundly, as burns brightly the flame striving for the fight ahead."* Vladimir Kramnik openly says that he himself is an intuitive player: *"Intuition is immediate awareness of the position, but this is difficult to explain logically. Intuition in a sense depends on knowledge; the more you accumulate, the better your intuition becomes... I myself am an intuitive player; my whole game is based on intuition. I simply reject certain variations or do not calculate them to the end, because I sense that they are incorrect."* [89]

It seems like nobody doubts the existence of intuition in chess, and that it is a necessity for the very strategy of the game, for a player´s tactics and ability to calculate different variations and endgame techniques. Beliavsky and Mikhalchishin explain that there are three types of intuitive decisions in chess: (1) combinative, (2) positional and (3) psychological (the sense of danger - predictions of the opponent's plan and taking the correct preventive measures). [89]

As we may conclude, intuition is one of the vital elements for success at playing chess, but even greater importance is given to intuition when playing the oriental game *go*[53]. Like chess, *go* is a game of skill - it has been described as being something like four chess games going on at once on the same board - but it differs from chess in many ways. The rules of *go* are very simple, and though, like chess, it is a challenge to players' analytical skills, there is far more room in *go* for intuition. The history of *go* stretches back some 3-4,000 years, and probably originated in China[54]. *Go* is a territorial game. The board,

---

53 The Japanese name for this game is *igo*, shortened to *go* in English and other European languages, but it has no relation to the English verb "to go".
54 Although it originated in central Asia and there are references to the game by Confucius [500 B.C.], historically it was in Japan that the game really flourished. Probably introduced there well before the 8th century A.D., *go* soon gained popularity at the Imperial Court and, from this auspicious beginning, took root in Japanese culture. [149]

marked with a grid of 19 lines by 19 lines, may be thought of as a piece of land to be shared between the two players. One player has a supply of black pieces, called stones, the other a supply of white pieces. The game starts with an empty board and the players take turns, each placing one stone on a vacant point during their turn. Unlike chess, black begins the game, and the stones are placed on the intersections of the lines rather than inside the squares. Once played, the stones are not moved. However, they may be surrounded and captured, in which case they are removed from the board as prisoners. As an intellectual challenge, *go* is extraordinary. The rules are very simple, yet there is great scope for intuition and experiment in a game of *go*, especially in the opening. Like chess, *go* has its opening strategies and tactics, but players can become quite strong even when they know no more than a few basic patterns. [90]

Gregor Butala is a multiple winner of the Slovenian National *Go* Championship, and president of the *Go* Association of Slovenia. He explained to us when speaking about intuition that his introduction to *go* was nothing less than pure intuition – he recognizes that now, but back then, he just had that feeling of rightness, which turned out to be correct for him, when he found himself "all in" in this ancient and respectable strategic game. But let´s see what he told us about intuition in the *go* game. *"Go is like chess, a game of strategy. In go, the pieces are all the same (just black or white) and they do not move around the board like in chess. That's the part which makes* go *easier (especially with regard to learning the rules), but as soon as we start to discover the game, we may see that* go *is much more complex than chess in terms of the variations of different moves. For instance, in chess there are only 20 possible opening moves, while in* go *there are 361 possible moves. As the game continues, the number of possible moves increases enormously, until you approach the end of the game. The variation and complexity of the game of* go *are what actually make intuition so important in the game. In terms of basics,* go *is primarily a rational game, but it's an undisputable fact that intuition brings good results in* go, *especially when a* go *player has already achieved a higher level of knowledge and is more experienced."* He says that, as in other games and sports, the players can be classified as those who are more intuitive and those which rely more on rational decision making. *"In my opinion, the most recognized intuitive* go *player would be the great Takemiya*

Masaki[55], known for his 'cosmic' go. If I had to put myself in one of those two groups, I would say that I like to be rational, because we are taught to be rational all our lives, but that playing by my 'gut feeling' always brings me a strong feeling to 'go ahead' and usually brings good results. Among many such situations, I can remember playing one particular game in the 37th World Go Championship (WAGC) in 2016. That game, I can say, was totally driven by my intuition during various moments. I could sense a very strong feeling of what the next move should be (it was a very unique feeling which leaves a deep impression on a man), and I was so convinced of the next move to play that I was literally forced to 'override' my rational part. I won that game, but not many games are like that, unfortunately."

Svetlana Valeryevna Shikshin, 3rd Dan professional *go* player and instructor, is one of the very few Western women to reach professional status (the first in Europe). Early on in her career, she became European Female Champion and in the year 2006, she became European Champion. When talking with her about her experiences with intuition, we discovered that they are very similar to those of the chess players we interviewed. *Go* players also uses intuition to determine the best possible moves, and only then do they perform rational calculations: this saves them a lot of time. According to Svetlana, intuition can be especially useful in the middle game: *"In go, people usually use intuition the most in the middle game. In the beginning of the game, players use common* fusekis *and* josekis *(standard plays in corners, which have been developed over the centuries). Players study famous openings and memorize* josekis *in order to get a good start, but in the middle game, there is more potential for being creative. So the middle game is most difficult and unpredictable".*

Shikshin also pointed out the case when she played at the European Pair *Go* Championship (a fast-paced tournament with a short time limit), which is based on teamwork (male and female play together and take turns in one game) and therefor even harder than playing the whole game on your own. *"Teammates can't discuss the game and if anyone plays out of turn, there is a penalty - 3 points. Sometimes, in a game like this,*

---

55 Japanese professional *go* player. By the time he was 15, he was already 5th Dan. He earned the nickname "9th-Dan killer" because he won several games against top-rated players. His famous "cosmic style" of *go* would become popular among fans. It focused on a large *'moyo'* in the center of the board. He's known for keeping a consistent record of winning titles. The longest period in which he did not hold a title has only been 4 years. He closed out 2005 with an impressive win of 16 straight games. [150]

it is not easy to understand what your partner is trying to do. So players use their intuition a lot."

The Role of Intuition in Blindness

"I close my eyes so I can see."

— Paul Gauguin

There is one very interesting field where our intuition can play a major role and can be of great help – blindness. While we are usually taught that we only have five senses, we believe that intuition is also a primary sense - the first sense (as we wrote back in the chapter *The Definition of Intuition*). One assumption that we had made prior to beginning our research for the *Intuition and Success* project was that intuition can take over some parts of the other senses if a person is deprived of them. Therefor, we began searching for some evidence to either confirm or disprove this hypothesis. Through our research, we have found numerous examples that have led us to confirm that assumption beyond any doubt. Several very distinguished blind people who are active in different fields have personally entrusted us with their testimonies, telling us of their experiences in this matter. The common thread that binds these people together, aside from their being successful and also deprived of sight, is their internal connection to intuition and their experience with it. We consider the pattern which has revealed itself to be firm proof of the interconnection between blindness and intuition, and our research has shown that intuition can be very useful in the case of blindness. Why this is true is still hard to say, but that it is true has become more than evident.

Esref Armagan is a blind painter, blind from birth. He has never been able to see or understand colors, yet he is a well-known artist whose incredible skills have attracted the attention of international art researchers and scientists. In 2004, Harvard University, impressed by this genius, invited him for brain and eye scans. The results of those tests surprised everyone, even the scientists. The brain's visual cortex, usually dark in the visually impaired, lit up when Esref touched an object and began drawing. After this, Esref became the subject of an article by the famous magazine, New Scientist. He didn't start out with the idea of becoming an artist: he just wanted to learn about the world around him.

> *"I believe intuition is very important... without it, art would not be whole, it would remain incomplete."*
>
> — Esref Armagan

He believes that intuition as a special feeling can best be sensed by the pure of heart, and that it is something that requires a lot of work to master. Besides his artwork, one of the most important uses of intuition for him is also when he is meeting people for the first time. *"Being blind, when I meet someone new, I must be aware of the tone of their voice, the way that they walk, the perfume they wear and any other details about them, and immediately analyze all of this information, but also listen to my internal voice, what message it will bring to me about that person."*

Another interesting example of using his intuition that Armagan explained to us is in connection with groups of people, an audience and even the physical place where he is at some particular moment: *"I speak in many places, and intuition helps me when I'm on the stage: I have an instant understanding of what kind of people I'm speaking to. That intuitive information about the place and the audience help me to adapt in the proper way."* This ability was clearly demonstrated to one of the authors (Ivan) when, in an interview which was done over Skype, Esref Armagan, without seeing me or knowing anything about me at that time, suddenly started describing the room where I was seated, and then began to describe me as a person; what I like and dislike, what places I like, what are my habits and so on. He did this with an incredible and almost frightening accuracy. He finished by saying: *"This is an example of the sixth sense, this is an example of my intuition."*

Another amazing person deprived of sight who finds intuition to be very helpful and believes that it plays a major role in her life is Christine Ha, a Blind Cook, Chef, a New York Times best-selling author, TV hostess and the first blind contestant and Winner of MasterChef U.S (on FOX, with Gordon Ramsay). She proved to be the best home cook among as many as 30,000 contestants across America. Gordon Ramsay commented: *"Honestly, I know chefs with Michelin stars that don't have palates like hers."* [91]

Christine has the amazing ability to cook using her other heightened senses, and we were wondering ourselves if she uses intuition as well and if intuition somehow helped her to reach her success. She confirmed our assumptions, saying that she is a much better cook today than she was when she still had her sight. *"I'm learning to trust my intuition more, after having lost my vision. I use my intuition whenever I have to make large or overwhelming decisions, or whenever I feel I don't have enough information to guide my decision-making skills. That's when I 'trust my gut,' as they say. I know my kitchen, my equipment and the foods I cook quite well, so intuition plays a major role in cooking at home,"* she told us, and also shared with us one of the interesting intuitive experiences that happened during her MasterChef competition: *"After doing poorly at a few challenges on my season of 'MasterChef U.S.', I decided to follow my intuition more when deciding on which dish to make during a challenge. At the beginning, I would think a lot about what sort of dishes the judges would like or what they would praise. When I was assigned to cook a salmon dish, I knew deep down that I only like to eat salmon raw and that I hated it cooked. However, I worried that the judges would say I'm not showing any cooking skills if I simply served the salmon raw. Therefore, I proceeded to bake the salmon, and it came out dry and horrible. The whole time I was cooking, I knew the dish would be bad, too, and that I would never want to eat what I was cooking. After that challenge, I told myself I would no longer concern myself so much with what I thought the judges wanted, but rather I'd just cook something that I myself would want to eat and enjoy. That's why, when I was in the semi-finals, I decided to cook southern fried chicken, and when the judges asked me how I was so brave to cook something as basic as fried chicken, I simply answered, 'I love fried chicken, and I only want to cook what I'd want to eat myself.' It turned out to be very good fried chicken, and the judges raved about it. That's when I moved on to the finals."*

Intuition can make your life meaningful, even when you are in the "deepest, darkest hole" of depression, as John Brambitt told us. Brambitt is a professional artist, author of an award-winning book, and currently works as a consultant for museums in developing programs that are designed to include everyone – no matter their ability or disability. Who would know better than he, who lost his vision and whose hopes of becoming a creative writing teacher were shattered. He sunk into a deep depression, and felt disconnected from everyone and everything. But then something amazing happened: he discovered painting, once again. As he explains, he felt this strong force inside of him that was pushing him to spend hours and hours every day to try to learn how to draw again – and he did. But not only that: he became good at it, and achieved commercial success. His art has been sold in over one hundred and twenty countries. *"Just because that's the way things look on paper, or that's the way that educated people think about something, doesn't make it real. Reality is within you, and will be revealed though your intuition when the right time comes,"* he says, and continues: *"On the conscious level, I was feeling like 'this is stupid, this doesn't make sense, why in the world am I doing this'; yet, there was a point when my intuition not only told me what to do, it pushed me forward, like 'you gotta do this, you gotta do this, it's not an option'. It felt almost like a compulsion. Thinking back, if I would have listened to my conscious mind rather than my inner voice, I would never have done that, I would never even have tried to go back into art, and my life would never have change the way it has."*

With regard to his artwork, intuition has proven to be of great importance and he relies on it a lot. *"In painting, you study and practice your skills. And after a certain time, that practice brings you to the point that you don't need to use your memory any more, you just follow your intuition. I even try to use the oddest parts of myself and put them in my work, and I noticed that those works somehow connect me with people, whether they like me or not - the painting connects us in some unexplained way. Intuition is like thinking on the unconscious level,"* he explains.

Over the past few years, he has learned to trust fully in his intuition, and he accepts almost every workshop he agrees to do just because it feels right to him, it looks right to something within him. And when he goes to such an event, everything turns out to be great. But he also points out that other times, when he goes to certain events despite an uncomfortable feeling from the very first moment, he soon gets some confirmation that he shouldn't be part of that event at all. He also finds intuition to be of great value when meeting people: *"After losing my sight, I have noticed that I have much better interaction with other people then when I still had my vision. I actually expected it to be the other way around, but I notice that I feel the connection more now, or I may even feel the lack of a connection with people sometimes. Strangely enough, for me, things seem to be much easier now: I actually can pick up on people intuitively much better than before. I have talked to other blind people or to people who are visually impaired and they have noticed the same thing."* Brambitt believes that life is amazing, that we get information from a lot of different sources, and that it would be silly of us to discount any of them: *"Any place we can get knowledge, inspiration or feelings from, we need to latch onto them, and intuition is a big part of this."*

Although we´ve already mentioned Intuition and Chess, there´s one form of chess playing that varies quite a bit from the regular game: Blindfold Chess. This is an interesting example of how "deprivation" of the sense of sight can make intuition flourish. Let´s look at the case of the "Blindfold King" - chess grandmaster Timur Gareyev. Chess is a game where intuition plays a welcome part, and when speaking about playing chess while blindfolded, one cannot imagine playing without relying heavily on intuition. Gareyev holds a world´s record for the greatest number of simultaneous chess games played at one time while blindfolded. He has scored an astonishing 35 wins, seven draws and six losses against very strong opponents (with a rating of up to 2200). He shared his insight with us on the role of intuition for his game: *"When I play blind chess, I really try to give all my attention and focus to each one of the games I´m playing, and try to memorize the information and keep it all in my head, and form the right strategy for each one of those games and so on. But the game itself, the biggest part of the game, is actually played through intuition."*

"Blindfold chess masters consistently report that what they visualize are not images of pieces or chessboards, but abstractions of these with minimal or no physical features. A typical report is, 'I do not visualize real pieces, but I know where they are.'" [92]

The bottom line is that when someone is deprived of their sense of sight, even voluntarily by using a blindfold, their intuition can become more accentuated than normal, not only replacing part of the information loss caused by the impairment, but actually going beyond the amount of information that was previously acquired by the their sight. This may also be the case with the loss of other physical senses, or with the use of flotation tanks for controlled sensory deprivation, which temporarily simulates the loss of physical contact with the external environment. Another similar way of closing off the outer world in order to stimulate the inner senses, especially intuition, is by simply closing our eyes, which is used in many forms of meditation. Anything that replaces our external awareness with internal awareness, whether accidentally or by choice, would seem to improve our contact with intuition.

Dr. Ivan Erenda ⊙ Aleksej Metelko

Intuition in Science

> *"I just knew I had to do it".*

> —Enrico Fermi

Dr. Robert Samuel Langer, Jr., the most cited engineer in history, who has also been awarded the Queen Elizabeth Prize for Engineering, told us that, in his opinion, intuition plays "a very important" role in scientific research because "it guides decisions". *"I was trying to develop a controlled-release polymer and things weren't working well. There were hundreds of possible ways to think about doing this, but it was an extremely hard problem. My intuition helped lead me to a way that worked (the right material for encapsulation, the right loading of the drug, the right processing conditions),"* describes Dr. Langer with regard to how he managed to solve this specific scientific problem with the help of intuition.

He also confided to us that he believes that intuition can be more effectively used when a person has set goals that represents a greater good, which is something we also firmly believe. When our objective is related to our own personal interest, we still get lots of help; but when the objective is to improve the lives of others, to protect the environment, etc., whatever it is that lies behind intuition seems to take a deeper interest and sends us more information and guidance. This is a very beautiful thing, and would seem to indicate that when our interests are for the advancement of the Whole, and not just for the advancement of the little part of that Whole which is us, the Whole sends us more assistance. The more we open ourselves to this influence in benefit of collective interests, the more this process becomes natural and normal for us, and the more our goals shift into doing what contributes to the collective best for everyone and everything.

As we can see, intuition is no stranger at all to the world of science, even hard science. We have already discussed this a little bit, but at this point we are entering even deeper waters. Some very interesting insights were shared with us by Dr. Federico Capasso, Harvard University professor and a prominent researcher in applied physics, who was one of the inventors of the quantum cascade laser during his work at Bell Laboratories, where he held several management positions, including Vice President of Physical Research. Being a scientist, Capasso believes in a combined approach to solving complex problems in science, using both rational and intuitive methods: *"Most often, the best decisions come when you combine both approaches, the intuitive and the rational. That is why I tell my students, 'If you want to be good scientists, there is an intuitive aspect and creativity, but then you have to find the facts, provide the analysis and so on...' How you approach the problem, how you think about problems, these are soft skills, but often make a big difference between someone being just an average scientist and a top scientist."* It was nothing less than strong intuitive insights, or "flashes" as he calls them, which led to the invention of the quantum cascade laser, which has become the most widely used source of mid-infrared radiation for chemical sensing and spectroscopy: *'It started with an idea; I want it to make a device where the electrons move down a slope and emit a photon. So I had this idea of a waterfall of electrons that in some way creates a waterfall of photons. So that was a very intuitive kind of thing, it was 'half-baked', not ready to consume yet, but it was a starting point for the work on the invention of the quantum cascade laser. Yes, it was a good example of intuition."*

Another good example of intuition in science would be Dr. Enrico Fermi´s experiment, for which he later won the Nobel Prize in Physics. Fermi was a physicist and the creator of the world's first nuclear reactor. This amazing and untold story was described to Capasso by one of Fermi's young collaborators. *'Fermi was bombarding the chemical elements with neutrons and was looking for radioactivity, and at some point, out of the blue, he said, 'I'm going to put this block of paraffin wax in front of the neutron beam'. It turned out that when neutrons were passed through paraffin wax, they induced a hundred times as much radioactivity as when they were emitted without the paraffin. That was really the moment of the beginning of the atomic age. So that was actually an example of an intuitive leap: he had absolutely no reason to use the paraffin. Later, he said, 'I just knew I had to do it'."*

V. Developing Intuition

S PIRITUAL LIFE, THE way we choose to look at the things our physical senses can´t show us, is very important for the development of mankind as a whole, for the development of intuition and for the success of each individual. Oskar Kogoj told us, *"Without experience, there is no development of the soul and no development of intuition. Intuition is the inner faculty we have, but we need to listen, we need to engage. Sometimes you need to ask directly: for example, in the evening before you go to sleep, ask a question, what interests you, what do you need to do, ask about your doubts, anything. You will receive the answer, sometimes immediately, sometimes after a time: sometimes it will pop up all of a sudden, and sometimes it will be disguised within the events around you that will reflect the answer."*

In this chapter, we will discuss what each and every one of us can do to create the most favorable conditions possible for tapping into our intuition more easily and more often. There are numerous different approaches and techniques, and multiple combinations thereof: preferably, you should choose those that you feel most comfortable with and which bring you the best results. Each and every one of us is a unique human being, and each and every one of us has their own individual connection to their intuition. So put some additional effort into finding the right channel for communicating with your intuition, and of course the right stimulus, the best approach for tapping into your intuition, early in the process of your exploration. Don't worry if you don't make huge progress in a short time: sometimes it does happen immediately, sometimes after a few days, weeks or even months of practice, but we have never heard of anyone who wasn't eventually able to get in tune with his intuition if he remained persistent. Don't forget, intuition is our first sense, the inborn faculty we all have access to, so be patient and open, and keep on trying.

Evolve Your Belief System

Leaving aside the aspect of our body and related genetic influences, as well as who we are as a soul, each and every one of us is shaped through many different circumstances and sees the worlds through multiple "filters" that have been in one way or another *imposed* upon us. Where we were born and when, who are our parents, our family members, who are other influential people and even animals that surround us, as well as the environment we live in (historical, religious and other aspects play a huge role) – all these together build and shape our general belief system. According to the Oxford dictionary, a belief system is *"a set of principles or tenets which together form the basis of a religion, philosophy, or moral code"*. Also considering the fact that we are not alike and that we are each an individual soul on our very own mission, full of specific desires and goals, we each have our very unique personal belief systems. These are based much more on individual experiences and on our "inner life" than on our external conditions, which may be complete opposites of each other. The inner life is what is most importance for intuition.

"Yo soy yo y mi circunstancia." [56]

—José Ortega y Gasset

In beliefs, we live, we move and we are [...] Beliefs constitute the base of our life, the land on which we live [...] All our conduct, including our intellectual life, depends on the system of our authentic beliefs. In them [...] all lies latent, as implications of whatever specifically we do or we think [...] The man, at heart, is his beliefs; or, equally, the deepest stratum of our life, the spirit that maintains and carries all the others, is formed by beliefs... [93]

---

56 (*"I am myself and my circumstances."*) [130]

What we have found through our past research, and which is confirmed by our professional and private experience, is that too many people fall into a trap where their current *circumstances* control their lives. They are living their lives in accordance with seemingly unchangeable circumstances rather than using their true and full potential, listening to their inner voices, acting on their feelings, taking a risk to do what they feel they need to do. People are too afraid of trying something new, something different. It is easiest to live according to old habits, but when did something extraordinarily joyful happen and last without our effort? Don't allow your circumstances to limit your beliefs, so you can't fulfill all your potentials, satisfy all your needs and desires and reach a higher state of yourself.

Bruce Lee was much more than just a fighter, an awesome martial artist and a great actor and film director; he was also a very gifted and dedicated philosopher. There is one quote attributed to him that says, *"To hell with circumstances; I create opportunities."* This reflects exactly what we are trying to show here in this chapter – sail to the edge of your beliefs and courageously go beyond them. You'll be positively surprised by the life that is waiting for you out there and how easy it actually is to overcome fear and uncertainty, once you start following your inner compass. It will guide you through rough waters, you have nothing to be afraid of; and it will continue to guide you to the next, better version of yourself, over and over again. You will enjoy a state of blissfulness and fulfillment; you are meant to be successful. Tapping into intuition and letting it guide your course, you finally become the captain of your ship. *"Empty your mind, be formless, shapeless – like water. Now you put water in a cup, it becomes the cup; you put water into a bottle, it becomes the bottle; you put it in a teapot, it becomes the teapot. Now water can flow or it can crash. Be water, my friend"* said Bruce Lee.

Our belief system is our perception of reality; it represents an explicit border for our world, the field of operations that is considered possible and which we are allowed to use. And as such, belief systems often limit us and hamper our evolution and growth.

Tip: Constantly work on evolving your belief system and keep moving the imaginary borders - you simply deserve a wider perspective and a blissful state of mind. Ask yourself, *"What if...?, What could be different?, What are the alternatives?"*.

From time to time in our lives, we come to a crossroads where we face a certain milestone, a challenge, a lesson to be learned, if you will. Usually, these are the moments when we must leave our old familiar world and move on to a better version of ourselves. *"I decided to move from the VW-Audi group to Kia-Hyundai in 2004. Looking through rational eyes, I went from a highly prosperous company, were I liked what I was doing and everything was just perfect, to a company which was behind their competition at that time in many ways, and I had no way of knowing what I could expect to find there. But deep inside, I knew that I had to leave my comfort zone and move on. And I can remember all my colleagues and my friends and relatives questioning me, 'why was I going to do that', and at that time I didn't have any logical explanation for them, or even for myself, but looking back from the perspective of today, I know that I did the right thing,"* recounted Pontus Fontaeus. The reward for your decision may or may not be instant. In many cases, it may take a while for your "new" life to unfold. In some cases, the results may come much later, even years or decades later, but it will come, that's for sure.

Yes, Henry Ford was right when he said *"Whether you think you can, or you think you can't – you're right."* This is especially true when someone thinks he can't, since in that case he will not even give it a try, or if he does, without proper beliefs to support him, he will have less chance to succeed.

Intention – Careful What You Wish For!

While working on a problem or facing a tough decision, how willing are you to systematically gather all the relevant facts and data? How willing are you to make an honest review of all possible options? How ready are you to face any type of feelings, regardless of whether they are pleasant or unpleasant? Are you willing to learn, to try to function in many different ways? How committed are you to making the best of any given situation?

Answering these questions will give you a "snapshot" of how strong your intention is, how willing you are to move forward, and how strong your desire is to succeed at whatever you are doing at the time.

Intention and willingness to act are the stages where most people fall. Having good ideas and high expectations but doing little or nothing is not a good recipe for achieving your long-term goals; it's just a shortcut leading nowhere. The opposite is also true: too much effort and forcing the results may lead to an intuition blackout.

Reality always resides somewhere between what you want and what you actually do to achieve your goal. By doing absolutely everything that you can in a certain situation and by constantly learning new things in order to be prepared for doing more and acting in different ways, your goals will be achieved faster, your intention will grow along the way and so will the end results. No matter how complex the situation may seem to be, you will always be able to achieve incredible results, and by doing that, your intuition will appear in many different ways and moments, showing you the way to act, giving you the needed impulses to build up your intention and your desire to succeed (assuming you're on the right path, of course).

However, there is one thing we need to clarify at this point: pushing yourself too much will do no good, especially if you put too much effort into the *wrong* direction, the *wrong* path. The famed law of attraction does work: getting yourself in a certain emotional state, visualizing the future, seeing and feeling the desired results, manifesting physical reality through mental activities may get you in the "achiever's state of mind" and may eventually result in getting what you wished for, but it is our opinion that this is still far from being the complete key to a Successful Life. Why? Simply because you might not want what you dreamed of, once you get it. In most cases, people eventually achieve what they want, they succeed, but at the same time, they are miserable, they are not fulfilled from within (remember the example of Robin Williams). So, take care what you wish for, it might come true. Also worth mentioning at this point is that when forcing things too much in one direction, doing too much thinking and making too much effort, you may completely block yourself from achieving the goal you are striving for. Overdosing with forceful effort may completely block your intuition, and you might start following the wrong path. So, always try to be aware of what you should really be working towards, and when your direction should change.

Awareness of the Present Moment

> *"If you are depressed, you are living in the past. If you are anxious, you are living in the future. If you are at peace, you are living in the present."*

> — Lao Tzu

Awareness of the present moment is another simple yet very effective method for connecting with yourself, and consequently, for developing your intuitive perception at the same time. It is especially appropriate to remember this when you are stuck in negative thoughts and feelings, over-analyzing past experiences or when you feel you are continuously falling into negativity, getting deeper and staying longer in that negative state of mind. What you want to do in this kind of situation is to switch that state of mind as quickly as possible.

One of *boosters* that will get you well on your way toward reaching that positive turnaround is to follow the next few steps:

⊃ Calm down with a few deep abdominal breaths (exhale twice as long as you inhale). Let your thoughts slowly calm down. You are like a mountain, still and mighty, and your thought are like clouds or the wind, they come and go. You will not be distracted in any way because you will not think about the clouds, you won't give them names or labels or judge them, they just are. Accept them and release them, and they are gone;

- ⊃ See yourself in your mind by imagining yourself from different perspectives, including from a bird´s perspective, for example. Feel the stillness of the moment;

- ⊃ Now, start observing yourself while imagining that you are frozen in time, knowing you are not in any hurry and you can discover all the details that look interesting to you;

- ⊃ Pay special attention to your body, to the muscle tensions and any possible discomfort in any part of the body. Awareness of your body is essential and absolutely necessary for reaching a full state of self-awareness. As soon as you are fully aware of your body, it will relax completely and you will be able to understand your thoughts and feelings much better. You will feel very light and may experience a sensation *of floating*, you may feel like your physical body is just one part of your greater being;

- ⊃ If doing this exercise when you are not alone, like on a plane or in a meeting, after you become aware of your own body, thoughts and feelings, try to sense your neighbors´ energies too, or even the energy of the entire group you are with;

- ⊃ After you feel awareness of your entire being on all levels, or of the group´s energy, stay silent and see if any ideas or signs come to mind. This relaxed, expanded state can be a doorway for your intuition to communicate with you;

- ⊃ After a while, when you feel ready, slowly return to your normal state of consciousness, without forgetting how you felt or what you learned during the exercise. You may wish to thank whatever Higher Mind you believe in for helping you to relax and make contact.

Experiencing awareness of the present moment, when you are conscious of your body, thoughts and emotions, empowers you with complete control over the situation. Pieces that seem to be completely unrelated at first glance will start to fit together perfectly, and you are able to see the frame of the wider perspective and the next steps. This is very important - when you establish a connection with your own inner self and when being in the state of awareness of the present moment, ask yourself: *"What is the next thing I need to do?"* or *"What is it that I need to put my focus on?"* or for example *"Where is my attention needed at this moment?"*

This is a simple yet very effective method, but its success depends on regular practice. Try to do this exercise every day, for a couple of weeks at least, not trying to change anything, but just observing. Dr. Maxwell Maltz wrote a book in 1960 called Psycho-Cybernetics, in which he stated that his patients took 21 days to get used to their new facial features after he performed plastic surgery on them, thus creating the modern myth that people need 21 days to create a habit or permanently fix a conditioned response. However, in 2009, a publication entitled "How long does it take to form a habit", by health psychology researcher Phillippa Lally, defined an average of 66 days for most people to build new behavioral patterns. Obviously, each individual case takes a specific time to form new habits, depending on a wide variety of factors. By practicing, you are gaining real experience of awareness on a daily basis, which leaves the doors wide open to your intuitive insights. On many occasions, you will get instant flashes, insights, ideas, inspirations. If not at that very moment, the answers are going to come after a certain time, be very sure of that.

Never victimize yourself again. Whatever you do when you are in a negative state of mind, avoid further negative reactions and activities, as these will only drown you deeper in quicksand. Become aware of the present moment and bring some *happy* thoughts into your mind.

Tip: Ask yourself, *"Why do I feel like this?"*, *"What is the next thing I need to do to shift myself out of this state?"*, *"What makes me happy, what fuels me, what is the driving force behind my joy?"*, *"What am I grateful for?"* and *"What can I learn from this situation?"*. Asking these questions will keep you in control of the situation, instead of leaving you in these devastating circumstances with the frustrating feeling of being powerless. This should be enough for you to escape from the initial negative reaction, and may even enable you to shift instantly to a more positive state of mind.

Positive Attitude Directly Affects Natural Perceptiveness

> *"We can complain that rose bushes have thorns, or we can rejoice because thorn bushes have roses."*

> — Anonymous

It's just as simple as that. Are you familiar with the joke about whether the cup is half full or the half empty? It goes like this: *"My therapist set half a glass of water in front of me. He asked if I was an optimist or a pessimist. So, I drank the water and told him I was a problem solver."*

A positively oriented person tends to be happier, healthier and more successful. Why is that so? Simply because of the way our universe is built and works. Scientists have begun to recognize that everything in the universe is made out of energy (something that many ancient cultures have known for milenia). Atoms, which are the basic building blocks of everything in the material universe, actually have no physical structure: in other words, not one physical thing in our universe has a physical structure. Everything you see around you is in fact energy. Lately, there have been quite a few studies confirming the "mind over matter" concept, suggesting that thoughts have a direct effect on matter. Our thoughts have the power to change the physical world. Amazing research in this field has been done by Lynne McTaggart, especially in her book *The Intention Experiment,* where she discusses how the world around us can be influenced by our thoughts and intentions. As Walt Disney once said, *"If you can dream it, you can do it."* Or, as Ralph Waldo Emerson put it, *"You are what you think all day long."* And we couldn't agree more. This is also the very basis on which the law of attraction works (in its broadest concept) – whatever we are focusing on, we can eventually attract into our lives. According to James Redfield (The Celestine Prophecy) and many others, attention is also energy. Deepak Chopra, Prem Baba, Satya Naryan Goenka and others have mentioned this concept in one form or another. This is why, once we develop an intention (this may even include what some call thought-forms), feeding it with the energy of our attention causes the manifestation of that intention, in a direct proportion to the energy we give it. A positive attitude towards life and everything connected with it can also bring us phenomenal results in correlation with intuition, because with a positive attitude we naturally become more perceptive and can tap into intuition much easier, while on the other hand, a negative attitude acts to inhibit intuition.

Nurturing Compassion Brings Massive Inner Changes

As already discussed in the chapter on *Ego,* compassion is a very effective way of counterbalancing our ego, as compassion for others can lower our ego, our self-centeredness, and vice versa, when the ego is diminished, compassion arrives from all sides. It´s similar to turning on the lights in a dark room, and who doesn't want to be (en)light(ened)?!

There is actually so much we could say about the value that compassion can bring to both the giver and the receiver, and consequently to the entire world around them, that this would require us to write an additional book; but in order to stay within the framework of our present work, we shall try to put it as simply as possible.According to some philosophies, all forms of attraction are based on the energy of love. Material attraction, the attraction of opposites, including sexual attraction, may be classified as physical love. But spiritual attraction, the attraction of similar energies, of individuals who recognize something in others which is part of a greater whole to which we all belong, this is the basis of compassion. Compassion transcends physical love, and can be understood as the highest form of love, understanding things from another person´s point of view and thus creating a special bridge between us. And this has a highly influential effect on our intuitiveness.

Different wounds that we carry inside of us are derived from a lack of love (either of ordinary physical love or of compassion). If you dig deep enough, you find that everything that is wrong with someone is somewhere, somehow associated with some lack of love. And the wounds inside can surface in many different ways, such as physical or mental illness. *"Just as food is needed for the body, love is needed for the soul."* When you feel love, you also feel that you are more than just the body and the mind. Compassion is the highest, the purest form of love.

Let's compare compassion and sex, for example: in this regard, we can see that sexual desire is not as deep or inspiring as compassion. In sex, the contact is basically physical, while in compassion, the contact is basically spiritual.[57] If we look through a spiritual prism, the sexual man is the poorest, while the compassionate man is far richer.

The man of compassion simply gives and has no restrictions, no limitation at all, not even waiting for you to thank him. He generously shares his energy with a tremendous love. With compassion, there comes a feeling of living rightly; you get this feeling that only now you have begun to live meaningfully. Compassion can also be understood as very therapeutic from this point of view. [94] Most people seem to only do good out of fear that they will be caught and punished (by the police or by God) for doing "evil". But this "feeling of living rightly" is a much healthier motivation for doing good than fear, knowing that you´re doing what should be done, and the way we know can be considered as a form of intuition. It´s like the flowers that bloom for the sake of blooming; they don't expect something in return, they simply give of their beauty. From this point of view, their existence can also be interpreted as being compassionate (whether or not anyone or anything else is there to experience it, to enjoy their beauty), and this simple and very plastic example can show the very essence of compassion – compassion transcends what we usually refer to as love.

"You can't get very far until you start doing something for somebody else."

—Melvin Jones

"What if these men," Melvin Jones[58] asked himself, *"who are successful because of their drive, intelligence and ambition, were to put their talents to work improving their communities?"* This is how the Lions Clubs International (LCI) was born, 100 years ago, [95] and later led to the Lions Clubs International Foundation (LCIF), the leading humanitarian organization in the world. *"Lions around the world are united by a great spirit of giving and dedication to helping others. As the official charitable organization of Lions Clubs International, a leading humanitarian organization, Lions Clubs International Foundation (LCIF) supports Lions' compassionate works by providing grant funding for their local and global humanitarian efforts."* Since

---

57 While sexual attraction may lead to spiritual attraction, the first is inferior to the last in terms of quality.

58 Melvin Jones was a prominent business leader from Chicago, who formed his own insurance agency. Later, he devoted himself fulltime to LCI.

its founding, LCIF has awarded more than 13,000 grants totaling over US$1 billion. During the fiscal year of 2015-2016, one of the accomplishments through the SightFirst program was to provide eye care services to more than 22 million people, improving 51 eye care facilities and training 23,643 eye care professionals. [96] Compassion knows no limits. And because a Lion expects nothing in return, he is like a blooming flower; he is a "man of compassion" who generously shares his energy. Compassion releases a powerful force for a positive change in both the one who gives and the one who receives.

It is very important to note that there is a huge difference between simply giving money and true compassion, as giving money by itself has less of an affect in comparison to the process of compassionate giving, where you give more than *just* money. What we are trying to say is that it is important *how* you give, how you express compassion, whether we are speaking of giving love, time, attention, skills or money. The very process of showing compassion also matters. Imagine a scenario where a man proposes to his beloved fiancée by nonchalantly flicking a ring at her from a distance, accompanied by some macho-style words. No explanation needed. And never hesitate over whether you should give, even when you know that you can't give *a lot*. As Buddha counseled, *"Give, even if you only have a little"*. It is the intention and the expression of compassion that matters the most. Give what you can, whether it is love, help, time or money. As a matter of fact, give as much as you can afford to give; even if it seems like so little to you, in the eyes of the receiver, it will most probably seem like a lot. Everyone can be a philanthropist, regardless of their income, as there is no minimum amount of compassion and empathy to be given.

> *"What we have done for ourselves alone dies with us; what we have done for others and the world remains and is immortal."*
>
> —Albert Pike[59]

---

59 Albert Pike was a lawyer, soldier and writer who played an active role in United States politics prior to the Civil War. He was a central figure in the development of Freemasonry and became the Sovereign Grand Commander of the Scottish Rite with the longest mandate in the history of the organisation. For years, his book *Morals and Dogma* (1871) was distributed to members of the Rite.

Nurture compassion and you will naturally open yourself to intuitive insight. Compassion leads to a better understanding of people within a specific situation, and through that, to improvements in communication and response in all situations.

Tip: Learn to hear your inner voice, be led by your heart and never stop giving – this way, you will always walk the right path and you will never walk alone.

How Useful are Meditation and Prayer?

When our body is relaxed, when there is no tension in our muscles, our inner sensory system gets permission to awaken and miracles can happen. We all remember the story of Archimedes; his discovery happened while lying in his tub, relaxing after the worries of the day. He was so excited that he ran into the streets naked, shouting, *"Eureka! Eureka!"*

Meditation has been in use for at least two and a half millennia, and probably much longer. Not only was it known in the East, but also in the West, and in many other different cultures around the world, including numerous African tribes. American Indians practiced a form of meditation similar to Japanese Zazen, and numerous shamans and healers utilized some sort of practice which could be labeled as meditation. [97]

During meditation, your body and mind are in a state where they are more sensitive to signals from your intuition, and in that state, it is much easier for intuition to break through the thick layers of the conscious mind.

Through techniques of deep meditation, a person can not only calm his mind and body, but can also reach a level where he can control vital body functions like the heartbeat and body temperature. Yogis are said to be capable of experiencing life beyond the physical plane, to become one with everything.

By using a yoga technique known as g Tum-mo, Buddhist monks are able to significantly raise their body heat by as much as 8.3°C (47° Fahrenheit) in their fingers and toes. In experiments conducted by Dr. Herbert Benson, monks sat calmly and completely unaffected by the chilly atmosphere. Then they were draped with ice-cold wet sheets and the unexpected happened – the wet sheets started to steam, and after about one hour they were completely dry. [98] [99]

Victoria Lynn Weston says that, for her, meditation is the number one method for tapping into intuition: *"For me, meditation helps me keep a clear mind, although intuition doesn't care how cluttered one's thinking is, or how busy you are."* She is also dedicated to walking, which she believes is also a great method for connecting to our intuition: *"Walking for me is great for connecting and listening to my intuition – just connecting with nature and being open to all my five senses, hearing the birds chirp, the wind ruffle leaves – it keeps me aware of my intuition and soul."* Victoria also entrusted us with one of her interesting experiences with intuition. She explains: *"In addition to being an intuitive consultant, I have produced documentaries, written screenplays. For example, while working on one screenplay, I had an intuition that Oscar-winning director, Oliver Stone, would be interested in my script. I focused on how to meet him: before pitching my script, I should say I had produced a successful documentary – so I had that credit – I sent a letter to schedule a pitch meeting and voilà, I had not one but two face-to-face meetings. My intuition was right, Oliver Stone was interested. However, he wasn't interested in buying my script. Two different things."*

Meditation is a very powerful way to shut down external and internal stimuli, which consequently allows you to enter a certain state of mind – definitely more receptive to intuitive signals. And the same goes for prayer: even though it is different in its very purpose and practice, one can easily draw a parallel between the two when taking into consideration chanting, repetition, stillness of body and the state of grace produced. If we may make a comparison, a prayer works like a mantra[60].

---

60 Mantras are melodic phrases with spiritual interpretations such as a human longing for truth, reality, light, immortality, peace, love, knowledge, etc. (they may or may not have a literal meaning). It is believed that the sounds produced while chanting mantras have psychological and spiritual powers, affecting a person´s vibratory level. Therefor it is believed that mantra meditation helps to induce an altered state of consciousness. The most widely spread and basic mantras are *Om* and *Ave Maria.*

This is how Lisa Nichols put it: *"If you want to make intuition a more useful tool, you have to sit still more often, you have to meditate more often, do breathwork and pray. Because when you pray, you ask for answers, but when you meditate you can hear the answers. So many times we pray but don't know where we are gonna get the answer from, and that's in your meditation time, that's in your breathwork time, that's when your intuition has enough space and enough quietness to talk to you."*

During every historic age, meditation and similar practices have been deeply connected with religious and ritual customs. The concept of meditation is interconnected with mystical experiences[61]. Christianity is far from ignorant concerning meditation; Saint Francis of Assis and Hildegard of Bingen, both well-known Christian mystics, advised believers that, in addition to prayer, they should also search and look deep inside themselves. [97]

The Desert Fathers, one of the oldest Christian orders, has been practicing Hesychast prayer, a *"meditative practice that was traditionally done in silence and with the eyes closed — 'empty of mental pictures' and visual concepts, but with the intense consciousness of God's presence."* [100]

"Silence is the beginning of the purification of the soul.... A mind undistracted by external things and not dispersed through the senses among worldly things, returns to itself..." [101]

Nobel Peace Prize winner, Dr. Shirin Ebadi, revealed to us how intuition had already played a very important role in her early life, and how it often changed the course of her life. She told us a story from her childhood when she was about 12 or 13 years old. Her mother became very ill, and she was very upset and went to pray. *"And I thought: 'Oh, nobody is really hearing me.' And suddenly I felt that somebody was hearing my voice, that my prayer was heard. I felt the presence of God, and that really changed my life. Because, if before that event I didn't have very strong faith in God, from that moment on, my faith became much stronger."*

Meditation and prayer are performed by different people with different motives – and for whatever reason you do them, they help. So if your motive is to strengthen the bond with your intuition, then yes, these two practices can be of help.

---

61 We belive that this is so because meditation provides access to a different level of consciousness where mystical experiences are more likely to occur than in our everyday state.

Changing the Perspective

Human perspective is far more important than we were ever taught, more than we can even imagine, and that's why it's very important to learn how to change it when the time for change comes. Our point of view is pretty much dependant on the beliefs we are nurturing, but that doesn't mean we must change our beliefs to look at something from a different perspective. At particular moments in our lives, we come to the point when it helps a lot if we are able see things and situations from different perspective (point of view).

From time to time, it happens that we just cannot find the right solution; we might be struggling with a certain issue for days, weeks, maybe even years. Not even the assistance of a professional advisor helps. What might be useful in that kind of situation is to play a little game with your mind – change your perspective.

It's very useful for someone to learn to be able to shift between two or more perspectives. This means, in the first place, that he has to be able to distance himself from his thoughts and feelings, to become as separated from the issue as possible; and secondly, once in this objective state of consciousness, he must be able to spark his imagination and visualization in order to *implement* a different perspective.

Using your inner guidance system, you can picture different possible scenarios and simultaneously pay attention to how you feel about each of them. This, for example, is how Angelo Vermeulen, space systems researcher, biologist, artist and keynote speaker gets in touch with his intuition - through "feeling" different scenarios. *"Sometimes picturing different potential scenarios and then sensing what feels 'right' is a good way to progress,"* says Vermeulen, who also shared how, at a certain point in his life, he "felt" that he needed to move from Belgium to the Netherlands, and how this turned out to be a great decision. *"Recently I moved from my hometown in Belgium to my university town in the Netherlands. There was a strong intuitive component to making this decision. Since I knew this was going to be a temporary move, with little possibility of renting out my apartment in Belgium, I wasn't sure that I would be able to handle this new situation financially. But at a certain point, I decided this was the way forward. There was some reasoning involved in the decision making (finalizing my PhD studies with more focus, etc.), but it also 'felt' like this was what I needed to do. It turned out to be a very good decision, through which I became a happier and more productive person."*

One might imagine how others sees this issue (either those who are related to the issue or those who are not related, or even some particular person whom you admire for his ability to overcome such obstacles) and how they would react if confronted with the issue. How would they proceed, what actions would they take or advise you to take? Try to develop this imaginary story even further, allowing yourself to seek answers from different perspectives. You'll be surprised by the results!

Deepening Self-Respect

Self-respect is certainly one of the most important aspect of our lives, directly interconnected to either beneficial or destructive self-behavior in the broadest sense. Only when we have deep self-respect can we start to fully love ourselves as the real person we are on the inside, distinct from the "mask" we wear for the outer world. The more energy and time we invest in deepening our self-respect, the more we feel connected with our true self, and then the miracle happens – we start to enjoy being ourselves. This kind of blissful state inevitably results in greater perceptiveness of our inner senses, and our body and mind drop their barriers against listening to the enlightening voice of intuition.

A great way to strengthen self-respect is to explore oneself, get to know yourself better, find out who you really are and what you really want, and stop striving for something that doesn't fit your true inner self and your true path to more meaningful life. Be honest with yourself. Jain 108 told us that, in his opinion intuition is not just knowledge to guide our material lives but it also brings Divine knowledge to guide our spiritual lives: *"The real purpose of intuition is to remember who we are, because we all get lost. We run our journey, and we are going through lots of different experiences, and sometimes we forget who we are, we forget our intuition, we don't listen to our gut feeling. We do things because we have to pay debts or pay the bank some money, and we are not really listening to our body or our higher self anymore. Intuition is not just knowledge to guide our material lives but it also brings Divine knowledge to guide our spiritual lives. Where we came from and what we should do are the questions, and the answers we get through intuition. So we have to go back inside, we have to meditate, we have to sit in the forest, we have to go back to the farm, we just have to stay connected. It's important that we remain whole, happy, healthy and connected, and we have to follow our passion; otherwise, the journey changes to something else, we become trapped."*

Will Smith explained in one interview that he has a mission statement which has stayed the same for the last few years now, and which says "improve lives". He said that he realized that the way to improve lives is to continually improve yourself. [102]

Intuition Modeling Technique

Try to model your intuitive process from start to finish by analyzing as much as possible your past intuitive situations. As we described before, every intuitive insight has certain signs, which can be organized into 4 main groups: (1) mental signs, which appear in our thoughts; (2) body signs or sudden specific physical symptoms; (3) signs from our environment; and (4) signs from our dreams.

Once you determine that you have had an intuitive experience sometime in the past, you should live through that event again, trying to notice in your imagination or memory all the feelings you experienced. Answering the following questions can help you:

- ⊃ What were the thoughts and feelings that you had before and during the moment of intuitive insight?
- ⊃ Which physical signs related to your intuitive experience can you remember most clearly?
- ⊃ Did you notice any interesting signs in your surroundings, like a sudden change in the weather or a word that you heard on the street?
- ⊃ What did you dream about during the nights before your insight came; were there any interesting details that you can remember? Did you sleep well or was it an agitated night, and can you remember any details about that?

By tracking and analyzing your intuitive experiences, sooner or later you'll be able to define your specific intuitive model, which is naturally changing all the time, according to your spiritual development and the intensity of your experiences. What kind of intuitive model you can expect and how it can change over time is described in the following account by one feminine participant in our research, who wished to remain anonymous.

An Intuitive Diary Allows Deeper Retrospection and Insights

"I really have learned I think how everything happens for a reason, and I am conscious of trying to look for the reason instead of the incident itself."

This is an excerpt from the Journal of Oprah Winfrey, (August 23, 1994), who has been a devoted diarist since the age of 15. [103]

Did you know that some of the most influential people in history kept detailed journals? Yes, at one point in their lives, they all happened to realize the transformational power of examining their inner thoughts with complete sincerity.

Along with Anne Frank, who might very well be the most famous diarist in history, there are many others from all walks of life: U.S. Presidents Harry Truman, George Washington and Thomas Jefferson, artist Andy Warhol, writers like Virginia Woolf, Franz Kafka, Ernest Hemingway and Oscar Wilde, musician Curt Cobain, and we could go on and on.

Also from the scientific point of view, there are many studies that indicate the positive effects of expressive writing. Anyone who is interested in the topic might want to understand the very nature of how our brain works. *"The act of writing accesses your left brain, which is analytical and rational. While your left brain is occupied, your right brain is free to create, intuit and feel. In sum, writing removes mental blocks and allows you to use all of your brainpower to better understand yourself, others and the world around you."* [104] Writing a diary offers multiple benefits. Not only does it help to chronicle your life, but it also brings out all the things that have traumatized your mind, and in that way it is quite beneficial from the therapeutic perspective - your diary becomes your faithful confidant and your most honest friend. Writing your thoughts on paper has a tremendous transformational power, but one of the biggest benefits is that it gives you the opportunity to reflect.

Depending on your goal, your diary should have a certain structure, meaning you are writing certain thoughts, answers and ideas related to the particular purpose of that diary.

Whether you are tracking your health or looking to achieve some advancement in your personal or business life, journaling is the perfect way to channel your thoughts, and one of the most liberating experiences one can have.

When talking about intuition and awareness, keeping your own personal intuitive diary can serve you as a precious tool on the path to intuitiveness – it offers you the luxury of retrospection. Recording your mental, emotional and physical sensations, keeping records of your dreams and being able to express yourself as freely as possible will give a tremendous boost to the development of your intuitiveness.

The great thing about journaling is that this private introspection is open to you 24 hours a day. You can look back and reflect on your deepest thoughts anytime you want. As Oscar Wilde once said: "I never travel without my diary. One should always have something sensational to read on the train."

Tip: Being truly honest is of the utmost importance in writing a diary: write it as if no one else will ever read it and hold nothing back.

Another crucial step to bring you closer to a better and more successful life is to overcome the fear of taking action when intuitiveness arises. You can only do that if you have built up the courage to follow your intuition. The biggest problem with fear in regard to intuition is the lack of trust, the lack of self-confidence. You are afraid to follow your intuition; you trust more in the opinions of others, or you trust only in what you can see. You can change that very quickly by analyzing your past experiences with intuition. Have you ever done this? How much time did you dedicate to investigating your intuitional experiences? Check your past experiences and find the pattern, analyze positive and negative events, list the moments when you had a good or bad premonition and compare these with what really happened later on, etc. You can do this in a variety of different ways, but what we have personally found to be a very practical and helpful method is making notes of the intuitive insights by keeping an intuitive diary. It really helps you to better understand and remember those valuable past intuitive experiences, as well as for retrospective analysis. If you are afraid of what might happen if you make a decision based on intuition, a good piece of advice might be to write down the exact reasons that make you afraid. Writing these down helps you to understand your "operating space" and to consciously look at them and clear them.

You will find more detailed instructions and simple steps on how to effectively write and use your own personal intuitive diary, making it your best possible assistant, in our upcoming book, which will enable you to start writing your intuitive diary immediately and in the most effective way.

The Dream Journal

We have already pointed out how dreams can directly or indirectly reveal visions, ideas and solutions to the problems that cause us stress - as was the case with Dmitri Mendeleev's periodic table of the elements, for example. The big secret is that this doesn't happen only to successful and famous people who we read about, it happens to all of us - the only difference between the two groups is that the first took their dreams more seriously.

Just like we discussed in relation to the intuitive diary, a great way to free your intuitiveness is to also start keeping records of your dreams, so you can reflect on them later, whenever it suits you. We would actually recommend that you keep records of your dreams in your intuitive diary (we will give detailed instructions in the upcoming book), so you can more easily compare the influence of one on the other. When reflecting on your dreams, you will notice that sometimes you will immediately see the meaning behind them, as if you had been *given* a direct message, while more often than not, you will have to dig deep into the symbolism of your dreams. Pay close attention to sensations and feelings linked with particular dreams and try to find an honest answer as to why these feelings appeared.

Raise Your Awareness

I N ORDER TO become more intuitive, we need to raise our awareness. We most certainly don't want to overlook the vision our inner life compass is enlightening us with, right? So we need to become more aware in order to recognize this moment: otherwise, it might happen that our brains will not detect it as something special.

There are many ways of practicing awareness, of entering and staying in a state of heightened awareness. One of the most important things is to maintain a relaxed state at all times, or at least to be able to put yourself in that kind of state prior to writing down your thoughts, because when you are relaxed, you are more receptive to intuitive signals. Your body and mind become calm, your thoughts become clearer, and in this special condition of inner peace, you will be more able to hear the voice of intuition.

It is also important to remain in the present moment. There are many different techniques for achieving this state. One of them is autosuggestion: for example, tell yourself, *"I'm aware of my breathing. I'm aware of my sensations. I'm aware of the place in which I am right now…"*, etc.

Pay attention to what your body is telling you. Observe your body – how do you feel? What does your body tell you about a certain issue or thought? How does it react to these issues or thoughts? Are there any thoughts you purposely don't want to hear or write down? Do you feel some special physical sensation? Is your body sending you any physical signals? Which kind of signals are these, and with which thoughts can you relate them?

"When I get a gut feeling, I pause for a moment and ask why I'm feeling that right now, and to what part of my life it is related. The answer does not always come right away, so I repeat this process until I find it."

— Gabriel Dechichi Barbar

Tip: He who seeks shall find. It's really as simple as that. Every one of us is a unique individual, and each of us has to find our own way to our intuition. Keep on searching.

It's not always easy to spot these signals. Sometimes, even listening to our feelings presents a problem, as Gabriel Dechichi Barbar told us: *"That's not as trivial as one might think, and I've seen many friends and pupils struggle to properly listen to their feelings, or even give up after failing to find answers a number of times. It's a deep self-knowledge process, and therefore not easy to master."*

"Something that has not been taught to you and blooms in you, that is intuition. Nobody has taught you, no school, no university, no college; nobody has said anything about it to you, it explodes in you - that is intuition. You need not go anywhere, you only need to go inside yourself." [69]

Writing your intuitive diary in this way, you will create a treasury of "unfiltered thoughts" for yourself, a great tool for recording and analyzing your inner guidance. When reflecting on them, you are able to re-live the events you experienced and process them without fear or stress: this is very important.

Franz Kafka, for example, believed that *"referring back to old journal entries — looking back on situations, life changes, old sufferings — gives one a kind of reassuring feeling. You look back on these situations and times — some 'which today would seem unbearable' — and you realize you lived, you survived. You were even able to write it all down! And doing so can lead to great wisdom about the self."*[105]

And where else will this lead you if not to your own blissfulness?! That's what it's all about.

As above, so below. Among the many ways to understand this classic phrase, we can understand it also as "what is in your mind will be in your life". The intention that you feed with the energy of attention materializes. Let's finish this chapter with the words of Oprah Winfrey, which carry a deep meaning. A wise reader will be filled with even greater enthusiasm. *"In my 40s, I got wiser. I started using journals to express my gratitude — and watched my blessings multiply. What you focus on expands."* [103]

Creative Expression and Playing Games

We've already mentioned how engaging in creative activities can help to calm your cognitive mind. Every activity connected with creative expression, like painting, drawing, playing an instrument or doing any other artistic activity works beneficially for you, as its source comes from the right hemisphere of the brain, which is also directly connected with intuition. Allow yourself to get involved in as many art-related activities as possible.

You can also test yourself with what are popularly called "guessing games", playing different intuitive games with the aim of training and developing your intuitiveness. For examples, open a book and try to *guess* the page number before looking at it. Instruct your kids to think of or write down a number from one to ten and try to *guess* it. Before opening a box of candies, try to *guess* the number of candies inside. Take a deck of cards and test yourself by *guessing* their colors. Try to *guess* the color of the dress or shirt your co-workers will wear tomorrow. When driving a car, try to *guess* the color of the next car that will pass in front of you or the direction in which it will continue. Use your own creativity to invent similar pastimes to train your intuition.

Small Daily Tasks Which Can Benefit Anyone

Would you be happy to hear that there are several simple tricks which require just a small amount of effort but can bring dramatic results with regard to developing your intuition? Prepare yourself for some "aha moments", as these little tricks do exist - we call them small daily tasks, and the key to successfully exploiting them lies in experimentation and persistence.

A major part of the path for developing intuition is constant experimentation – you will find some of the exercises more joyful and effective than others, and that's totally okay; just make those that most agree with you count, and change others to better suit yourself. The hardest thing is to break the daily pattern, to escape your daily routine; everything else will be easier. Set your phone alarm to remind you of your daily task, if necessary. Try to spend a day without any planned activities (and no planning for tomorrow); you'll be surprised how liberating that is.

Do more things with your left hand (as it is directly connected to the right hemisphere of the brain, which is the "home" of intuition). Try to draw or write something with your left hand and pay attention to other ordinary things that you do throughout the day like: phone typing, unlocking doors, arranging your hair, fastening the buttons on your shirt, brushing your teeth, etc. The change of habit alone will help you to become more conscious of what you´re doing, as well as helping you activate the intuitive side of your brain.

Engage in repetitive and creative activities as they can both calm your cognitive mind and open you up to intuition. Draw, paint, write a poem, run, play an instrument, etc.

One of the questions that we asked Drago Plecko was if he could share some "daily exercise routine" which can help develop intuition, and this is what he had to say about it: *'In the last ten years, I have developed non-typical exercises that reinforce intuition, and some are known (in slightly different versions) in many schools of Buddhism and other traditions. Conscious walking is one of them: it must be perfectly rhythmic so that the intervals between the impulses which reach the neurons can be completely predictable in duration (this helps with the process of awareness). Concentrating on the parts of your tongue, you can master the relationship between the body and the psyche, and with that, change distorted signals; while the exercise that stimulates the so-called 'God module'* [62] *inside the skull (just above the left ear) directly promotes the work of the pineal*

---

62 Vilayanur Ramachandran, Ph.D., distinguished professor and director of the *Center for Brain and Cognition* at the University of California, San Diego, announced that he had discovered the 'God Module' in the brain, which could be responsible for man's evolutionary instinct to believe in religion. These and other studies gave birth to a new field of brain science - neurotheology, the cognitive neuroscience of religious experience and spirituality.

gland and develops intuition. There are also some mudras[63] where touching the tip of the tongue and the nose improves the coordination of various brain areas."

Do you ever experience the feeling of knowing what might happen in the future? Got a feeling about which football team will win? Getting a premonition that something good or bad is going to happen? Write it down and check it out sometime later to see if your hunch was right.

Several internet sources estimate that an adult makes about 35,000 decisions each day, with varying degrees of consciousness involved. That gives us a lot of maneuvering space for experimentation.

"Don't think. Feel. It's like a finger pointing at the moon. Do not concentrate on the finger, or you will miss all of the heavenly glory."

— Bruce Lee

When you make a decision, try not to think about it, but feel it instead. Learn to differentiate between the two processes: you'll find it extremely useful. When we asked Drago Plecko about his personal experience with intuition, he said: *"Whenever intuition played a crucial role in my life, it first came to me as a feeling, and only from this feeling was the understanding derived."*

Another version of this exercise is to apply it to sensing things about people you've never met before. Prior to meeting someone, avoid learning anything about them. Then see what kind of information you can acquire just from observing, sensing and feeling their energetic field? As time goes by, you will realize you simply know certain things about them that you couldn't possibly explain. That is part of the power of intuitive insight.

In closing, it must be said that trying too hard to tun3e into your intuitional abilities may have the opposite results. Forcing your intuition may actually keep it away. Be aware of all the aspects we have talked about, and just allow your intuition to find a way to reach you instead of pushing too hard to make something happen. Your intuition is there, and it will begin to appear once you open the door and begin to keep an eye out for it.

---

63 Mudra is a symbolic or ritual gesture (mostly performed with hands and fingers) in Hinduism and Buddhism. In yoga for example, mudras are used to stimulate different parts of the body to affect the flow of prana (life energy) in the body.

PART III

VI. Back to the Future

Intuition vs. Artificial Intelligence;
How Can Mankind Survive
the Upcoming AI?

WHEN OUR ANCESTORS faced the First Industrial Revolution that occurred with the emergence of the iron and textile industries during the 18th and 19th centuries, they had to deal with many newborn economic and social challenges. The most significant technological achievement at that time was the development of the steam engine. Later, with the emerging Second Industrial Revolution between 1870 and 1914, they had to cope with new challenges, mostly driven by electricity, petroleum and steel. Some of the most significant technological contributions of the Second Industrial Revolution were the internal combustion engine, moving assembly line, lightbulb and telephone. History shows the scale on which these inventions changed our everyday lives and the ways in which the world changed. Consequently, we had to overcome new obstacles that came along, and it wasn't an easy thing to do.

Then, in the second half of the 20th century, the time came for our forefathers to lead the way through the next generation of challenges brought about by the Third Industrial Revolution, also known as the Digital Revolution. This represented the emergence of digital technology, the rise of telecommunications and the appearance of the personal computer and internet. It may be easier for most of us to relate with this period, since it was happening during our lifetimes. The challenges directly affected our lives, in "real time". Just think about how, all of a sudden, our jobs changed due to these new technological advances.

We have become able to perform many types of work from anywhere in the world, having access to enormous amounts of information from any location at any hour, "magical" capacities that were undreamed of 50 years ago.

Looking at the present, we are already entering the so-called Fourth Industrial Revolution, Industry 4.0 or 4IR, which is understood to be a new era of different technological breakthroughs in a number of fields, including the Internet of Things (IoT), automation and robotics, artificial intelligence (AI), biotechnology, nanotechnology, quantum computing, autonomous vehicles, blockchain, etc. This incipient 4IR is based on smart systems, new ways in which technology is becoming embedded within society, and even within the human body itself. The scale on which 4IR is changing (and will continue to change) the world is unprecedented. We can only imagine how our lives will change in the next few decades. So we find ourselves living in an interesting time, with rapidly advancing technology and the Fourth Industrial Revolution on one side, and growing global human awareness and the use of latent human potentials on the other - both capable of dramatically changing the world.

Digital technologies are becoming more and more sophisticated and integrated in our everyday lives. "Machines" are getting smarter every day, and although the current level of AI is still in the early stages, we can no longer fool ourselves into avoiding the conclusion that it already plays a major role in our lives, affecting everything from how we live and work to how we entertain ourselves. Narrow intelligence is already built into many of our machines. Just think of how we communicate – the majority of today´s communication goes through digitally managed channels.

We are already entrusting our lives to AI – did you ever hear someone express a doubt about the smart safety systems built into our cars, motorcycles and other vehicles? People simply get behind the wheel and drive – their trust is complete. Not to mention the airline flights, during which most of the time we are in the hands of the autopilot. Even take-off and landing are no longer a question; under certain circumstances, pilots do use this automated assistance. So what really keeps you safe and secure while you´re enjoying a delicious meal 10,000 feet above the ground is nothing but our "baby" AI. Artificial Intelligence is also quite integrated in stock-market trading, and some very interesting studies are taking place in medical diagnosis. *"Machine learning significantly improves accuracy of cardiovascular risk prediction, increasing the number of patients identified who could benefit from preventive treatment, while avoiding unnecessary treatment of others."* [106]

Methods like this, if or when implemented, could save millions of lives per year.

Another key indicator that shows why AI will continue to develop is the fact that by 2020, over 50 per cent of the workforce is expected to be members of Generation Y (born between 1977-1994), who have grown up connected, collaborative and mobile. [107] Their lifestyle will demand innovation and novelties, and we believe that it will cause an additional push on advancing AI.

We are entering the future of completely autonomously self-driving vehicles, devices with powerful predictive capabilities, advanced voice translation, speech recognition, behavioral algorithms and suggestions (computer based decision making) installed in our everyday devices, tools, homes… And this is only the beginning; soon, it will also be installed in our bodies.

AI Is the Next Big Thing

AI is expected by many to be the main driver of economic and productive growth during the next 20 years or so. Investments in AI are growing fast in many areas of business. There will be *"a greater than 300% increase in investment in cognitive computing in 2017 compared with 2016."* [108]

"In 2017, the global AI market is expected to be worth approximately 2.42 billion U.S. dollars." And it is predicted to reach 59.75 billion U.S. dollars in 2025. [109]

According to a PwC report, AI will contribute as much as $15.7 trillion to the world economy by 2030. To get a better picture, that's more than the current combined output of China and India. [110] But AI is not something new: It had its first serious beginnings about 70 years ago, and from that time on, thanks to devoted scientists such as Alan Turing, John McCarthy, Marvin Minsky and others, it has been slowly but steadily growing. But the very foundations of AI were already present in antiquity, with myths where mechanical men appear and stories about artificial beings endowed with intelligence or consciousness by master craftsman.

In the words of Pamela McCorduck, AI began with an ancient wish to forge the gods. [111]

But the real progress in AI began with advances in machine learning (*"the ability to learn without being explicitly programmed in order to analyze data and solve problems without the manual programming of specific functions"*) and deep learning (*"the area of machine learning with the objective of mimicking the brain by constructing artificial neural networks"*), where computers are more and more able to recognize patterns, sounds, images, texts, etc. [112]

Artificial Neural Networks (ANNs) are able to mimic the way in which the human brain works. They do not just look for single patterns of information, they are able to look for layers of patterns simultaneously. That's how voice translation and speech recognition are becoming much more efficient. [113] Nevertheless, the recent NASA discovery of the Kepler-90 solar system, which with its eight planets, at first glance represents a miniature version of our own solar system, was actually discovered by an AI program. Christopher Shallue, a senior software engineer at Google Brain, and Andrew Vanderburg, a NASA Sagan Postdoctoral Fellow at the University of Texas at Austin, trained the AI program that utilizes ANNs modeled after our brains to identify planets from the Kepler database. [114]

The list of things humans can do better than computers is getting smaller and smaller. And one of the next big steps in AI is going to take place with the merging of certain AI applications with the human, and we mean this literally. You might not even be aware of it, but in a way, this process has already started.

Elon Musk puts it very simple by saying, *"We're already a cyborg. You have a digital version of yourself, a partial version of yourself online in the form of your emails, your social media, and all the things that you do, and you basically have super powers with your computer and your phone and the applications that are there. You have more power than the president of the United States had 20 years ago. You can answer any question, you can video conference with anyone, anywhere. You can send messages to millions of people instantly. Just do incredible things."* [115]

And the merging of digital intelligence in some kind of symbiotic way with the human is going to rapidly continue, making us more and more superhuman. Ironically enough, as we shall discuss later in this chapter, this might also be one of the solutions to rival AI.

"By the 2030s, Kurzweil predicts, we will be cyborgs, with nanobots the size of blood cells connecting us to synthetic neocortices in the cloud, giving us access to virtual reality and augmented reality from within our own nervous systems. Nanobots in our veins and arteries will cure diseases and heal our bodies from the inside." [116]

With the growing trend of digital information created by humans, would you be surprised if some day it will reach a magnitude similar to the biological information in the biosphere? In 2014, the quantity of digital information has reached about 5 zettabytes (5×10^{21} bytes), which is 500 times more than the individual genomes of every human on the planet, and that could be encoded by approximately 1×10^{19} bytes. The total amount of DNA contained in all of the cells on Earth is estimated to be about 1.325×10^{37} bytes of information. With the current rate of digital storage growth, the digital information will rival the total amount of DNA contained in all of the cells on Earth in about 110 years. [117]

A very likely consequence of the further development of AI in the "near" future is that a lot of jobs will be replaced by AI. According to a paper, *The Future of Employment,* by Dr. Carl B. Frey and Dr. Michael Osborne from Oxford University, 47 per cent of total US employment is in the high risk range. [118] Also, Kai-Fu Lee, one of the top tech voices in China, believes that robots are likely to replace 50 percent of all jobs in the next decade. He said that AI is the *"singular thing that will be larger than all of human tech revolutions added together, including electricity, [the] industrial revolution, internet, mobile internet — because AI is pervasive. It is the decision engine that will replace people, not one on one, but one with many."* He added that AI capabilities are way higher than those of humans. High-end jobs like white-collar workers and radiologists are also at risk. [119]

According to the UKCES (the UK Commission for Employment and Skills) report on Jobs and Skills in 2030, *"the future AI applications could take over stock and financial markets completely, almost entirely foregoing human input… leading to the creation of new jobs in the area of personal training and assistance… leading to a new focus on interpersonal skills in formerly purely technical and other occupations (in health care, e.g., a shift from medical diagnosis to working with patients)."* [107]

When Will We Face Human-Level AI (AGI)?

We don't need to dig any deeper, it's pretty obvious where we are headed. With the further development of artificial intelligence (AI), we are reaching the point where we will be able to create self-improving human-level AI. Leading authorities in the field of AI have no doubt that, in some particular time in the future, it will reach the level of a human being.

Actually we are speaking about AGI (Artificial General Intelligence) or strong AI, which can be understood as the intelligence of a machine that could successfully perform any intellectual task that a human being can. [120] And that raises many important questions; existential questions, as a matter of fact.

The point in time when this will happen is popularly known by the term "technological singularity" or simply "singularity". Singularity *"is the hypothesis that the invention of artificial superintelligence will abruptly trigger runaway technological growth, resulting in unfathomable changes to human civilization."* [121]

"According to this hypothesis, an upgradable intelligent agent (such as a computer running software-based artificial general intelligence) would enter a "runaway reaction" of self-improvement cycles, with each new and more intelligent generation appearing more and more rapidly, causing an intelligence explosion and resulting in a powerful superintelligence that would, qualitatively, far surpass all human intelligence." [122]

Speculation about this decisive moment in human history has long been visible in science fiction writing, and is the predominant theme of serial movies such as Terminator and Matrix.

It's hard to give a clear prediction; no one knows for sure what the future holds, but some prominent experts are very clear in their previsions.

Raymond Kurzweil, for example, predicted that computers will pass the Turing Test[64] by 2029 (he came to this conclusion using Moore's Law[65]), and that later on the exponential growth in computing

---

64 The Turing Test is a test of a machine's ability to exhibit intelligent behavior equivalent to, or indistinguishable from, that of a human, developed by and named after famed computer pioneer Alan Turing in 1950. [151]

65 Moore's Law refers to an observation made by Intel co-founder Gordon Moore in 1965, who noticed that the number of transistors per square inch on integrated circuits had doubled every year since their invention. The law predicts that this trend will continue into the foreseeable future. [152]

capacity will lead to the Singularity. *"I set the date for the Singularity - representing a profound and disruptive transformation in human capability - as 2045"* says Kurzweil in his book *The Singularity Is Near* [123].

Although people like to predict the exact date for this Singularity, it is quite possible that it will not be a sudden event, but rather that it will gradually expand over a certain period of time. Nevertheless, once this happens, we have to understand that there will be no going back.

As Bart Selman, professor of Computer Science at Cornell University, said: *"It will be the first time we've made machines that can think better than us, and that will make it much harder to predict what they will do. And, more worryingly, whether we can control them."* [124]

Can We Win the Race?

Humanity is facing two big problems with regards to AI: the technological dilemma on the one hand, and the problem of ethics on other. Deciding on how to proceed in each direction is completely dependent on us, humans, at least for now.

As Raymond Kurzweil said at the Beneficial AI 2017 Conference: *"I don't think we can solve the problem just technologically. Imagine that we've done our job perfectly and we've created the most safe, beneficial AI possible, but we let the political system become totalitarian and evil, either evil world government or even just a portion of the globe… it's not gonna work out well, and so part of the struggle is the area of politics and social policy."* [125] Before we can successfully reach human-level AI with sufficient ethics, we as humanity need to solve our own ethical questions. And another side of the coin is that even if we solve the question of who is going to be in control of the super-intelligent AI, what if this AGI gains conscious, stops "obeying" its master and starts to impose its own will — not necessarily evil, but with possibly devastating consequences. It's possible that AGI could treat us with the same disregard as we treat other species.

Elon Musk believes that we are either headed towards super intelligence or the end of civilization. [125] With a deep understanding of AI and its benefits, Musk also warns the world that, at the same time, it also represents our greatest existential threat.

According to Musk, in an age when AI threatens to become widespread, humans would be useless. We would be like "pets" for them, like a house cat is to us. [115] Of course he doesn't believe that AI will develop a will of its own some time very soon, so currently he is more concerned about someone who might use it in a bad way and cause an unstable situation. [126]

"Can we build AI without losing control over it?" is the title of a TED-talk given by Samuel B. Harris, in which he points out key issues related to AI and the general fear of machines taking over humanity that probably resonates with the majority of the population. Harris is concerned about the time when machines will be able to improve themselves and be so much more competent that we are that the slightest divergence between their goals and our own could destroy us. The very first sentence with which he started his talk seemed to be particularly interesting: *"I'm going to talk about the failure of intuition that many of us suffer from. It's really a failure to detect a certain kind of danger."* [127]

We will discuss more about the relevance of intuition in connection to AI later in this chapter; but yes, what he said about the failure of intuition is true. But we need to add that it's not the rule for everyone. Why does this happen? When pure "intellect" and "knowledge" (reasoning) rules, there is less room for intuition, and as we shall see, in the future it will be of crucial importance to change this imbalance.

Will we be able to retain control over a higher intelligence than our own? Will we became "pets" of the AI? How can humanity prepare for that moment and escape human obsolescence? What can we do as individuals?

The First Steps Have Been Taken

We believe humanity can retain superiority over AI. Since there is no way we can ever reverse the process we've started (or as Samuel Harris says, *"The train is already out of the station, and there's no brake to pull"*), we must look for ways to live with it. [127]

The solution is to raise our awareness, to adjust and take steps towards possible solutions to the above-mentioned issues now, and we must succeed in a relatively short time.

Actually, the very first step has already been made with the OpenAI initiative. Perceiving the urgent need for higher awareness of the AI issue, Elon Musk co-founded the non-profit AI research company called OpenAI, which freely collaborates with other institutions and researchers by making its patents and research open to the public – in this way, he wants to ease the possible negative consequences of the future of AI.

Musk believes in the democratization of AI: *"The best of the available alternatives that I can come up with… is that we achieve democratization of AI technology. Meaning that no one company or small set of individuals has control over advanced AI technology."* [126]

When speaking about humanity on a time scale, let's take a look into the human evolutionary process. Would there be any possibility of intervening in the name of a better future? Alongside the democratization of AI, Musk is also the one who has repeatedly emphasized the need for humans to evolve. The idea behind this is to improve the neural link between humans and AI, when merging AI technology with human systems.

He launched a company called Neuralink which is focusing on *"creating devices that can be implanted in the human brain, with the eventual purpose of helping human beings merge with software and keep pace with advancements in artificial intelligence. These enhancements could improve memory or allow for more direct interfacing with computing devices".* [128] At the 2017 World Government Summit in Dubai, Musk stated that with the so-called "neural lace" inside our skulls, one could flash data from his brain, wirelessly, to any digital device or other computing power in the cloud. He estimates a first meaningful partial-brain interface will occur around 2022. [129]

The logic is quite simple: as machines get more and more human, humans should become more and more like machines. It does make sense, but we must not overlook further development of human capabilities as well – we believe that, in the first place, a human must become more human, too, meaning that he should first exploit his human potential to its fullest. What we have in mind is the development of our capabilities of emotional intelligence, compassion, empathy and intuition as a showpiece.

In the first place, this development must occur in order to successfully counterbalance the loss of job opportunities in the future, and secondly, to promote the very survival of the human race.

According to Kai-Fu Lee, the jobs which will be lost in the future can only be replaced by service-type jobs. He emphasizes the *"people-to-people connection. How to heal all the souls who no longer feel they have a way towards self-realization."* Lee also points out philanthropy as a future occupation, referring to hospitals and orphanages. He believes we need to regard service as a first-class job, and to focus on the area where machines will never be able to act, or, in his own words, *"touching someone's heart with your heart"*. [119] We must be ready to act in the ways in which machines never can. The jobs that are most likely to be secure in the future are those which contain a great deal of creativity, a holistic approach, empathy, emotional intelligence and jobs with different executive responsibilities that require deeper insights. Over time, more and more future jobs will not require as much skill with analytics, logic, reasoning, and "knowing the numbers"; they will require a more intuitive approach.

Brain lateralization is the idea that each of our brain hemispheres controls or is specialized in certain skills or types of behavior. Although the two hemispheres are connected and in interaction at all times, certain functions can be performed mainly in one specific hemisphere.

The left half of the brain is more logical, analytical, rational, verbal, math/science oriented and connected to linear thinking and sequencing, while the right half is more creative, intuitive, holistic, non-verbal, art oriented, and connected to feelings, visualization and imagination.

Left-Brain Functions	**Right-Brain Functions**
Reasoning	**Intuition**
Logic	Creativity
Analytic thought	Holistic thought
Science and math	Art awareness
Language	Non-verbal
Written	Imagination
Numbers skills	Insight

Can you spot the pattern? The majority of the most impactful job skills for the future are directly related to the functions of the right brain hemisphere.

We believe that we can apply the same principle for our future in general, especially in connection with AI. Our advantage over AI lies in nurturing the skills located within the domain of the right hemisphere of our brain.

Intuition - Showpiece of the "Parallel Agenda"

> *"Even though the future seems far away, it is actually beginning right now."*

—Mattie Stepanek

We all want the change to be for the better. It is therefore of crucial importance that, alongside technological development, mankind starts systematically developing consciousness in its broadest sense, and nurtures and exploits in-born human capabilities – with intuition as a driving force at the forefront. In the not-so-distant future, intuition may become the one single defining faculty left to us humans.

We can't just sit by and watch, we need to engage. Humanity must not be satisfied with *"it might be a good idea to start developing our human potentials"* anymore, because the time has come for us to take a stand. That "good idea" must be seen as an urgent necessity - we must develop and master the existing potentials of humanity itself – especially those which are "hidden" to the naked eye and which are the most powerful. Through continuous research, more and more has become known about intuition, so we have acquired a certain amount of knowledge concerning this subject. Maybe we don't know all of its secrets, and maybe we'll never know and understanding its deepest foundations, but maybe that is how it´s meant to be. Maybe we will never be able to comprehend it, maybe we dont have the right "equipment" for that. But that doesnt really matter: most of us also don´t have a deep understanding of computers, for example, but we all know how to use them, and their benefits to our lives...

Intuition is a different realm of internal activity that is not dependent on intellect, although it can penetrate it. The fact of the matter is that a higher reality can penetrate a lower reality, but the lower cannot penetrate the higher. Mystics say that there are three levels of reality: the known, the unknown, and the unknowable. *"Intellect is involved with the known and the unknown, not with the unknowable. And intuition works with the unknowable, with that which cannot be known."* [69]

You can feel it, use it and benefit from it, but you can´t find a reasonable explanation for it. Intuition as our inner guide is all around us, it's here, offering us instant insight, the right direction, the path. The "communication" channel exists, and what's even more fascinating, it works, which we prove in this very book. But in order to use it, you have to be aware of it, in tune with it: as is the case with any other faculty, practice makes perfect, and it takes courage to follow where it leads. Let's transform the negative energy of our ego into the positive energy of intuition. Let's exploit this immense fountain of enlightenment.

Intuition as a powerful force within us is the best possible answer to the potential threats of AI, both from the perspective of the process of building an AGI and from the perspective of rivaling that AGI. Actually, what we believe is that, in the far future, the faculty of intuition might be the one single faculty left to humans. It is its uniqueness and distinctiveness that will, in our opinion, result in intuition being the only competence that an AGI could never "learn". AGI will never be able to "tap into intuition", as it is a connection to an even higher level of reality, beyond the reach of any machine.

Regardless of what the future holds, whether we imagine the worst-case scenario in which machines rule the world or a more benign scenario where humanity is challenged with human-cyborg evolution, we must develop, maintain and sharpen our capacity for intuition. In any case, intuition will help us make our lives more meaningful, regardless of the system and environment in which we will come to live. That is why it is so important and different from other faculties. It's not just something that "might be a good idea"; we MUST nurture our intuition now, include the use of this faculty as a basic concept in our global culture and pave the way for future generations who will need it even more.

Of course, we cannot expect this transition to happen overnight. Our estimate is that the time needed to successfully and systematically integrate the concept of intuition into worldwide human culture as a fundamental way of life will take at least one generation (25 years), if not more. This would be sufficient time for humanity to totally dominate such a capacity and for humans to become completely in tune with themselves as individuals and as a society. We see this period of actively rising awareness and mastery of the human potential in its broadest sense as needing to happen at least one generation (or

25 years) before the Singularity, or to be more precise, prior to the peak of the Singularity. We call this concept a "Period of a Parallel Agenda", or simply "Parallel Agenda", and we are introducing it here for the very first time. So, as seen through the prism of future human talents, people-to-people skills and competencies, we must give serious attention to intuition and systematically implement it into our everyday lives. In this way, we will also gradually be able to get in tune with our collective intuition, to perceive the collective purpose of life on a larger scale. In other words, a period of Parallel Agenda can be understood as our means of self-preservation, our planetary life-insurance plan.

Remember these words, attributed to Charles Darwin: *"It is not the most intellectual of the species that survives; it is not the strongest that survives; but the species that survives is the one that is best able to adapt and adjust to the changing environment in which it finds itself."* Only when we learned to use our instinct to its fullest potential were we able to survive the cruel laws of savage nature. Later on, through the use and development of our intellect, we were able to rise to become the civilization we are today. It isn´t perfect, but we are still here. And now, once again, we are in a period of transition to a new era, to a future where we will be threatened by new challenges. We are living in a time when we need to focus our attention and efforts on the next stage and tap into the highest level of consciousness – intuition. Intuition itself will show us the way, will lead us further: it is the next big step in our evolutionary process. *"Evolution is simply the capacity to register meanings that are "already there". Blue and green existed, even if Xenophanes could not distinguish between them. Wer are evolving into a universe that becomes progressively more fascinating as we learn to register new vibrations. No doubt in another thousand years, human beings will see a dazzling universe "with a dozen colours that do not exist for us"… Man has reached a point in his evolution where he must graduate from clocks to wathces, from the large to the subtle. He must turn increasingly inward. That is, he must turn to the hidden levels of his being,…to meanings and vibrations that have so far been too fine to grasp."* [70] It's just that simple.

VII. What Feels Like the End is Often the Beginning

"Now this is not the end. It is not even the beginning of the end. But it is, perhaps, the end of the beginning."

—Winston Churchill

YOU´VE JUST FINISHED reading "Intuition and Success". You´ve seen the results of the years of research we have performed, giving dozens of examples of successful people who´ve learned to use the inner guidance of their intuition to help them make the key decisions that have kept them from being just another dissatisfied resident on the planet Earth and has helped them discover their "mission" in life and/or become successful at doing what their heart desires. You´ve been given a variety of explanations about what intuition is and is not. You´ve heard several possibilities concerning where it may come from: the "dark continent" of the subconscious mind, that most mysterious level of our individual psyche which is still being mapped and studied; a collective field of consciousness, the uncharted mental territory where we all may be connected; or some higher power, as proposed in all religions and mystical philosophies. And you´ve been given some of the techniques for developing your own connection with the part of you that knows what you should do, including APE (Analyzing Past Experiences), observing when you´ve already made use of intuition in your life.

And you´ve seen that ALL OF US have access to this intuitive orientation – it is part of our natural birthright as human beings. While the only thing we know for certain is that we know very little, it would seem apparent that reality is greater than we presently think. In this book, we have striven to avoid classifying intuition and other innate (but often latent) human capacities as being "supernatural" – to use Osho´s terminology once more, many details concerning intuition are presently unknown to modern society, but they are not unknowable. The same can be said of humanity´s past – whatever happened long ago, whatever memories we have lost of a time when our intuitive link may have been stronger, we have never lost our sensitivity to the influence of intuition - we just lost our belief in it. Well, as we have shown throughout this book, WE STILL BELIEVE!

As we have tried to show, intuition can benefit everything we do. In business, intuitive leadership based on trusting that inexplicable "gut feeling" makes all the difference between making right and wrong decisions about who to hire, what products or services to offer, and how to instantly react to each moment. In everything from science to sports, intuition influences how and when we should make or change our plans and strategies, and gives us the ideas we need to achieve our goals. In art and design, it leads us to discover the most beautiful and useful ways to be creative. But one of its main revelations to us has to do with what aspects of our lives really SHOULD be improved and strengthened, and which aspects should be abandoned in favor of others which will take us closer to the real goals in our lives. It´s easy for us to accept the traditional path in life - grow up, get an education, use this education to get a job or enter a career, use this job or career to acquire a fortune, use this fortune to consume goods and services and stay in step with what is fashionable, and thus contribute to the continuity of a market of production and consumption. But this chain of stages is not necessarily the path to success. True success comes from knowing yourself more intimately, from discovering your heart´s true desire, and from achieving that desire. And who can tell your heart´s true desire better than your heart itself, your inner guide, your intuition?

Your heart is the key to your intuition. While certain influences have spent centuries teaching us that our head, our intelligence, our rational thought processes are the only real guides we have to lead us to success (just as they have told us that success can only be measured by wealth and power), many people, including those interviewed here, have found that listening to their heart has been their best guide. The heart is also the key to love, the uniting force in life, whether we limit it to connecting us with one single person or allow it to open us to a connection with everything around us. And the heart can lead us to compassion, the form of universal love that permits us to know what things might be like from another person´s point of view, to "walk a mile in our brother´s shoes", to understand why they do what they do and to choose to accept and forgive things that might otherwise lead to conflict. So let´s learn to trust our hearts more, to achieve a greater love for all and to allow that love to show us the path to success.

Another key concept we have presented is that, instead of waiting for intuition to appear in the latter part of our lives, we should reorganize certain aspects of our education or social conditioning so that intuition is learned and applied in our youth. Instead of considering Financial and Social Success to be the foundations for life and the goals which we should program ourselves to achieve early in life, leaving Spiritual Success and internal gratification for our latter days, we can invert this ingrained pattern and teach our children to pursue Spiritual Success, self-knowledge and trust in their inner connection from the beginning of their lives. This redefinition of what constitutes a successful life, represented by the Hourglass diagram, can have an enormous impact on our understanding of what is truly important, our early discovery of how each of us should plan our futures, and our capacity for improving our world through long-range sustainable goals which will benefit the whole, all while we are still young and full of the energy needed to implement these improvements.

Now we come to the single most important point of all – PRACTICE! All the bright ideas in the world mean nothing if we don´t use them. We must find the strength, the will, to apply what we´ve learned in theory and use it in our lives. This concept has two basic aspects – practice to develop your intuition, and practice what your intuition reveals to you to become successful. You can make your own personalized plan for quieting the internal and external noise and distractions that don´t let you hear your inner voice, thus acquiring a lifestyle that gives you more room for being open to your intuition. As often as possible, ignore the outside world and look within yourself.

Practice the techniques revealed in this book: and when you begin to hear what your deepest self is telling you, follow its clues and DO what it indicates. The more it perceives that you´re taking it seriously and making use of the ideas and information it sends you, the more your intuition will grow. And it is in this sense that finishing this book is only the beginning – if you seriously want to improve your life through intuition, now is the time to begin employing what you´ve learned.

While there is really only one course that can teach us how to recognize and use our intuition – life itself, the "School of Hard Knocks", as some call it – this book offers many tips and techniques that can be applied in practice. Try them out, see which you´re attracted to or what variations come to mind. But whatever method you choose, USE IT! Repeat it constantly and pay attention to the results: even the smallest hint of guidance that pays off may be the first step on the road to expanding your own internal contact. You are your own laboratory, so experiment!

The main rule to remember is that intuition makes its own rules (or so it seems, because we still don´t know all the variables involved), so paying attention, trial and error, and familiarity through repetition, will eventually show you which rules and methods apply for YOUR Intuitive Guidance System. By showing your intuition that you´re interested and trying to open your contact with it, it will react and work to bridge the gap from its side too. And sooner or later, you will break through.

One point that was emphasized in several parts of "Intuition and Success" is that your motives also have an influence on the quality of your contact with your intuition. Just because your only interest is to advance your position in this material world doesn´t mean that intuition will not bring you ideas of how to achieve that goal. But the more you connect with the big picture, offering to make your contribution to improving the world and helping others, recognizing that we are all part of one big family and that by helping others we are also making the world a better place for ourselves, the more your intuition will act to help. Once again, the heart is the key – working simultaneously on increasing your ability for compassion and your intuitive abilities, your inner guide will be motivated to help you more.

The prognosis for life on Earth which we give at the end of this book may seem unlikely to some. But if we look closely at the rate of technological advancement over the past few centuries, and compare it to how fast things are now changing from year to year, or from day to day, we come to realize that control of most factors in life by AI (Artificial Intelligence) in the near future is not just the fantasy of someone watching too many science fiction movies. Humans as we are today may in all likelihood become obsolete in a world where machines can do everything better than we can. And it is within this disheartening scenario that intuition shines forth as a ray of hope and offers a potential insurance policy against our future unimportance. We may discover that the success of the human race as a whole depends on our intuitive skills. If we can once more develop our inner connection with "that which knows" as a Parallel Agenda to the short-term plan of more pleasure and comfort, we may be able to guarantee our place in the scheme of things to come. To repeat a quote from Oscar Kogoj (page 169), *"If more people would rely on their inner voice... all of humanity could make a giant leap forward."* And even if you aren´t convinced of the need for stronger intuitive abilities for future generations, at least try to discover the benefits of intuition for your own life, and maybe some of what you learn will still help someone else in years to come.

About the Authors

Dr. Ivan Erenda

 Ivan graduated from the University of Ljubljana, Slovenia, with a Bachelor of Science in Chemical Technology. After obtaining his degree, he continued on to postgraduate school to obtain his Master's degree in International and Diplomatic Studies and a Doctoral degree in Quality Management on the topic of INTUITIVE DECISION MAKING. He is the author/co-author of several different academic papers.

He works as a successful top-level manager in the highly demanding automotive industry, where he has over five years of experience managing large groups of people (500+) and over 10 years of experience managing medium-sized groups of people (100+). Guided by true leaders and shaped by several leadership positions, he has developed and sharpened his intuitive abilities. His research interests include business management, crisis management, psychology and psychic phenomena.

Ivan currently lives with his family in Novo mesto, Slovenia. He is an advanced Tai Chi Chuan practitioner and active member of the Lions Club Novo Mesto, supporting different humanitarian actions.

Aleksej Metelko, BSc (Econ), WTP

 Aleksej graduated from the University of Maribor, Slovenia, with a Bachelor's degree in Marketing. He completed vocational training at ITM Worldwide, earning a diploma in International Trade Management at the Master's level and fulfilled all requirements prescribed by the IATTO (International Association of Trade Training Organizations) for the designation of World Trade Professional (WTP).

He is a well-rounded business professional and strategic thinker with a proven track record of managing international sales and marketing (5+ years) and managing business development (10+ years), organizing workshops and working as a mentor for startup entrepreneurs. Aleksej has been researching personal development and spiritual growth from an early age, sharpening and applying his intuitive skills throughout his business and personal life.

Aleksej is an author and editor with more than 200 published articles, and an active member of the Lions Club Novo mesto, contributing to a variety of humanitarian projects.

Resources

We invite you to share your thoughts about *Intuition and Success:*

You are welcome to join the social media discussion and find further information about the authors and their work here:

www.inner-success.com

www.facebook.com/IntuitionAndSuccess
www.facebook.com/ivan.erenda.1
www.facebook.com/aleksej.metelko

www.twitter.com/intuitionsucces
www.twitter.com/IvanErenda
www.twitter.com/AleksejMetelko

www.linkedin.com/groups/12102159
www.linkedin.com/in/ivanerenda
www.linkedin.com/in/aleksejmetelko

ivan.erenda@gmail.com
aleksej.metelko@gmail.com

Also From
Dr. Ivan Erenda and Aleksej Metelko

Intuition: Quotes and Reflections
World's Largest Treasury of
Intuition Sayings

With 621 quotes and reflections from 415 authors, this book contains the world's largest treasury of intuition sayings and offers immediate insight into the most powerful words of wisdom on intuition (some of them were exclusively published in this book).

Reading the book "Intuition Quotes and Reflections" will open the door for instant insight into the greatest words of wisdom on intuition

AVAILABLE AT AMAZON: http://amzn.to/2FtKXIk

References

[1] M. F. Callan, "Robert Redford: The Biography," 2011, ISBN: 978-1-84737-778-4.

[2] P. Weidinger, "10 Famous People Who Avoided Death on 9/11," 2011. [Online]. Available: https:/listverse.com/2011/12/12/10-famous-people-who-avoided-death-on-911/. [Accessed January 2017].

[3] M. Park, "Small choices, saved lives: Near misses of 9/11," 2011. [Online]. Available: http://edition.cnn.com/2011/US/09/03/near.death.decisions/index.html. [Accessed January 2017].

[4] C. Ellison, "Opera Recalls A Hero's Life, Love and Song," 2011. [Online]. Available: https://www.nytimes.com/2011/09/04/arts/music/heart-of-a-soldier-opera-about-rick-rescorla-911-hero.html. [Accessed January 2017].

[5] "http://archived.parapsych.org/members/r_d_nelson.html".

[6] P. Bancel and R. Nelson, "The Global Consciousness Project," 2008. [Online]. Available: http://noosphere.princeton.edu/papers/pdf/GCP.Events.Mar08.prepress.pdf. [Accessed 25 4 2017].

[7] R. Nelson and P. Bancel, "Effect of mass consciousness: changes in random data during global events," *Explore,* p. 373, 2011.

[8]   B. Ware, The Top Five Regrets of the Dying, Hay House, Inc., 2012.

[9]   L. A. Robinson, Put your intuition to work, Wayne, Nj: The Career Press, 2016.

[10]   D. Piętka , "The Concept of Intuition and Its Role in Plato and Aristotle," *ORGANON 47:2015.*

[11]   Y. Tang, Confucianism, Buddhism, Daoism, Christianity and Chinese Culture, 2015, ISBN: 978-3-662-45533-3.

[12]   "Immanuel Kant Quotes About Intuition," [Online]. Available: http://www.azquotes.com/author/7722-Immanuel_Kant/tag/intuition. [Accessed February 2017].

[13]   U. Malaspina and V. Font, "The role of intuition in the solving of optimization problems," *Educational Studies in Mathematics, Vol. 75, No. 1 (September 2010),* pp. 107-130.

[14]   R. Highfield, "Female intuition put to the test," *Electronic Telegraph,* 30 March 1995.

[15]   "Matty Mullins Quotes," [Online]. Available: https://www.goodreads.com/quotes/1005688-the-only-person-you-should-try-to-be-better-than. [Accessed February 2017].

[16]   Sadhguru, Inner Engineering: A Yogi's Guide to Joy, New York: Penguin Random House LLC, 2016.

[17]   M. Zimmerman, "The Nervous System in the Context of Information Theory," *Human Physiology,* vol. 82, pp. 166-173, 1989.

[18]   J. Fox, "Harvard Business Review," [Online]. Available: https://hbr.org/2014/06/instinct-can-beat-analytical-thinking. [Accessed May 2017].

[19]   N. E. Collinge, "The Laws of Indo-European," 1985.

[20]   "The guardian," [Online]. Available: https://www.theguardian.com. [Accessed 23 5 2017].

[21]   D. C. Nix, The Field of Being: Collected Thoughts on the Evolution of Human Consciousness, New York Bloomington: iUniverse, Inc., 2009.

[22]   L. Mctaggart, The Field: The Quest for the Secret Force of the Universe, New York: Harper Collins Publishers, 2003, ISBN: 978-0-06143518-8.

[23]   T. Dimitrov, 50 Nobel laureates and other great scientists who belive in God, 1995-2008.

[24]   "25 Famous Scientists Who Believed in God," [Online]. Available: https://www.famousscientists.org/25-famous-scientists-who-believed-in-god/. [Accessed May 2017].

[25]   http://www.worldometers.info, 7.3.2017.

[26]   C. Petitmengin, The Intuitive Experience. Published in F. Varela and J. Shear (Eds) (1999), The View from Within. First-person approaches to the study of consciousness (London: Imprint Academic), pp. 43-77, 1999.

[27]   G. P. L.-F. J. a. S.-S. E. Hodgkinson, "Intuition: A fundamental bridging construct in the behavioural sciences," *British Journal of Psychology (2008), 99, 1–27.*

[28]   C. a. S.-S. E. Akinci, "Intuition in Management Research: A Historical Review.," *International Journal of Management Reviews, 14 (1), pp.104-122.,* 2012.

[29]   W. Hart, "Dualism, in Samuel Guttenplan (org) A Companion to the Philosophy of Mind, Blackwell, Oxford.," 1996.

[30]   H. W. Puner, Sigmund Freud: His Life and Mind. Retrieved 1 November 2017..

[31]   C. Jung, Synchronicity: An Acausal Connecting Principle, Princeton, New Jersey: : Princeton University Press. p. 8., 1973.

[32]   A. Yiassemides, Time and Timelessness; Temporality in the theory of Carl Jung, New York: Routledge, 2014.

[33]   C. G. Jung, Synchronicity: An Acausal Connecting Principle, New York: Routledge, 2010, ISBN: 978-0-415-13649-5.

[34]   C. I. i. A. C. a. S.-S. E. Barnard, "Intuition in Management Research: A Historical Review," *International Journal of Management Reviews,* Vols. 14 (1),, pp. pp. 104-122.

[35] G. P. Hodgkinson, J. Langan-Fox and E. Sadler-Smith, "Intuition: A fundamental bridging construct in the behavioural sciences," *British Journal of Psychology (2008), 99, 1–27*.

[36] K. Turner, "Psychology Today," [Online]. Available: https://www.psychologytoday.com/us/blog/radical-re-mission/201405/the-science-behind-intuition. [Accessed May 2017].

[37] "Lufityanto, G., Donkin, C., & Pearson, J. (2016). Measuring Intuition: Nonconscious Emotional Information Boosts Decision Accuracy and Confidence. Psychological Science. doi: 10.1177/0956797616629403, retrieved from Intuition – It's More Than a Feeling," [Online]. Available: https://www.psychologicalscience.org/news/minds-business/intuition-its-more-than-a-feeling.html.

[38] R. J. Davidson and A. Lutz, "Buddha's Brain: Neuroplasticity and Meditation," *IEEE Signal Processing Magazine,* September, 2007.

[39] S. Lazar, "How Meditation Can Reshape Our Brains, TEDxCambridge 2011," [Online]. Available: https://www.youtube.com/watch?v=m8rRzTtP7Tc. [Accessed January 2018].

[40] E. Taub, "American Psychological Association," [Online]. Available: http://www.apa.org/action/careers/health/edward-taub.aspx. [Accessed December 2017].

[41] M. Merzenich, "Growing evidence of brain plasticity, TED," [Online]. Available: https://www.ted.com/talks/michael_merzenich_on_the_elastic_brain. [Accessed March 2018].

[42] J. E. Pretz, J. B. Brookings, L. A. Carlson, T. Keiter Humbert, M. Roy, M. Jones and D. Memmert, "Development and Validation of a New Measure of Intuition: The Types of Intuition Scale," *Journal of Behavioral Decision Making,* vol. 27, p. 454–467, 2014.

[43] A. F. Fields, "Decision-Making using Organizational Engineering Methodology," Wayne Huizenga Graduate School of Business and Entrepreneurship of Nova Southeastern University, 2001.

[44] E. Dane and M. D. Pratt, "Conceptualizing and Measuring Intuition: A Review of Recent Trends," *International Review of Industrial and Organizational Psychology,* vol. 24, 2009.

[45] R. McCraty, Science of the Heart - Exploring the Role of the Heart in Human Performance, ISBN 978-1-5136-0636-1, vol. Volume 2, Boulder Creek: HeartMath Institute, 2015.

[46] "Heart Intelligence," [Online]. Available: https://www.heartmath.org/articles-of-the-heart/the-math-of-heartmath/heart-intelligence/. [Accessed August 2017].

[47] L. Marks, "Heart Power," [Online]. Available: http://www.healingheartpower.com/. [Accessed December 2017].

[48] I. Burling, "Does your heart actually feel emotion?," [Online]. Available: https://www.quora.com/Does-your-heart-actually-feel-emotion. [Accessed December 2017].

[49] H. Herlin, Skrivne moci nadcutnega, Ljubljana: Cankarjeva zalozba (Kocevski tisk), 1982.

[50] H. Palmer, Inner Knowing: Consciousness, Creativity, Insight, and Intuition, New York City: J.P. Tarcher/Putnam., 1998.

[51] J. Wolff, Your Creative Writing Masterclass, St Ives: Clays Ltd., 2012, ISBN: 978-1-85788-578-1.

[52] K. S. Rao, "Life and work of the Mathemagician Srinivasa Ramanujan".

[53] P. Baksa, "The Zero Point Field: How Thoughts Become Matter?," [Online]. Available: https://www.huffingtonpost.com/peter-baksa/zero-point-field_b_913831.html. [Accessed December 2017].

[54] "http://www.sheldrake.org/," [Online]. Available: https://blogs.scientificamerican.com/cross-check/scientific-heretic rupert-sheldrake-on-morphic-fields-psychic-dogs-and-other-mysteries/. [Accessed 25 4 2017].

[55]   M. Kelly, "Princeton University - Ants build 'living' bridges with their bodies, speak volumes about group intelligence," [Online]. Available: https://www.princeton.edu/news/2015/11/30/ants-build-living-bridges-their-bodies-speak-volumes-about-group-intelligence. [Accessed August 2017].

[56]   E. Dane and M. G. Pratt, "Exploring intuition and its role in managerial decision making," *Academy of Management Review*, vol. 32, p. 33–54, 2007.

[57]   W. Isaacson, Steve Jobs, New York: Simon & Schuster, 2011, ISBN 9781451648553.

[58]   I. Fontaine, "Emotional intelligence, intuitive intelligence : the end of IQ hegemony," [Online]. Available: https://histoired-intuition.com/2014/02/12/emotional-intelligence-intuitive-intelligence-end-iq-hegemony/. [Accessed November 2017].

[59]   J. Owen, How to Manage, Glasgow: Bell & Brain Ltd., 2009, ISBN: 978-0-273-72698-2.

[60]   "How Much Do We Love Television? Let Us Count the Ways.," *The New York Times*, July 4, 2016.

[61]   Osho, "Die O Yogi Die; The Essence of Existance," [Online]. Available: http://www.osho.com/iosho/library/read-book/online-library-ego-gorakh-die-c44bce7a-691?p=56c7d7103a-38d7ec8236916e0ad98ca5. [Accessed January 2018].

[62]   S. Smith, "Newsweek," [Online]. Available: http://www.newsweek.com/will-smith-hollywoods-most-power-ful-actor-97341. [Accessed March 2018].

[63]   "Goodreads," [Online]. Available: https://www.goodreads.com/quotes/700545-fear-is-not-real-it-is-a-product-of-thoughts . [Accessed January 2018].

[64]   "Thich Nhat Hanh, Transform Your Fear," [Online]. Available: https://www.youtube.com/watch?v=CrSUgK_IgZE. [Accessed November 2017].

[65]   T. N. Hanh, The heart of the Buddha's teaching, New York: Harmony Books, 1999.

[66]   K. Hiss, "The Scary Things That Happen to Your Brain When You're Stressed—And How to Calm Down," [Online]. Available: https://www.rd.com/health/wellness/effects-of-stress-brain/1/. [Accessed December 2017].

[67]   M. Castleman, "37 Ways to Make Managing Stress Much Easier," [Online]. Available: https://www.rd.com/health/wellness/stress-management-tips/. [Accessed December 2017].

[68]   S. Kronen, "Elephant Journal: Jim Carrey & his "Spiritual Awakening"," [Online]. Available: http://www.notey.com/@elephantjournal_unofficial/external/18508142/wtf-jim-carrey-his-%E2%80%9Cspiritual-awakening-%E2%80%9D.html. [Accessed November 2017].

[69]   Osho, Intuition: Knowing Beyond Logic, 2001, Osho,, St. Martin's Press , 2001, ISBN: 0-312-27567-6.

[70]   C. Wilson, The Occult, Frogmore, St Albans: Granada Publishing Limited, 1973.

[71]   "Master Happiness - Tony Robbins | Inside Quest #40," [Online]. Available: https://www.youtube.com/watch?v=_Sf3vMMErwg. [Accessed April 2018].

[72]   I. Erenda, M. Mesko and B. Bukovec, "Intuitive decision-making and leadership competencies of managers in Slovenian automotive industry," *Journal of Universal Excellence,* Vols. Vol. 3, No.2, p. pp. 87–101, June 2014, Vol. 3.

[73]   T. Anshul and A. Yukti , "The Recruitment of Intuitive Managers," *European Journal of Business and Management,* Vols. Vol.7, No.4, pp. pp. 305-308, 2015.

[74]   C. C. Miller and D. R. Ireland, "Intuition in Strategic Decision Making: Friend or Foe in the Fast-Paced 21st Century?," *Academy of Management Executive, 2005, Vol. 19, No. I.*

[75]   R. Fenker and J. Zoota, Intuitive retail modelling: Does science have anything to offer?, Journal of Corporate Real Estate, Vol. 3 Issue: 3,pp. 248-259, 2001.

[76]   K. Husejnovic, "Boscarol o milenijcih," [Online]. Available: https://www.24ur.com/novice/slovenija/boscarol-in-milenijci.html?focus=1. [Accessed December 2017].

[77] R. Branson, Losing My Virginity, London: Virgin Books, 2009.

[78] P. Dourado, The 60 Second Leader: Everything You Need to Know About Leadership, in 60 second bites, Chichester: Capstone Publishing Ltd., 2007.

[79] "Sports coach UK Research Summary 8," [Online]. Available: https://www.ukcoaching.org/sites/default/files/no8%20 Intution%20and%20coaching.pdf. [Accessed December 2017].

[80] Melissa, "The Interesting Thing About Gut Instincts," [Online]. Available: http://www.jumpstartyourdreamlife. com/gut-instinct-2/. [Accessed December 2017].

[81] "Wikipedia: Zmago Sagadin," [Online]. Available: https:// sl.wikipedia.org/wiki/Zmago_Sagadin . [Accessed December 2017].

[82] "Interesting Chess facts," [Online]. Available: https://www. Chess.com/blog/keshushivang/interesting-Chess-facts2   . [Accessed January 2018].

[83] N. Wolchover, "Popular Science: How Many Different Ways Can a Chess Game Unfold?," [Online]. Available: https:// www.popsci.com/science/article/2010-12/fyi-how-many- different-ways-can-chess-game-unfold. [Accessed January 2018].

[84] "Wikipedia: Garry Kasparov," [Online]. Available: https:// en.wikipedia.org/wiki/Garry_Kasparov. [Accessed January 2018].

[85] "Wikipedia: Carlsen Magnus," [Online]. Available: https:// en.wikipedia.org/wiki/Magnus_Carlsen. [Accessed January 2018].

[86] "Goalcast," [Online]. Available: https://www.goalcast. com/2017/03/13/Chess-grandmaster-garry-kasparov-let- intuition-guide-you/. [Accessed January 2018].

[87] B. Wall, "Chess Intuition," [Online]. Available: http://billwall. phpwebhosting.com/articles/Intuition.htm.   [Accessed February 2018].

[88]   V. Beim, The Enigma of Chess Intuition: Can You Mobilize Hidden Forces in Your Chess?, Alkmaar: New In Chess, 2012, ISBN: 978-5691-379-3.

[89]   A. Beliavsky and A. Mikhalchishin, Secrets of chess intuition, London: Gambit, 2002, ISBN: 1901983528 9781901983524.

[90]   "Briish GO Association: Why is Go Special?," [Online]. Available: https://www.britgo.org/intro/intro1.html. [Accessed January 2018].

[91]   "The Blind Cook," [Online]. Available: http://www. theblindcook.com/about/. [Accessed December 2017].

[92]   E. Hearst and J. Knott, Blindfold chess : history, psychology, techniques, champions, world records, and important games, London: Jefferson, N.C. : McFarland & Co., 2009.

[93]   J. Usó-Doménech and J. Nescolarde-Selva, "What are belief systems?," p. 147–152, Volume 21, Issue 1 2016.

[94]   Osho, Compassion: The Ultimate Flowering of Love, New York: St. Martin's Griffin, 2007, ISBN: 978-0-312-36568-4.

[95]   "Lions International: Melvin Jones Biography," [Online]. Available: http://www.lionsclubs.org/EN/who-we-are/ mission-and-history/melvin-jones.php. [Accessed March 2018].

[96]   "Lions International: About LCIF," [Online]. Available: http://www.lcif.org/EN/about-lcif/index.php.   [Accessed March 2018].

[97]   A. P. Kezele, Sinhroniciteta: prebujanje Celote, Ljubljana: Chiara, 2016, ISBN: 978-961-94116-0-5.

[98]   H. Benson, J. W. Lehmann, M. S. Malhotra, R. F. Goldman, J. Hopkins and M. D. Epstein, "Body temperature changes during the practice of g Tum-mo yoga," *Nature - International Journal of Science,* vol. Vol. 295, p. pp. 234–236, 1982.

[99]   J. Bush, "Explained: How Tibetan Monks Use Meditation to Raise Their Body Temperature," [Online]. Available: https:// www.buzzworthy.com/monks-raise-body-temperature/. [Accessed March 2018].

[100]   W. Kallistos, The Inner Kingdom, New York: St. Vladimir's Seminary Press, 2000, ISBN: 0-88141-209-0.

[101] "Orthodox Mysticism: Teachings of the Desert Fathers," [Online]. Available: http://esoterictexts.tripod.com/DesertFathers.htm. [Accessed November 2017].

[102] "Inspiring Interview of Will Smith - How To Face Fear," [Online]. Available: https://www.youtube.com/watch?v=IRpi1NwHOac. [Accessed May 2017].

[103] "Oprah: An Exclusive Look at Oprah's Journals," [Online]. Available: http://www.oprah.com/spirit/oprahs-private-journals-diary-excerpts. [Accessed February 2018].

[104] M. Purcell, "Psych Central: The Health Benefits of Journaling," [Online]. Available: https://psychcentral.com/lib/the-health-benefits-of-journaling/. [Accessed February 2018].

[105] "Endpaper: 7 Truths About Keeping a Diary From 10 Brilliant Minds," [Online]. Available: http://blog.paperblanks.com/2013/01/7-truths-about-keeping-a-diary-from-10-brilliant-minds/. [Accessed December 2017].

[106] W. F. Stephen, J. Reps , J. Kai , J. M. Garibaldi and N. Qureshi , "Plos: Can machine-learning improve cardiovascular risk prediction using routine clinical data?," [Online]. Available: http://journals.plos.org/plosone/article?id=10.1371/journal.pone.0174944. [Accessed September 2017].

[107] E. Störmer, C. Patscha, J. Prende, M. Rhisiart, P. Glover and H. Beck, "The Future of Work: Jobs and Skills in 2030," [Online]. Available: https://assets.publishing.service.gov.uk/government/uploads/system/uploads/attachment_data/file/303334/er84-the-future-of-work-evidence-report.pdf. [Accessed October 2017].

[108] J. McCormick, "Predictions 2017: Artificial Intelligence Will Drive The Insights Revolution," [Online]. Available: https://go.forrester.com/wp-content/uploads/Forrester_Predictions_2017_-Artificial_Intelligence_Will_Drive_The_Insights_Revolution.pdf. [Accessed October 2017].

[109] "Statista: Revenues from the artificial intelligence," [Online]. Available: https://www.statista.com/statistics/607716/worldwide-artificial-intelligence-market-revenues/. [Accessed October 2017].

[110] "Bloomberg News: AI Will Add $15.7 Trillion to the Global Economy," [Online]. Available: https://www.bloomberg.com/news/articles/2017-06-28/ai-seen-adding-15-7-trillion-as-game-changer-for-global-economy. [Accessed October 2017].

[111] P. McCorduck, Machines Who Think - A Personal Inquiry into the History and Prospects of Artificial Intelligence, Natick, MA: A. K. Peters, Ltd., 2004, ISBN: 1-56881-205-1.

[112] "Investing In Artificial Intelligence - Economic Growth And Stock Picking," [Online]. Available: https://seekingalpha.com/article/4063499-investing-artificial-intelligence-economic-growth-stock-picking. [Accessed October 2017].

[113] "Shortlist Magazine: Is AI the beginning of the end of mankind?," [Online]. Available: http://thefutureofai.blogspot.si/2015/06/shortlist-magazine-tech-is-ai-beginning.html#!/2015/06/shortlist-magazine-tech-is-ai-beginning.html. [Accessed October 2017].

[114] P. Perry , "NASA's A.I. Discovers a Second Solar System With 8 Planets, Just Like Ours," [Online]. Available: http://bigthink.com/philip-perry/nasa-has-discovered-a-new-exoplanet-using-ai. [Accessed October 2017].

[115] "Code Conference 2016: Elon Musk interviewed by Kara Swisher and Walt Mossberg," [Online]. Available: https://www.youtube.com/watch?v=wsixsRI-Sz4. [Accessed November 2017].

[116] M. Dowd, "Elon Musk's Billion-Dollar Crusade to Stop the A.I. Apocalypse," [Online]. Available: https://www.vanityfair.com/news/2017/03/elon-musk-billion-dollar-crusade-to-stop-ai-space-x. [Accessed November 2017].

[117] M. R. Gillings, M. Hilbert and D. J. Kemp, "Information in the Biosphere: Biological and Digital Worlds," *Trends in Ecology and Evolution,* Vols. March, Vol. 31, Issue 3., 2016.

[118] C. B. Frey and M. A. Osborne, "The Future of Employment: How Subsceptible Are Jobs to Computerisation?," 2013. [Online]. Available: https://www.oxfordmartin.ox.ac.uk/downloads/academic/future-of-employment.pdf. [Accessed November 2017].

[119] S. Yan, "CNBC: Artificial intelligence will replace half of all jobs in the next decade, says widely followed technologist," [Online]. Available: https://www.cnbc.com/2017/04/27/kai-fu-lee-robots-will-replace-half-of-all-jobs.html. [Accessed November 2017].

[120] A. Scott , "Wearing Your Intelligence: How to Apply Artificial Intelligence in Wearables and IoT," [Online]. Available: https://www.wired.com/insights/2014/12/wearing-your-intelligence/. [Accessed November 2017].

[121] A. H. Eden, J. H. Moor, J. H. Soraker and E. Steinhart, Singularity Hypotheses: A Scientific and Philosophical Assessment, Heidelberg NY Dordrecht London: Springer, 2012, ISBN: 978-3-642-32559-5.

[122] "Wikipedia: Technological singularity," [Online]. Available: https://en.wikipedia.org/wiki/Technological_singularity#cite_note-mathematical-3. [Accessed November 2017].

[123] R. Kurzweil, The Singularity Is Near: When Humans Transcend Biology, New York: Viking, 2005, ISBN: 978-0-670-03384-3.

[124] "Is AI the beginning of the end of mankind?," [Online]. Available: http://www.shortlist.com/tech/is-ai-the-beginning-of-the-end-of-mankind. [Accessed November 2017].

[125] "Superintelligence: Science or Fiction, The beneficial AI 2017 Conference," [Online]. Available: https://www.youtube.com/watch?v=h0962biiZa4. [Accessed November 2017].

[126] "Y Combinator: Elon Musk Interview - How to Build the Future," [Online]. Available: https://www.ycombinator.com/future/elon/. [Accessed November 2017].

[127] "TED Talk: Can we build AI without losing control over it?," [Online]. Available: https://www.ted.com/talks/sam_harris_can_we_build_ai_without_losing_control_over_it/transcript?language=en#t-1000. [Accessed November 2017].

[128]   "The Verge: Elon Musk launches Neuralink, a venture to merge the human brain with AI," [Online]. Available: https://www.theverge.com/2017/3/27/15077864/elon-musk-neuralink-brain-computer-interface-ai-cyborgs. [Accessed December 2017].

[129]   "World Government Summit 2017," [Online]. Available: https://www.youtube.com/watch?v=GGwRIzQvU-k. [Accessed December 2017].

[130]   J. Ortega y Gasset, Obras Completas, Vol. I. Ed., Madrid: Taurus/Fundación José Ortega y Gasset, 2004.

[131]   (. http://archived.parapsych.org/members/r_d_nelson.html.

[132]   J. Haves, C. W. Allinson and S. J. Armstrong, "Intuition, women managers and gendered stereotypes," *Personnel Review,* no. Personnel Review, Vol. 33 Issue: 4, pp.403-417, pp. 403-417, 2004.

[133]

[134]   D. Skaret, "Eminent Canadian Women's Perceptions of Intuition," 1993.

[135]   A. M. Hayashi, "When to trust your gut," *Harvard Business Review, 79(2): 59–65,* 2001.

[136]   T. Stumbrys, D. Erlacher and M. Schredl, "Reliability and stability of lucid dream and nightmare frequency scales," *International Journal of Dream Research, 6(2), 53–56.,* 2013.

[137]   T. Stumbrys and D. Erlacher, "Mindfulness and Lucid Dream Frequency Predicts the Ability to Control Lucid Dreams," *Imagination, Cognition and Personality 2017, Vol. 36(3) 229–239.*

[138]   R. A. Baer, "Mindfulness training as a clinical intervention: A conceptual and empirical review," *Clinical Psychology: Science and Practice, 10(2), 125–143.,* 2003.

[139]   "February," [Online].

[140]   "Merriam Webster Dictionary," [Online]. Available: https://www.merriam-webster.com/. [Accessed March 2017].

[141]   Z. Mihajlovic Slavinski, "Spiritual Technology," [Online]. Available: http://spiritual-technology.com/?p=10. [Accessed March 2017].

[142]   "International Remote Viewing Association," [Online]. Available: http://www.irva.org/. [Accessed April 2017].

[143]   B. C. Olsen, Modern Esoteric: Beyond Our Senses, San Francisco: Consortium of Collective Consciousness Publishing, 2018.

[144]   "Guinness World Records," [Online]. Available: http://www.guinnessworldrecords.com/world-records/fastest-serve-of-a-tennis-ball-(male). [Accessed December 2017].

[145]   "Guinness World Records," [Online]. Available: http://www.guinnessworldrecords.com/world-records/fastest-badminton-hit-in-competition-(male)/. [Accessed December 2017].

[146]   "Encyclopedia Britannica: Nepal earthquake of 2015," [Online]. Available: https://www.britannica.com/topic/Nepal-earthquake-of-2015. [Accessed December 2017].

[147]   "Wikipedia: Davis Cup," [Online]. Available: https://en.wikipedia.org/wiki/Davis_Cup. [Accessed December 2017].

[148]   "Firstpost," [Online]. Available: http://www.firstpost.com/sports/lin-dan-ivanisevic-clijsters-the-best-wild-cards-winners-ever-1025815.html. [Accessed December 2017].

[149]   "British GO Association: A Brief History of Go," [Online]. Available: https://www.britgo.org/intro/history. [Accessed February 2018].

[150]   "Wikipedia: Masaki Takemiya," [Online]. Available: https://en.wikipedia.org/wiki/Masaki_Takemiya. [Accessed January 2018].

[151]   A. Turing, "The Alan Turing Internet Scrapbook," [Online]. Available: http://www.turing.org.uk/scrapbook/test.html. [Accessed November 2017].

[152]   "Investopedia: Moore's Law," [Online]. Available: https://www.investopedia.com/terms/m/mooreslaw.asp#ixzz52q3X8CVg. [Accessed November 2017].